A HOUSE DIVIDED

Studies in Judaism and Christianity

Exploration of Issues in the Contemporary Dialogue Between Christians and Jews

Editor in Chief for
Stimulus Books
Helga Croner

Editors
Lawrence Boadt, C.S.P.
Helga Croner
David Dalin
Leon Klenicki
John Koenig
Kevin A. Lynch, C.S.P.
Richard C. Sparks, C.S.P.

 A STIMULUS BOOK

A HOUSE DIVIDED

The Parting of the Ways Between Synagogue and Church

Vincent Martin

A STIMULUS BOOK

PAULIST PRESS ◆ NEW YORK ◆ MAHWAH

The Publisher gratefully acknowledges use of the following material: excerpts from *St. Justin Martyr, The Dialogue with Trypho,* translated by Thomas B. Falls in the Fathers of the Church Series,Volume 6; Washington, D.C.: Catholic University Press, Inc., copyright © by Ludwig Schopp.

Library of Congress Cataloging-in-Publication Data

Martin, Vincent, 1912-
   A house divided : the parting of the ways between synagogue and church / by Vincent Martin.
      p.   cm.—(Studies in Judaism and Christianity) (A Stimulus book)
   Includes bibliographical references and index.
   ISBN 0-8091-3569-8
   1. Judaism (Christian theology)—History of doctrines—Early church, ca. 30-600. 2.Church history—Primitive and early church, ca. 30-600. 3. Christianity and other religions—Judaism. 4. Judaism—Relations—Christianity. I. Title. II. Series.
BT93.M38 1995   95-3020
261.2′6—dc20   CIP

Published by Paulist Press
997 Macarthur Boulevard
Mahwah, NJ 07430

Printed and bound in the United States of America

Contents

Dedication

To the many friends,
Jews and Christians,
who nurtured my study
of our common roots.

Introduction

A quite unexpected by-product of Hitler's madness was a reorientation of the relations between Jews and Christians from latent animosity toward open and candid dialogue. The results have been impressive, more so since they were not anticipated. After a quarter of a century of serious efforts, however, the dialogue is showing signs of uneasiness among the participants. Some of them question its present agenda and would like to explore new topics. Others wonder if much real progress is still possible; they feel that the only task ahead is the dissemination among Jews and Christians of the new concepts and attitudes already developed in circles of specialists.

To explain this lowering of expectations we need to go back to the social context in which the dialogue started. After World War II the immediate motivation on the Jewish side was a latent anxiety about survival, kept alive by the specter of a possible new SHO'AH in the future, a Hitlerian-like holocaust. Never again! Such a strong commitment was a very understandable motivation. On the other hand, some Christian leaders were experiencing at that time a vague sense of guilt about their prudent silence during the Nazi persecution. They were worrying about the pervasiveness of antisemitism in Christian societies, an antisemitism which had offered a fertile soil to the growth of Hitlerism and the carrying out of the "final solution."

Given this social context it is not surprising that the dialogue was mostly concerned with the full acceptance of the Jewish people into the life of Western society, not only in legal terms, but also as full social partners. The religious dimension of the problem was not ignored, but it was more or less de-emphasized as neither side knew how to handle their religious past in this new situation of dialogue. The common frame of reference in the mutual efforts toward comprehension had to be humanistic and not religious.

This humanistic approach has remained a significant aspect of the Jewish-Christian dialogue for the last twenty-five years. It had to be humanistic because no other frame of reference was available to old spiritual ene-

mies who were seeking some common values to share. The dialogue was
intended to heal and not to increase the mutual hurt. But this approach
implied serious limitations from the start. These limitations are now becoming more conscious.

Rabbi Joseph B. Soloveitchick, the leading halachist of our times, in an
article published in TRADITION 1964, had reminded the Orthodox Jews that
the various religious experiences are incommensurable. The inner life of faith
is not to be exposed in the public arena; it is a mysterious relationship of the
soul with the living God. Dialogue between Jews and Christians can be welcomed only for the solution of the social and political problems encountered
by Jews and Christians in the human environment in which they need to live
as good neighbors.

Rabbi Henry Siegman, an Orthodox rabbi who played an important role at
the beginning of the official dialogue between Judaism and the Catholic
Church, gave a very sensitive and knowledgeable analysis of the ongoing dialogue in THE JOURNAL OF ECUMENICAL STUDIES, 1978: "A Decade
of Catholic-Jewish Relations."[1] Rabbi Henry Siegman stressed the difference
of agendas between the two partners in the dialogue. What impels the
Christians to dialogue with Jews is "the mystery of the Jewish rejection of
Christianity."[2] But "for the Jew the problematic of Christian-Jewish relations
is determined by a history of Christian attitudes and actions toward the Jews
which diminished their humanity and inflicted on them suffering and martyrdom."[3] Beyond such problems he also agreed that the profoundly personal and
intimate experience of faith must remain foreign to the dialogue. Rabbi
Siegman, however, was confident that some kind of dialogue will remain possible as long as the partners are aware that they are coming to each other with
different agendas and are remaining open to each other's concerns.

The danger is that a purely humanistic dialogue will cure only a few symp-
toms and leave untouched the roots of the disease. Even if the dialogue
achieved "a sincere examination of the Christian conscience on the subject of
antisemitism" (a task not yet completed) and respected "the theological
dimension of the Jewish relationship to the Land of Israel" (another task not
yet completed),[4] there is little chance that the deep animosity between Jews
and Christians would suddenly dissolve into friendly and cooperative relations. The affair of the Carmel of Auschwitz revealed the depth of antagonistic feelings in the Jewish subconscious, and today in many Christian Churches
anti-Judaism is still embedded in worship and homiletics, with foreseeable
consequences on the attitudes of the average Christian. How could the dialogue overcome the sequels of a very painful history without addressing the

religious attitudes which in fact have conditioned, and are still conditioning, the relations between the two communities?

In the introduction to his recent THE CHRISTIAN PROBLEM,[5] Stuart E. Rosenberg remarks: "Vast progress had indeed been made in the last two decades which has advanced the cause of mutual understanding between Christians and Jews. Yet we are really only at the beginning. There are still large preserves and pockets of confusion and misunderstanding which we must jointly address and enlighten."[6] "This is the time to come forward at last, not merely with a fleeting Church resolution here, a liberal Vatican document there, which 'proclaim' 'anti-Jewishness' as 'un-Christian,' but with a thorough investigation and review of the basic adversarial character of Christianity versus the Jews and their religion."[7] Not to be too one-sided such a thorough investigation could also review the basic adversarial character of Rabbinic Judaism toward the Christians and their religion. If the task is urgent, the challenge is forbidding. How to render it truly constructive and not destructive?

The following essays will investigate the mutual adversarial character of Jewish-Christian relations at its source, i.e., in the progressive and painful parting of the ways between Rabbinic Judaism and Apostolic Christianity during the first century. A perusal of Justin Martyr's DIALOGUE WITH TRYPHO inclines one to think that the Synagogue and the Church were already completely estranged from each other by the middle of the second century. The progressive differentiation in belief, ritual and organization was an important factor in this complete estrangement. However, the crucial factor that will mark and, to a great extent, condition Jewish-Christian relations in subsequent centuries was the early crystallization of deeply felt antagonistic feelings which arose during the bitter separation between the two communities.

The ordinary tools of a social scientist are not available for the study of religious attitudes in the first century. The only source of information available is the remaining literature analyzed by exegetes and historians. However, so much has been analyzed and even discovered during the last hundred years that a minimal effort at reconstruction may provide a sketch of the origin, the structure and the processes of change of these religious attitudes.

The approach in these essays accordingly will not be exegetical, theological, or even historical, but rather broadly sociological. It is not a story of events, but an effort at entering into the experience of the actors of a great religious drama, trying to understand how and why they acted as they did. There is no doubt that God's Spirit was actively present in this religious drama, but his mysterious activity is never revealed to the social scientist.

A Glossary of Hebrew Terms

'ADON	Sir, lord.
'ADONAI	(my lords), Lord God.
'AGGADAH	the non-legal portion of the traditional teaching (history, moral maxims, prophecy).
'AHARIT HA-YAMIM	the end of days, the millennium.
'ALENU	closing prayer of the daily services.
'AM HA-ARETZ	the ordinary people of the land.
'AMIDAH	(standing position), the daily prayer of Eighteen Benedictions.
'AM NIFRAD	the people set apart.
ANAWIM	the poor ones.
ASHKENAZI	German, Eastern European Jew.
BAAL SHEM TOV	master of the good name, the Charismatic Leader of modern Hasidim.
BEIT MIDRASH	house of study.
BERIT	circumcision, covenant.
BIRKAT HA-MINIM	blessing (against) heretics.
EL	god.
ELOHIM	(gods), Lord God.
'EMET	verity, faithfulness
GOY	nation, non-Jew.
GOYIM	the nations.
HACHAM	a wise man.
HALACHAH	the legal portion of the traditional teaching (from HALACH, to go).
HANUKKAH	an 8-day holiday in December commemorating the rededication of the Temple.
HASID	pious, devotee.

HASIDIM	Jewish sect in 2nd century B.C.E. Jewish mystical sect in Eastern Europe, circa 1750.
HAVURAH(OT)	group(s), company.
HESED	loving-kindness.
HILLEL	sage, early 1st c., lenient interpretation.
HURBAN	the "Catastrophe," the destruction of the Jerusalem Temple by Titus in 70 C.E.
KABBALA	medieval system of Jewish theosophy, mysticism and thaumaturgy.
KADDISH	memorial prayer for the dead.
KASHRUT	ritual observance of dietary laws.
KIBBUTZ	communal settlement.
KIDDUSH HA-SHEM	sanctification of the Name, martyrdom.
KINNERET	lyre, Sea of Galilee.
MAR	Sir in Aramaic.
MARAN	our lord in Aramaic.
MERKAVAH	chariot (of Ezekiel).
MIDRASH	biblical homily.
MIN(IM)	kind, gender, heretic(s).
MISHNAH	collection of halachic oral traditions (the Oral Law) compiled about 200 C.E.
MITZVA, MITZVOT	commandment(s), precept(s).
NASI	president, head of the Sanhedrin.
'OMER	the counting of 7 weeks from Easter to Pentecost.
PESACH	Passover.
PIRKEI AVOT	the tractate "Fathers" in the MISHNAH. A collection of ethical words of wisdom.
QUMRAN	residence of the Essenes on the NW shore of the Dead Sea.
SEPHARDI	Spanish, Spanish-Portuguese Jew.
SHALOM	peace.
SHALOM 'ALEICHEM	peace be with you.
SHAMMAI	sage, early 1st c., stringent in Law.
SHAVUOT	the Feast of Weeks, Pentecost.
SHECHINAH	the Divine Presence.
SHEMA ISRAEL	Deuteronomy 6:4-9. Israel's confession of faith.
SHO'AH	the "Holocaust," the killing of six million Jews by Hitler.
SHOMER MITZVOT	the one who keeps the commandments, an observant Jew.

SIDDUR	the daily prayer book.
TAEB	Prophet-Messiah of the Samaritans.
TALMUD	the MISHNAH with an authoritative commentary.
TANACH	Torah-Prophets-Writings, Hebrew Scriptures.
TORAH	the Pentateuch, or all the authoritative teaching of Judaism, written or oral.
TOSEPHTA	authoritative tractates which had not found a place in the MISHNAH.
TZADIK	a just one (righteous, pious, kind).
YETZER HA-TOV	the instinct to do good.
YETZER HA-RA'	the instinct to do evil.

I. Our Common Heritage

The rupture of friendly relations between Judaism and Christianity did not occur at some point in their later history, but at the very beginning, though a century elapsed before the rupture became total and final. There is an unavoidable consequence to this historical fact. In the conduct of a religious dialogue, a common frame of reference, mutually understandable and acceptable to Jews and Christians, will be found only if the Christians are willing to go beyond their own history and explore their Jewish roots. As Jews and Christians accept the Hebrew Scriptures as divine revelation, such a requirement does not seem to present any difficulty. Recently, many walls have been destroyed and many bridges built among exegetes of different persuasions. The academic dialogue is healthy and thriving. However, many Jews involved in non-academic dialogues insist that, while we may read the same texts together, we do not understand them in the same way. They are quite right. We always receive and understand God's words in and through our own religious tradition, the Oral Law for Jews, the teachings of the Fathers for Christians. Another way, however, remains open to us. With the resources of historiography we can try to recreate the religious life of God's people at the time of Jesus of Nazareth. We face only one serious difficulty; that period was a very untidy one, a time of troubles. Judaism was being pulled in many different directions. Josephus writes of the Sadducees, the Pharisees, the Essenes and the Zealots; there were the Hellenist Jews and the Parthian Jews. If there was no question about who was a Jew, there were many questions about what Judaism was and what it ought to be.

Upon closer examination, we will discover underneath this extreme pluralism a solid core of common belief and practice. The existing pluralism did not come from a wave of syncretism as had happened in the past, but from the spiritual richness of Judaism itself, and from the extremely trying circumstances of the social and political situation. The solidity of the inner core was a legacy of the preceding period, a period of relative peace in the aftermath of the exile in Babylon. It had not been a time for brilliant creativity or daring exploration, but for survival and for trying to bring into some unity, or at least some kind of integration and harmony, the many different traditions which had nourished the religious life of Israel before and during the exile. Such was the period from the restoration of the walls of Jerusalem under Nehemiah in 445 B.C.E. to the onset of the Great Persecution initiated by Antiochus IV Epiphanes and the Maccabean revolt in 167 B.C.E. The early years under Persian hegemony were the formative years. The conquest by Alexander the Great in 333 B.C.E. and the intrusion of Greek culture into many areas of the Middle East did not, at first, disturb the equilibrium reached by the small community of returnees who had settled in and around Jerusalem. It is the life of this small community that we need to rediscover and somehow to recreate in spirit.

Theirs was a world quite different from the world of the Patriarchs, the sojourn in the desert, the conquest of Canaan, the time of the monarchy, the schism between Israel and Judah, the painful and intensely creative period of the exile in Babylon. The national life was centered on the rebuilt Temple in Jerusalem, and the High Priest had emerged as the leader of the nation. The great figure who symbolized and at the same time was the most efficient agent of this restoration was Ezra, the father of Judaism, i.e., of the religion of Israel revived in a new garb among the remnant of the tribe of Judah. An Aaronic priest, working in the spirit of Ezekiel, he was totally committed to an ideal of holiness. His great contribution to the survival of his people was to replace the authority of the king with the authority of a book. Biblical critics argue about his role in the gathering and editing of the five books of Moses into the Torah. He certainly created in the people a new respect for the Law. The holiness that had been centered on the Temple now became diffused in the community through the observance of the commandments. The Torah, being at the same time a religious code, a civil code and a criminal code, was destined to shape every aspect of Jewish life.

From a religion of revelation Judaism had become a religion of interpretation. The voice of prophecy had become silent; the scribe emerged as an important religious figure who not only transmitted the written Torah but also explained it on the basis of the oral tradition. Beautiful psalms and a variety of religious books called the WRITINGS appeared. The Bible, the Word of God to Israel as proclaimed in the Law and the Prophets, became also the Word of Israel addressed to God in poetry, meditation and quest for Wisdom. God was not simply the particular god of Israel, nor the first and strongest among the gods, but the One God who is uniquely transcendent, looking down on heaven and earth whose sole creator he is. Nevertheless, God remained close to Israel and dwelt in their midst in the Holy Temple. They called him "our Father," and Israel was "his son." From all the nations, for reasons unexplained, God had set his heart on them and had chosen "the fewest of all peoples" (Deut 7:7) to be his very own, a priestly kingdom and a holy nation (Exod 19:5–6).

At Sinai the people of Israel had accepted the covenant God had initiated with their father Abraham. Many pages of the Scriptures, however, are witnesses to Israel's breaking of this covenant. Israel's original sin was the worship of the golden calf (Exod 32). At the time of the prophet Elijah only 7,000 in Israel had not bent the knee before Baal (1 Kgs 19:18). King Manasseh built altars to the whole array of heaven in the two courts of the Temple, and caused his son to pass through fire. He practiced soothsaying and magic, etc. (2 Kgs 21:5–9). The prophet Jeremiah confronted the Jerusalemites with their disloyalty to the living God: there were as many gods in Judah as there were towns and as many altars to Baal as there were streets in Jerusalem (Jer 11:13). The verdict of the Lord Sabaoth was not surprising:

> The house of Israel and the house of Judah have broken the covenant that I made with their ancestors. Therefore, thus says the Lord, assuredly I am going to bring disaster upon them that they cannot escape; though they cry out to me, I will not listen to them (Jer 11:10–11).

But, in his great mercy, the Lord declared later through the prophet Jeremiah:

> The days are surely coming, says the Lord, when I will make a new covenant with the house of Israel and the house of Judah. It will not be like the covenant that I made with their ancestors when I took them by the hand to bring them out of the land of Egypt—a covenant that they broke…I will put my law within them, and I will write it on their hearts; and I will be their God, and they shall be my people (Jer 31:31–33).

Was not Early Judaism, in the wake of the renewal begun by Ezra, the fulfillment of this prophecy of Jeremiah? There were many signs, at that period, of a new heart and a new spirit among the people. The humiliations, the pains, and also the shock experienced face to face with an exuberant religious life in the land of Babylon must have led many to a deep soul searching. Through God's care and guidance, the people had slowly returned to their maker and let his Spirit write his words not only on their lips but also on their hearts. Somewhere, among the multitude of nations and their variegated worship of religious shadows, the living God could rejoice in a tiny community who "knew" him, was listening to his Word, and was willing to be challenged by his holiness.

A great price was demanded from them. In what seems to us a monstrous, if not an outrightly immoral, decision, Ezra obliged all men from the community of the exiles who had married foreign wives to put them away from them along with their children (Ezra 10). This was part of a general policy intended to create a wall of separation between Jews and Gentiles. In time the strict observance of the dietary laws, of the Sabbaths and Festivals, not to mention circumcision, abhorrent to the Greeks, would build strong barriers to normal social contacts with the pagans. Until then, God had let his people mingle freely with the neighboring nations. We know the result. In the contest of influence between himself and the false gods, God had often lost. Finally the time had come for God to withdraw his distracted children into solitude that they might discover and learn where spiritual strength could be found. And this time God won. When the test came with the sudden and unexpected persecution of Antiochus Epiphanes, the majority of the people remained loyal to the living God. The popular revolt led by the Maccabees was religious and not political. The symbol of its victory was Hanukkah, the purification and rededication of the Temple. The heroic figures of the Maccabean martyrs, the first KIDDUSH HA-SHEM (i.e., "Sanctification of the Name" through willingness to die for God's honor), were God's seal of approval on the religious life rebuilt on Judea's hills by the spiritual heirs of Ezra.

It would be a mistake, however, to conceive of this spiritual reconstruction in early Judaism as equivalent to the frame of reference of modern Orthodox Judaism. Not only would it leave uninterested those Jews who at present are the most involved in the dialogue, but it would ignore the very obvious differences between Temple Judaism and Rabbinic Judaism, the Judaism which emerged from the burning of the Temple and the destruction of the Holy City. A Judaism centered on sacrifices and worship in the Temple was not identical with a later Judaism which would be centered on the synagogue and the study of TORAH. The authority of the priest called to duty by God in the covenant of Levi was not identical with the authority of the scribe whom tradition would come to recognize as occupying the chair of Moses.

Jews and Christians, for different reasons, will have to make serious efforts to reconstruct objectively the life of their spiritual ancestors. From where they now stand, they could try using a method successfully developed by phenomenology to probe into their own collective consciousness, putting in parentheses one historical element after the other until they reached the period of Early Judaism. If at the end of this process of reduction they could agree on the same objective memory, they would have found a well-articulated frame of reference which could offer a basis for a genuine religious dialogue.

The first lines of PIRKE AVOT are intriguing:

> Moses received the Law from Sinai and handed it down to Joshua, and Joshua to the elders, and the elders to the prophets, and the prophets handed it down to the men of the Great Assembly.[8]

Who were the men of the Great Assembly, about which we have no historical record? A note of the editor explains that "the great synagogue was a body of 120 elders, judges, prophets, sages, teachers and scribes who returned from exile with Ezra." Concerning them the tradition remains very vague. Nevertheless, as a symbol, the Great Synagogue permanently reminds us of the unique role played in salvation history by the community of exiles who returned to Jerusalem and the hills of Judea. It has been the source, the fountainhead, of this unique religious stream which in time would part into Rabbinic Judaism and Early Christianity. The two relate to each other as two sisters or two brothers, Rabbinic Judaism being naturally the older brother. The younger brother has left the paternal home and has tried to become universal. Neither can deny that today, as tomorrow, they are and will be carrying a common heritage in the many facets of their religious personality.

It is this common heritage, to the extent that it is still alive in Judaism and Christianity and has not become stifled under ideological accretions or historical mishaps, that could offer a simple but sufficient frame of reference to start a genuine religious dialogue between Jews and Christians, a dialogue intended not to convince, but to open the way to mutual understanding and respect.

II. Mutual Disappointment

Jesus' Jewishness was not a problem for his contemporaries. Born of a Jewish mother, circumcised on the eighth day, raised in an observant family, as a child and a teenager he slowly absorbed the religious traditions and the life style of a community shaped by the values of early Temple Judaism. The culture and the society in which someone is born are not simply her or his earliest human environment; they are also part and parcel of the structure of her or his personality. Our mother tongue is more than words spoken around us; it is our own speech through which we express and know ourselves. Whatever our approach to the mystery of Jesus' personality, any attempt at separating and isolating him from his people and his culture is simply nonsense. If there was any originality in Jesus' teaching and life, it sprang within the context of a Near Eastern society and was fed with all the spiritual resources of Temple Judaism. Modern Jewish and Israeli writers who have overcome centuries of prejudice and have been able to encounter Jesus directly in the synoptic Gospels are struck by his Jewishness. They perceive in him a certain quality which we GOYIM seem unable to detect. Jesus is a member of their family. We are not.

We know nothing about the private life of Jesus of Nazareth, Yeshua Ben Yosef. We know him only as a public figure who for a very short time—from one to three years—became a focus of attention, first in Galilee and then in Jerusalem. Today there is an emerging consensus among exegetes that we are able to know something about the historical Jesus, though what, and how much, will remain a bone of contention for years to come. However, thanks to some ascertained facts or acknowledged sayings, we are able to meet a religious personality at the same time completely Jewish and distinctly unique. The first question for the historian will not be "What does Jesus mean to us today?" but rather "What did he mean to his contemporaries?" What was the immediate perception of this uncommon figure, first among the common people in far-away Galilee, and then to the members of the religious establishment in the heart of Judaism, in Jerusalem?

The fact that the first public act of Jesus had been to visit the Jordan Valley to be baptized by John, son of Zechariah, is significant. Not only did John introduce him to some of his disciples, but Jesus for his part acknowledged the proclamation of John and made it his own: "Repent, for the kingdom of heaven has come near" (Matt 3:2; 4:17). In so doing he publicly accepted messianism as the context of his career. At the same time, he was creating for us a very difficult problem of interpretation. What did messianism mean to the common people listening to him in the synagogues of Galilee? What did it mean to Jesus himself? What would it mean later to his disciples when they called him no longer master, teacher or rabbi, but lord and messiah?

1. THE ELECTION OF ISRAEL

Before we discuss this difficult topic of messianism, an important word of caution is necessary. Messianism is not the core, the essence, the raison d'être of Judaism. The Torah barely mentions it. It came into existence only through the oracles of the Prophets. Christians distort the Hebrew Scriptures when they read them only in terms of "preparation for" or "types of" something else. In the words of the prophet Micah, Judaism is what the Lord is asking of Israel: "to do justice, and to love kindness, and to walk humbly with your God" (Micah 6:8) and to do it NOW. If the past is what made us and the future is what remains in the hands of the Lord, the present is the existential moment of our encounter, as a person or as a community, with the living God. Judaism finds its raison d'être in nothing else except its election by God to be his people. When God sought to establish an interpersonal relationship between himself and humanity, he chose a particular people and set it apart to become the light of the nations. In Moab, beyond the Jordan, Moses told the Israelites:

> For you are a people holy to the Lord your God; the Lord your God has chosen you out of all the peoples on earth to be his people, his treasured possession. It was not because you were more numerous than any other people that the Lord set his heart on you and chose you—for you were the fewest of all peoples. It was because the Lord loved you and kept the oath that he swore to your ancestors...(Deut 7:6–8).

Many today, even some Jews, find themselves unable to receive this word spoken by Moses in the name of the living God. Could God be capricious? Are the Israelites, though very few in number, a more gifted and more attractive specimen of humanity? The election of Israel seems to go against the grain. From the time of the French Revolution a deep sensitivity to equality has been slowly spreading across the world. Though we are witnessing a strong revival of tribalism, communalism, ethnicity, nationalism and even religion as principles of social identity, it is always understood that no group is or could be superior to one's own. Societies structured around unequal privileges are progressively disappearing. On the other hand, people might not be in such a hurry to condemn the concept of election if they would continue to read the text of Deuteronomy:

> Therefore, observe diligently the commandment—the statutes, and the ordinances—that I am commanding you today (Deut 7:11).

God chose Israel not for what it was at the time of its first election, but for what it could become with God's constant nurture and the people's faithful consent. God was offering his people a very rigorous way, indeed, not an easy way of life.

Can we conceive the election of a particular people as the most pragmatic method available to God for achieving a personal relationship with humanity? God could have addressed himself directly to every nation without any show of favoritism. At least, he could have spoken through those personalities who shaped the spirit of the great civilizations, men like Buddha, Confucius, Socrates, etc., rather than through Moses. God's intention in choosing Israel was not to improve human culture; his children could try their own hands at becoming civilized. He wanted only to be known as a personal being, and, once he had found or created moral integrity among his creatures, establish a permanent bond of mutual love:

> Hear O Israel: The Lord is our God, the Lord alone. You shall love the Lord your God with all your heart, and with all your soul, and with all your might (Deut 6:4–5).

Most of the giant steps in human evolution have been taken in one or two points on planet earth, from where they have been diffused into larger and larger areas. All forms of the alphabet, for example, have a common origin in the Middle East. In cultural development, as in technological development, the creation of a prototype is supremely important. Its quality and perfection will condition all future development. Following the same method, God selected one people among all the nations to become the archetype of his personal relationship with humanity. At the appropriate time, when the conditions were ripe, after reminding the Israelites of the signs and wonders which accompanied their salvation from Egypt, God offered them the privilege of becoming his people:

> Now therefore, if you obey my voice and keep my covenant, you shall be my treasured possession out of all the peoples. Indeed, the whole earth is mine, but you shall be for me a priestly kingdom and a holy nation (Exod 19:5).

After the exile in Babylon, the work of the leaders of the Great Assembly had been so effective that a spiritual perception of the holiness of God—of his justice and his mercy—had become ingrained in the life of Israel, together with a clear awareness of the call to be holy as the Lord is holy. The worship of idols had completely disappeared from the Land of Israel. KIDDUSH HA-SHEM, the sanctification of God's Name, was, and has truly remained, the core, the essence of Judaism. It is the first petition of the KADDISH as well as of the OUR FATHER, "Hallowed be thy Name." The messianic hope, "Thy Kingdom come," is only the second petition. It must be studied and understood in the context of the sanctification of the Name. If the latter was not always mentioned in messianic texts, the reason is that being like a second nature it easily remains subconscious in a Jewish mind.

2. MESSIANISM

The relationship between the sanctification of the Name and messianism is, nevertheless, intimate. The covenant which links God and Israel is more than a legal structure; it is a process in time. God is not in time, but people are, becoming, changing, and always able to reaffirm or to reject prior commitments. The history of the covenant, or sacred history, does not depend solely on the HESED and EMET of God, on his love and fidelity, but also on women's and men's obedience or initiative, as well as on their reluctance and sometimes even their rebelliousness. In fact, God's sovereignty is not always acknowledged, and often is acknowledged with the lips only and not with the heart. Classical prophecy had convinced Israel that some day, on THE DAY OF THE LORD, this tension between the will of God and the human will would be definitively resolved. By a manifestation of power God would crush all his enemies; this meant the enemies of Israel outside and all the wicked souls inside the House of Israel. At the same time God would display such an abundance of loving-kindness that Israel would finally turn to God with all its heart, all its soul and all its might. A final and decisive intervention of God in history was beyond doubt; the question remained when and how.

In periods of peace, security, and political autonomy, the hope for such a decisive intervention somehow receded and remained a simple silver lining on the horizon of time. Such was the case during the period of the Great Assembly, the formative period of Temple Judaism, and again after the revolt of Bar Kochba, during the formative period of Rabbinic Judaism. However, at other times, such as the bloody massacres by the Crusaders, or in answer to the expulsion from Spain and the fires of the Inquisition, messianic hopes surged again with great strength. It is not surprising that in the troubled times during which Jesus was born, the period between the onset of the Great Persecution under Antiochus Epiphanes and the final destruction of Jerusalem under Emperor Hadrian, a revitalized hope gripped Jewish imagination, causing much tension, anxiety and political upheaval. It is this period characterized by such heightened messianism—and also by a new pluralism in spirituality and social structure—that forms the bridge between early Temple Judaism and Rabbinic Judaism. It is occasionally referred to as Late Judaism.

As was to be expected during such a troubled period the basic question surfaced: What kind of decisive intervention by the Almighty was Israel to expect and when? There was a variety of opinions, attitudes and imaginative scenarios. Underneath most of them it was possible to discern two main orientations. The oldest one went back to classical prophetism. It tended to see God's intervention as happening in the world of our daily experience. God would finally put this world of ours in proper order, as hoped for in the 'ALENU prayer, "when the world shall be perfected under the reign of the Almighty." The glorious promises of the great prophets would finally be realized in a very tangible manner and all abominations removed from the earth. This would bring a happy ending to human history. The other trend was pessimistic. It went back to apocalyptic prophecy, which came into its own at the time of the Great Persecution in the middle of the 2nd century B.C.E. There was a feeling that everything had been tried in vain. Not only the human race but even nature was beyond repair. God would have to destroy this world and make a new heaven and a new earth in which evil would not exist. The birth of such a new world was colorfully described in the abundant apocalyptic literature of the time, in which images had taken the place of concepts.

These two opposite orientations can be illustrated by the two possible translations of the Hebrew term for the far distant future: 'AHARIT HA-YAMIM. It can be translated "the last days," meaning the last period of history, or alternatively "the end of days," meaning the period beyond history. These two ideal types allow for various kinds of concrete combinations. Maimonides in the twelfth century crystallized Jewish tradition in terms of first the messianic age (the last days), followed later by eternal life (the end of days).

Though perfecting this world or creating a new world is ultimately the work of God, nevertheless, in many scenarios God would achieve his purpose through the agency of an "anointed one," a "christ," be he king, priest, prophet, or a combination of these. The Essenes, for example, were expecting the coming of a prophet, followed by two messiahs, the anointed High Priest, meaning the Messiah of Aaron, and the anointed King, meaning the Davidic Messiah, the two working hand in hand. What was really important was the establishment of the perfect sovereignty of God with or without a christ.

During the period of Temple Judaism there were no opinion polls to tell us which messianic orientation was most generally accepted. There is a large consensus among Jewish and Christian historians that at the beginning of the first century C.E. many in Israel looked forward to an imminent intervention of God in political and military terms. They expected a descendant of David to appear, to overthrow the yoke of Roman occupation, and to make Jerusalem the political center of the world. The priestly aristocracy and the cosmopolitan merchant class might have preferred that nothing would ever happen, while the impatient zealots were already taking matters into their own hands; but the majority was probably looking forward to the coming of a King Messiah who would restore the kingdom to Israel. Were there many hoping for a radical end of times, for proximate death and resurrection, for a heavenly Jerusalem? It is not known. The fact that apocalyptic literature was taboo in Rabbinic Judaism, and was preserved mostly by Christian hands, does not mean that it had not been widely read in the period before the Jewish Wars. Still, the apocalyptic vision seemed to express a minor trend compared to a more mundane messianism.

John, son of Zechariah, was probably one of those who were looking toward an apocalyptic end in the near future. His baptism with water was a preparation for a baptism with fire. His appeal to the masses was pressing: "Repent, for the kingdom of Heaven has come near" (Matt 3:2). This proclamation was not well received by the religious authorities in Jerusalem; they were not convinced and they refused to believe in him (Mark 11:31). According to Flavius Joseph, Herod the Tetrarch:

> . . .who feared lest the great influence John had over the people might put into his power and inclination to raise a rebellion (for they seemed ready to do any thing he should advise), thought it best, by putting him to death, to prevent any mischief he might cause, and not bring himself into difficulties by sparing a man who might make him repent of it when it should be too late. Accordingly he was sent a prisoner, out of Herod's suspicious temper, to Macherus...and was there put to death.[1]

3. THE MESSIANISM OF JESUS OF NAZARETH

If at the beginning of his public life Jesus of Nazareth seemed to speak and act in the footsteps of John, very quickly real differences appeared in the details of their activities. John's voice crying in the wilderness was calling people to come to him to be baptized. Jesus was visiting the country towns of Galilee, speaking in the synagogues on Shabbat and accepting invitations to private homes:

> For John came neither eating nor drinking, and they say, "He has a demon"; the Son of Man came eating and drinking, and they say, "Look, a glutton and a drunkard, a friend of the tax collectors and sinners!" (Matt 11:18–19).

John had put special emphasis on baptism to achieve spiritual and bodily purity; Jesus was known rather as a healer and teacher. Were such differences significant? Were they perceived by those who were curious or sympathetic toward Jesus?

Jesus' favorite expression was "Kingdom of God," not "kingdom of the Messiah." Can we say confidently that its meaning was obvious to his listeners? Given the paucity of historical documents, it is difficult to ascertain the current signification of the term. The best supposition remains that the expression evoked the vision of a new age in the image of the glorious past under David and Solomon. Just moments before Jesus' departure the apostles were still asking: "Lord, has the time come for you to restore the kingdom to Israel?" (Acts 1:6). From this text we can conclude that to his followers Jesus was first a prophet of the restoration of Israel, a prophet of the last days, rather than a prophet of the end of history. To validate this affirmation we will need to deal satisfactorily with the undeniable streaks of radical eschatology present in the teaching of Jesus, because they seem to challenge any earthly hope for the restoration of the kingdom to Israel.

As noted, in passing from the anonymity of a life in Nazareth to the limelight of a life of healing and teaching, the first act of Jesus was to receive baptism from John, son of Zechariah. By this act he accepted the task of working publicly, if not in the framework, at least against a background of radical eschatology. He expected that some day all would be made new (cf. Matt 19:28), and that the Son of Man coming in glory on Judgment Day would discriminate between the just and the wicked (Matt 25:31-46). The style of the eschatological discourses (Matt 24, Mark 13, Luke 21) is indeed very different from that of many parables, but the proclamation of the eschaton is echoed in the lessons of many of these. The end of time had to be expected, the time of the harvest, the drawing in of the fishing nets, the finding of the hidden treasure or the pearl of great value, the welcoming of the bridegroom with the closing of the door, etc. When all this will happen, however, remains God's secret. Jesus simply acknowledged his ignorance about the time of the end:

> But about that day or hour no one knows, neither the angels in heaven, nor the Son, but only the Father (Mark 13:32).

Those who acknowledged that Jesus of Nazareth had been graced by God with the gift of prophecy might have compared his vision of the future with the vision of the great prophets of Israel. They saw the immediate future (blessing or curse) against the background of the end of days, THE DAY OF THE LORD, the time when God's sovereignty will be fully acknowledged by all or, as Paul would say later, "so that God may be all in all" (1 Cor 15:28). To excise from the Gospels the texts which mention Jesus' vision of the end of days is a priori exegesis. It was possible for Jesus to have a prophetic vision of "the end of days" and still focus on what was for him the near future, "the last days," the time of his immediate involvement in the history of his people.

That his present role was messianic and not eschatological appears in a text which some might read as unimportant: "The Pharisees came and began to argue with him, asking him for a sign from heaven, to test him" (Mark 8:11–12). The Pharisees must have demanded a cosmic sign in the tradition of the apocalyptic literature, not some healing or exorcism. At the request for a sign Jesus showed some impatience. "Why does this generation ask for a sign? Truly I tell you, no sign shall be given to this generation" (Mark 8:12). Jesus' answer would make no sense if the requested sign referred to some healing activity. In the parallel text of Matthew, the evangelist adds: "...no sign will be given to it except the sign of the prophet Jonah" (Matt 12:39). Matthew has already lost the context of Jesus' saying; he interprets the sign of Jonah as a sign of Jesus' resurrection. However, the fact that Jesus later affirmed, "...there is something greater than Jonah here...and there is something greater than Solomon here" (Matt 12:41–42), indicates that the original meaning given to the incident by Jesus himself was not in terms of his future resurrection, but rather in terms of his own mission, a mission similar to the activities of Jonah and Solomon, the prophet who preached repentance and the king who was the perfect teacher of wisdom. Therefore Jesus was hoping to appear to his contemporaries less as a prophet of the end of history than as the central actor in the future restoration of the kingdom to Israel.

The figure of Solomon must have appeared out of context to Jesus' listeners. Solomon was not a typical messianic figure. The liberation of Israel would bring to mind the wonderful interventions of God in history rather than the mystery of Divine Wisdom, or the wise administration of a kingdom. Any proclamation of the imminence of God's Kingdom would evoke the figure of King David, or at least some strong military or political figure. As previously noted, liberation from the yoke of Roman occupation was at that time the core of the people's aspirations. If the end of this world, the "end of days," had been around the corner, liberation from the Roman yoke would have become superfluous. On the contrary, if God's intervention was to usher in "the last days," the final period of history, the liberation of Israel remained supremely important. Jesus, however, was a pacifist. At the time of his arrest he proclaimed, "Put your sword back into its place; for all who take the sword will perish by the sword" (Matt 26:52). It would not be surprising if Judas Iscariot and others among his disciples wondered and worried about his ability to lead a successful military campaign.

Moreover, Jesus himself seemed to discourage any idea that he was a political Messiah—notwithstanding the very strong Davidic messianism in Luke's Gospel of the infancy. The fourth Gospel might have kept alive the memory of an authentic incident after the miracle of the loaves:

> When the people saw the sign that he had done, they began to say, "This is indeed the prophet who is to come into the world." When Jesus realized that they were about to come and take him by force to make him king, he withdrew again to the mountain by himself (John 6:14–15).

The so-called messianic secret which runs through most of Mark's Gospel is a clear confirmation of Jesus' attitude. Jesus simply refused to identify in any way with the dynastic messianism of Proto-Isaiah or with any politico-military movement which would achieve the liberation of Israel and the inauguration of God's sovereignty through the forcible expulsion of the Romans from the land. In this serious matter Jesus and the majority of his brothers and sisters were not quite on the same wavelength.

If Jesus drew back from the title KING MESSIAH, was he without any messianic consciousness whatsoever? E. P. Sanders in JESUS AND JUDAISM, after a critical analysis of Jesus' activity rather than his teaching, states: "Most of the things which we know about Jesus with virtually complete certainty fit rather neatly into the category of a prophet of Jewish restoration."[2] He illustrates this statement with four points:

1. Jesus began his career as a follower of John.

2. He chose 12 disciples who later would argue about their position in the government of the kingdom.

3. The cleansing of the temple was not an act of purification or edification, but a sign of the coming of a new or renewed temple in the new age.

4. Immediately after the resurrection, the disciples worked within the framework of Jewish restoration expectation.

Sanders moreover recognizes that Jesus manifested a clear awareness of his central role in this process of restoration, which would end by a mighty act of God in the near future. On the other hand, Jesus never gave any description of how God would exercise his sovereignty in a purified and renewed Israel, nor of the human agents who were to be employed to help God achieve his purpose.

Perhaps Jesus revealed his vision concerning the restoration of the kingdom to Israel only to a few disciples. "To you it has been given to know the secrets of the kingdom of heaven, but to them it has not been given" (Matt 13:11). Does this mean that Jesus had an esoteric teaching, reserved for an intimate circle of disciples, and different from what he taught sympathizers and crowds? If we combine this possibility with the fact that some of the sayings and parables of Jesus, transmitted orally for a few years, have come to us as isolated units extricated from their setting, it becomes extremely difficult to chronicle the development of Jesus' teaching. Whether speaking to the crowds, or privately to his own disciples, Jesus seems to have only progressively disclosed what was in his mind and heart. We have to wait for his farewell address at the Last Supper to hear the disciples saying, "Yes, now you are speaking plainly, not in any figure of speech!" (John 16:29).

4. JESUS AND THE COMMON PEOPLE

It is difficult to precisely evaluate the impact of Jesus' teaching among the 'AM HA-ARETZ, the common people, our main interest in this section. In his preaching at large, was Jesus presenting anything more than an urgent appeal to return to God, to become good Jews, sincere and generous, and to trust in God who was soon going to visit his people with power? His healings and exorcisms might have been signs that God was starting to manifest his messianic power in the life of Israel. The day of salvation was at hand. John, son of Zechariah, had spoken of judgment. Jesus was speaking of hope, of good news. At the beginning of his ministry he had said, "Those who are well have no need of a physician, but those who are sick; I have come to call not the righteous, but sinners" (Mark 2:17). And it was "to the lost sheep of the house of Israel" (Matt 10:6) that the twelve were sent on a mission. Was the

Jesus movement anything more than a revival movement in preparation for some hoped-for messianic event?

There are indubitable signs that Jesus occasionally pointed toward something else, particularly in conversation with close disciples. These hints at a new interpretation of Judaism are hard to analyze. Some lead us to probe the nature of Jesus' spirituality and personality; others introduce us furtively into his vision of the kingdom, of the expected new age. All exegetes agree that Jesus was an intensely religious person. He was totally God-oriented and preferred nothing whatsoever to the will of God. In a sense this attitude was the perfect expression of the sanctification of the Name, of the binding power of the covenant. To this intense love of the living God, Jesus joined an effortless love of neighbor. For him love of God and love of neighbor were in perfect harmony. This once granted, can we affirm that the same harmony existed between his love of God and a possible love of the world, world understood not in the Johannine sense of the congregation of sinners, but in the sense of the multifaceted splendor of creation, especially in its humanistic expressions?

In his classic JESUS OF NAZARETH, Joseph Klausner never tires of insisting that Judaism is the way of life of one particular nation, that it is a culture and a society in which the sacred and the profane are not parallel or alternate, but fused into a theocratic unity—despite the malaise of modern Zionism vis-à-vis the traditional religion. The parable of the lilies of the field is beautifully poetic, but can a "nation" live simply by trusting in God without worrying about tomorrow? In a Jewish context, a religious doctrine which would focus exclusively on the relation of each individual with his God and his neighbor, a relation presented moreover in purely ethical or mystical terms, would sound strange and unreal. The prophetic style, even of John, son of Zechariah, was always to interpellate the whole nation, or at least its leaders. Was the imminent coming of the Kingdom of God, of God's sovereignty, concerning only the welfare of the individual Jew, or also specifically the welfare of all the people which God had chosen for his own?

Jesus did not project an ascetic image. He did not invite his disciples to fast; he accepted invitations to banquets. On the other hand, his ethical ideal was quite rigorous. The rich must not only give alms, they must share their wealth with the poor. The one who is attacked must turn the other cheek. Marriage was indissoluble, and continence for the sake of the Kingdom was highly praised. The taking of oaths and the fostering of quarrels were prohibited. Finally, the hated Roman soldier, the enemy, must be loved. There was such a reversal of values here, the last becoming the first, that one may wonder if Jesus was speaking of the immediate application of these precepts in everyday life, or was preparing rather his close disciples to teach and lead the people later when the Kingdom would have come, and God's gracious intervention would have changed the hearts of men and women as promised by Jeremiah and Ezekiel. It has been shown by Klausner that for each one of Jesus' new precepts a parallel saying can be found somewhere in MISHNAH, TALMUD, MIDRASH, or SIDDUR. What is unique is the way these various precepts, when they are brought together, form a new GESTALT, a new spirit, what Klausner called "an exaggerated Judaism."[3] The question then arises: how much of this "exaggerated Judaism" was communicated to the masses, the 'AM HA-ARETZ, listening to Jesus? Possibly very little; enough, however, to create a feeling of awe and otherness. Jesus offered mere glimpses of a new age, a new social order. Though it would be a reality of this world, it would have enough unfamiliar characteristics to be described by E. P. Sanders as other-worldly, not otherworldly-heavenly, but rather otherworldly earthly.[4]

Those brought up in the Christian tradition will always find it hard to enter into the historical world in which Jesus lived and into his own history as it really took form. The reason is simple. What was primary in Jesus' earthly life became secondary for his disciples after his resurrection, and what was secondary became primary. J. Ramsey Michael suggests the possibility of an emerging consensus in interpretation if all exegetes would recognize that, "In many different ways Jesus affirms the traditional Jewish expectations, yet he gives them what Henry James would call a 'turn of the screw,' a new twist that shocks his hearers and in some respect calls their behavior and world view into question."[5] In the teaching of the Apostles this new twist would eventually lead to a reversal of perspectives. From God-centered the Kingdom became Messiah-centered, from being Israel-centered it became Gentile-centered, and from looking toward an approaching liberation it became some kind of realized eschatology.

Here we are concerned with the proclamation of the Kingdom not as it was understood after the Resurrection, but at the time when Jesus was still sharing our present human condition. It was a Jewish event in a purely Jewish context. With his contemporaries Jesus was looking toward and hoping for the imminent breaking in of the full sovereignty of God. We saw that he could not fully share the immobilism of the Sadducean priesthood, nor the fantastic scenarios of the apocalyptists, nor the more sober expectations of a military-political overthrow of the Roman occupation. Was there anything left? Geza Vermes, the noted Jewish scholar at Oxford, suggests the existence of a fourth trend in messianism. In JESUS AND THE WORLD OF JUDAISM he wrote:

> It was largely an exilic and postexilic phenomenon, attested already by
> Deutero and Trito-Isaiah in the second half of the sixth century BC....(Isa

60:1–6). A pure and sanctified Israel was to draw the Gentiles to God. The manifestation of God's sovereignty over his own was to serve as a magnet for the rest.[6]

Geza Vermes does not develop this messianic concept, which remained a minor trend in Judaism. From all the books of the Hebrew Scriptures, the Deutero-Trito Isaiah is the closest to the spirit of Jesus of Nazareth. Luke used Isaiah 61 to introduce Jesus' ministry (Luke 4:18), and Jesus himself quoted Isaiah to answer the doubts of John, the son of Zechariah (Matt 11:4, Luke 7:22). In Deuteronomy Moses had promised, "The Lord your God will raise up for you a prophet like me from among your own people; you shall heed such a prophet" (Deut 18:15). The Messiah, the Deliverer, would manifest himself in the role of a prophet. For the Samaritans the future Messiah, the TAEB, was characterized as a prophet rather than a warrior.

If such a messianic conception had existed in Israel at the time of Jesus—and it would have been among a very small minority—Jesus would have found it very congenial. We can surmise that in his late twenties he had an inaugural vision, similar to the calls of Isaiah, Jeremiah or Ezekiel, a profound mystical experience in which God disclosed to him that, though the end of time had not yet come, he would give him the Spirit without reserve to usher in the restoration of Israel, establish the kingdom of the last days, secure the ingathering of the exiles (Isa 60:4), and make Jerusalem the mother of all nations (Isa 2:3). Jesus was to win not by the sword but by the Spirit. At the appropriate time there would be a powerful manifestation of the Spirit as promised by the prophet Joel, but this visible manifestation had first to be prepared. It would happen in the framework of the covenant, which meant not as an act of pure grace, of God acting alone, but as an act of synergy, of divine and human activity. It was to be a theo-anthropic activity. God's Messiah and God's people had to play their part in it. That is why, on the basis of the eschatological consciousness which had been greatly strengthened by the mission of John, son of Zechariah, Jesus would have to prepare all of Israel to become in time recipients of the gifts of the Spirit. They had to learn to assume their full responsibility and to fulfill the tasks God was calling them to.

It is obvious that in such a vision of spiritual messianism the central role had to be played by the religious authorities of the house of Israel. Jesus always recognized the authority of the High Priest and of the sons of Aaron. Concerning the emerging spiritual power of the scribes, Jesus had said, "The scribes and the Pharisees sit on Moses' seat; therefore do whatever they teach you and follow it" (Matt 23:2–3). For Jesus to convince these authorities of the nature of his mission and to have them ready to receive God's visitation was the core of his prophetic role. Given the religious structure of Israel at that time, there was little probability that the majority of the people would have accepted Jesus' charismatic leadership without the approval of these religious authorities, who were sometimes criticized but still highly respected. This question is so important that it will have to be discussed in another section.

We know that such an approval never came. This abstention kept the common people hesitant, attracted to Jesus as a man of God, but confused about his mission. Suddenly a crisis erupted after a sermon in the synagogue at Capernaum, as recorded at the end of chapter six in the Gospel of John. After many of his disciples had heard it, they said, "This teaching is difficult; who can accept it?" (John 6:60). After this crisis many of his disciples left him. Following this incident Jesus left Galilee and resolutely took the road to Jerusalem (Luke 9:51); he expected mostly hardship and had to face the probability of martyrdom. The little group of his faithful followers became more closely knit. Many in the crowd were still curious or admiring, but somehow the masses were not entering into the spiritual magnetism of Jesus' personality. He seemed to be a question more than an answer. Nowhere, however, do we find any negative attitude toward him among the AM HA-ARETZ. Those who did not become his devout disciples kept a certain psychological distance from him. They respected him, were certainly grateful for his healings but, notwithstanding his tireless efforts, they had not been able to enter into his vision of the Kingdom of God.

In announcing the good news of the Kingdom Jesus was insisting: Wait and be vigilant. At the hour you do not expect, it will be here. Be always ready! And they waited with hope and apprehension. They waited, they waited...and the Kingdom never came. Then the one who had awakened genuine hopes died a miserable death at the hands of the Romans without any sign whatsoever of divine intervention. "But we had hoped that he was the one to redeem Israel" (Luke 24:21). They, the ordinary people, never rejected him. He had given them honest hopes. These hopes did not materialize, and once more the 'AM HA-ARETZ were disappointed.

Jesus also had hopes. He had hoped that his own people would go with him faithfully through the pangs of the coming of the Messiah. He died disappointed, alone with God. This was probably his greatest suffering.

III. The Story of a No

A religious dialogue between Jews and Christians will never get very far if it leaves out of consideration the primitive source of their mutual repudiation, i.e., the conflict between Jesus of Nazareth and the legitimate religious authorities of Israel. Rabbi Henry Siegman has remarked very perceptively[1] that what impels Christians to dialogue with Jews is the mystery of the Jewish rejection of Christianity. We argued in the last chapter that the 'AM HA-ARETZ, the common people, did not reject Jesus; they wondered at his teaching, shared his hope for the imminent coming of God's Kingdom, and were disappointed by his miserable end. The same cannot be said of the religious leaders. Their attitude seems to have become increasingly negative. Given their position in the religious structure of Judaism, this attitude could not but have a deep influence on those who were hesitating to become followers of Jesus.

At that time the religious authorities were the only remaining national authorities in Israel. Of the three traditional institutions of the earlier periods— monarchy, priesthood and prophecy—only the priesthood had survived. The House of David faded away after Zerubbabel. The Hasmoneans and Herodian dynasties, not being Davidic, notwithstanding some brilliant political successes, had never built a deep legitimacy among the religious people. Meanwhile Rome had conquered and was ruling from above. After Ezra the great voice of prophecy had become completely silent. (The book of Daniel is not a prophetic book in the Hebrew canon.) For already 400 years—a long time—the only religious authority had been the priesthood as the custodian of the Law and the sole mediator between God and Israel. The man who was transmitting the Law in writing, and also translating it orally from Hebrew to Aramaic, explaining— even interpreting—to the people its often obscure meaning, the SOFER or scribe, became increasingly important for the well-being of Jewish society. A scribal authority, parallel but inferior to the priestly authority, emerged out of the requirements of everyday life. Its influence increased with the growth of education and literacy. The scribe became the teacher of the people and the judge who would declare the Law in particular cases. When the authority of the priesthood disappeared with the destruction of the Temple, the scribe was ready to become the rabbi, the spiritual leader of the community.

Priest and scribe refer to religious roles with specific authority. Sadducee and Pharisee, on the other hand, refer to specific attitudes in matters of doctrine, spirituality, and ritual. Their protagonists formed cliques and political groupings involved in intense rivalry. Judaism at that time was genuinely pluralistic. The Essenes and Zealots were on the fringe. Most of the priests were Sadducees and most of the scribes, except those working in the Temple, Pharisees. The scribe-Pharisees, less strong in Jerusalem, were the predominant influence in the outlying districts. They were the first religious authority Jesus encountered during his preaching in Galilee. Later on in Jerusalem his encounter would be principally with the Sadducees, the Temple clergy.

1. THE AUTHORITY OF JESUS OF NAZARETH

There is a serious obstacle, not easily overcome, in the quest for the exact relation between Jesus and the religious establishment. The Gospels, except possibly that of Mark, were written after the destruction of the Temple, at a time when all religious parties were in the process of disappearing, except for the Pharisees and the Nazarenes, i.e., the Jewish Christians. Judaism was reemerging in a new form, synagogue-centered rather than Temple-centered. There was a tense, sometimes bitter, relationship between this renewed Judaism and the new way of the Nazarenes. It is not surprising that the Christian oral tradition, and later its written tradition, instinctively selected among the incidents and sayings in the life of Jesus those which witnessed to negative attitudes toward scribes and Pharisees, although these had been sporadic and directed toward a few controversialists. Today there is a near consensus among exegetes that the animosity between Synagogue and Church at the end of the first century A.D. was of a different nature than the animosity between Jesus and the legitimate religious leaders of Israel. It is important for all of us, Jews and Christians, to reconstruct the original situation, and, if possible, to discover the nature of that small tear in the fabric of Temple Judaism which very quickly was to become a deepening rent.

How did Jesus appear to the scribe-Pharisees when his preaching started to attract huge crowds? Jesus was a Jew, but he was not a Judean. He was a Galilean who had grown up in Nazareth. "Can anything good come out of Nazareth?" (John 1:46). Galilee had been judaized for little more than a century. We must not project back into the time of Jesus the prosperity and literacy of the Jewish Galilean community of the second to the sixth century C.E. In the first century it was still a pioneering land, cut off from Judea by Samaria, with a non-Jewish population along the coast in the west and another one in the east, in the Decapolis. Religious and cultural activities were low-key, but Jewish self-consciousness was very high. Galilee was a hotbed of zealotry and rebellion. It is not surprising that to the sophisticated Jerusalemites the Galileans appeared uncouth and boorish. This was a strike against Jesus, at least when he encountered scribes who had come from Judea.

More serious was the fact that Jesus was an autodidact. He must have learned to read and write at the local synagogue in Nazareth. There is no sign that he attended a BEIT MIDRASH, and not the slightest indication that he had been the disciple of a respected master. (Even Paul claimed that he studied under Gamaliel, Acts 22:3.) If it had been otherwise, Jesus would have referred to the fact in order to get the ear of his listeners. People admired his wisdom, the apropos of his repartees and the beauty of his style, but he spoke only in parables and aphorisms and did not argue in the customary manner of the scribes. He may have been very effective in exhorting the people to a better life, but according to the criteria of scribes and scholars, he could not speak with authority. We know how autodidacts are received by professionals who have had to take all the steps of a long training. They might be received on account of their excellence, but they never really belong. With the priestly authorities Jesus, as a member of the tribe of Judah, had no link whatsoever. Being neither priest nor scribe, he could in no way be regarded as belonging to the religious establishment. He was a HASID, an especially pious and devout layman, who could proclaim a religious message only on the basis of his moral or charismatic authority.

Paradoxically it was the success of Pharisaism which gave Jesus the possibility of proclaiming his own message. Pharisaism was not an organization or a set of doctrines, but a spiritual movement with specific aspirations which could take different forms. It had its origin in a little-known movement existing before the Great Persecution. These HASIDIM, the pious ones, gave the Maccabees a nucleus of courageous and enthusiastic fighters who, against great odds, were able to lift from Israel the yoke of the heathen. Restoration, reconstruction, renovation, even reform, were in the air. The old aristocratic priestly families were satisfied with the purification of the Temple, a return to the status quo and, later, various political compromises with the powers that be. The progressive, creative elements, however, were looking for a more authentic religious life. Soon they came to split from the Hasmonaean dynasty and then among themselves. The heirs of Judas Maccabee had become too secular and too political. Power corrupts! Simeon, the brother of Judas, accepted the title of High Priest, though his priestly family was not in the lineage of Zadok. A group of priests led by the Teacher of Righteousness declared the Temple in Jerusalem polluted, struggled against the Wicked Priest, and established on the shore of the Dead Sea, at Qumran, a community of the "True Israel," the Essenes, centered on true worship and priestly authority.

Those who were later called the Pharisees, "the separated ones," went in the other direction. They were laymen who wanted to extend the holiness of Temple worship into everyday life by asking the laity to observe the laws of ritual purity imposed on the priests, to strictly observe the Sabbath, to fulfill all the obligations of tithing, etc. It was a democratization of religious life emphasizing the personal relation of the individual with God. In opposition to the Sadducees they encouraged learning and creativity in the development of Jewish Law, accepting an Oral Law parallel to the Written Torah. Modern Jewish scholarship has been able to redress the blanket condemnation of Pharisaism common to all Christian traditions. (The Webster New World Dictionary gives as the second definition of pharisaic, "self-righteous, sanctimonious.") Certainly there were bad Pharisees; some are described and condemned in the TALMUD itself. But the great figures of Hillel, Shammai, Gamaliel and the saintly Rabbi Akiva, the martyr, were shining examples of the depth of religious life created by God's Spirit in and through this strand of Judaism. In the JEROME BIBLICAL COMMENTARY we read: "...it must be admitted that the Gospel evaluation of the Pharisees, since it emerged from an apologetic context, is far too negative and does not give the Pharisees sufficient credibility for being a constructive spiritual force."[2]

2. THE PHARISEES' RESPONSE

If modern criticism builds a favorable picture of the Pharisaic movement and of its unique role in saving Judaism from extinction, how can we explain the unfriendly relationship between Jesus of Nazareth and some of the contemporary Pharisees? The Gospels, influenced by later disputes, do not give us an exact picture; nevertheless, the fact remains that a certain tension existed between some Pharisees and the Jesus movement. Paradoxically, most historians would classify Jesus as a Pharisee. All agree he was not a Sadducee, an Essene, or a Zealot. He believed in the Oral Law, the resurrection, the personal relationship with God, and most other Pharisaic tenets. The fact that some Pharisees did not like him was no surprise. We can always find some bad apples in the basket of most religious traditions, including the Christian ones. But what about the good Pharisees? There must have been something in Jesus' behavior or teaching which made even good Pharisees recoil from him.

Rather than one factor which alone would explain this negative attitude, we will probably find a constellation of different factors, some of greater and others of minor importance. We have already mentioned Jesus' Galilean origin and his status as an autodidact. These were minor factors. More important could be the differences in temperament and in attitude toward the Law.

The Pharisees were perfectionists. They needed to know exactly what is right and what is wrong. They were interested in details. They wanted holiness to be experienced in every aspect of secular life in order to achieve harmony between the will of God and human activity. From the history of monastic life we have learned what happens when a spirit of absolute perfection bewitches the soul of some monastic leader or reformer. He needs detailed rules, and not only rules but also regulations, procedures, customaries, ceremonials, etc., in which external behavior is emphasized and human beings become spiritual machines deprived of spiritual spontaneity. Religious communities which are strong and lasting always face the risk of this kind of alienation. The richness and complexity of religious life attained by Temple Judaism at the time of Jesus made this a very real danger. Jesus did not condemn external observances, far from it (Matt 23:23), but he insisted that outward behavior be the expression of internal dispositions. He seems to have been allergic to any form of alienation; hence his emphasis on sincerity and his aversion for hypocrisy. He lived fully the SHEMA ISRAEL, the command to love with all your heart, all your soul and all your might. He did not seem to welcome an excessive number of regulations. He wanted a certain spiritual space for the soul to breathe freely, and he was not anxious to extend to all Israel the rules of ritual purity which were appropriate for priestly service in the Temple. Consequently, there were enough small differences in life-style between the Pharisees and Jesus that they would be unwilling to identify with each other.

The attitude toward the Law is a more important and more difficult problem, given the Law's centrality in the religious life of Israel. We must absolutely avoid projecting into Jesus' situation the problem Paul faced as apostle to the Gentiles. This error has poisoned modern exegesis. All the contemporary Jewish writers who have studied the life of Jesus agree that he was SHOMER MITZVOT, an observant Jew, who de facto lived consciously according to HALACHAH. We have a clear text in the introduction to the Sermon on the Mount in the gospel of Matthew:

> Do not think that I have come to abolish the law or the prophets; I have come not to abolish but to fulfill. For truly I tell you, until heaven and earth pass away, not one letter, not one stroke of a letter, will pass from the law until all is accomplished (Matt 5:17-18).

A parallel text without context seems lost in the gospel of Luke, who wrote for the Gentiles, but the text must have come from tradition, "It is easier for heaven and earth to pass away, than for one stroke of a letter in the law to be dropped" (Luke 16:17). Jesus never conducted himself in opposition to the Written Law. A few times he contradicted it in his teaching, as in the case concerning divorce, but he based his ruling on other texts of the Torah and his intention was to make the observance of the Law not easier but more stringent. These few cases remain the exceptions which confirm the rule.

The real problem was Jesus' attitude vis-à-vis the Oral Law which the Pharisees considered as sacred as the Written Law and as equally given to Moses on Mount Sinai. It would not be put in writing in the MISHNAH and TOSEPHTA until 200 years after the time of Jesus. The history of this legal codification remains obscure. As known by Jesus it might still have had a flexibility which became lost in the subsequent period. Without any doubt Jesus expressed personal opinions on such borderline matters as do's and don'ts in the observance of the Sabbath, the completion of vows, and the extension of the rules of purity. In these matters Jesus tended to be more lenient than the Pharisees, and seemed to exclude a strict regimentation of religious life. In all these rulings the main question was on what authority this self-made man was basing his legal decisions. He had only one ground to stand on, the moral authority of a HACHAM, a wise and holy man.

Exegetes have pinpointed an area in the behavior and teaching of Jesus which could cause not only annoyance or irritation, but genuine hurt to the spiritual sensitivity of the average Pharisee: Jesus' attitude toward sinners. He was not afraid to approach them or to be approached by them. He was not reproaching or rejecting, but friendly and inspiring. John, son of Zechariah, had been harshly condemning. Concerning the Apostles, E. P. Sanders in JESUS AND JUDAISM writes, "A high tolerance for sinners was not characteristic of the early church, as far as we know it."[3] Jesus' attitude and behavior were, in fact, very unusual. The Pharisees' opposition is generally explained by Jesus' publicly breaking the rules of ritual purity. Was it truly a matter of ritual purity? The Pharisees were very well able to see the difference between a ritual omission and a real moral fault. We can surmise that for them the sight of Jesus in table fellowship with some 'AM HA-ARETZ would naturally arouse contempt, but the sight of Jesus eating with tax collectors and public sinners would arouse not simply contempt but moral indignation.

It was the great prophets of Israel who awoke in humanity the experience of sin. Human life is often a long history of failures, but in most societies men and women do not sin, they simply lose face on account of their mistakes and bear the legal consequences of their acts. It is only Judaism and its daughter religions which have linked social and personal behavior with the holiness of God. Genuine sensitivity to human integrity is sui generis; it does not need to be upheld by rational, aesthetic, social, or even religious values. In Judaism, however, the moral and religious aspects of human behavior are inseparably united: "You shall be holy, for I the Lord your God am holy" (Lev 19:2). This call from God is the leitmotif of the Mosaic revelation. Israel in her history developed a deep moral sense, and her religion has been aptly called ethical monotheism. Surprisingly for some, her original prayer book, the Psalter, in at least a third of the psalms, is like a school of hatred—a special hatred indeed—hatred of the wicked who emerges as the personal enemy of God and of the just. A more permissive moral sense in the twentieth century might hinder us from fully sharing in the sentiments of the psalmist. Jesus as well as the Pharisees was well attuned to this moral sensitivity. Even in our age of liberalism the ordinary churchgoer would still feel uncomfortable if the local bishop was discovered becoming chummy with Mafia leaders and tainted politicians, or the local pastor was starting to frequent shady bars supposedly to bring back to God the lost sheep.

It was the prophets who had initiated a moral division in the house of Israel by separating the wicked from the just. In so doing they had destroyed the perfect unity of the nation by creating one or various groups which did not belong fully to God's people. Until then only individuals had been acknowledged as sinners rejected by God. In Temple Judaism the Pharisees and the Essenes tended to monopolize holiness for themselves. Without speaking of monasticism, many Christian Churches have experienced similar trends toward holiness marked by exclusivism. The Pharisees were very conscious of their being the true Israel. The 'AM HA-ARETZ were to be pitied, but sinners were to be hated and kept at a distance the way today we keep at a distance a person with an infectious disease.

Jesus was never accused of being personally wicked, but his behavior was puzzling. He did not simply preach repentance; he approached sinners, welcomed them (Luke 15:3), sat at the same table (Mark 2:15), let a scarlet woman anoint and kiss his feet (Luke 7:36-50), admonished Peter to pardon seventy-seven times (Matt 18:21), and told his listeners that "the tax collectors and prostitutes are going into the kingdom of God ahead of you" (Matt 21:31). It is easy to imagine the reaction of some pious Pharisees at hearing such statements and witnessing such behavior. Their mentality, as their name implied (the separated ones), was one of exclusion of others and inclusion of their own. They could not deny that Jesus was an observant Jew, nor could they consider him a Sadducee, Essene or Zealot, but they could not include him in their own circle. Though he was too sophisticated to be an 'AM HA-

ARETZ, many could not see in him a builder of the true Israel; he might even endanger its future. His friendly relations with tax collectors and sinners, whose actual repentance was not always very clear, indicated that he was not "coming from God." Some even accused him of being a deceiver, casting out devils in the name of Beelzebul, the prince of the devils (Matt 12:24). Jesus had said, "Those who are well have no need of a physician, but those who are sick....For I have come to call not the righteous but sinners" (Matt 9:12-13). In the society in which Jesus was born it was not easy to be at the same time the friend of the virtuous and of the sinners. To the extent that for his listeners it was inconceivable that someone could at the same time hate the sin and love the sinner, Jesus' moral authority was becoming questionable.

It would take about fifty years for the Pharisaic movement to take a completely negative attitude toward the Jesus movement. New factors would come into play. At the time of Jesus some Pharisees were attracted to his teaching (Mark 12:28–34); some, like Nicodemus, may have visited him in secret (John 3); some, like Gamaliel, thought it better to leave Jesus' disciples alone (Acts 5:34–39). It remains that for the average Pharisee Jesus must have looked like a non-conformist. Moreover, by choosing twelve disciples as future leaders of a restored Israel and allowing the rising of a popular movement among the 'AM HA-ARETZ, he appeared as a potential rival. He was to be contradicted or even fought against in disputed matters, but there is no clear evidence that the bulk of the Pharisees ever wanted to eliminate him. At that time Judaism was basically pluralistic. The fight was a family quarrel which was not lacking any of the customary Jewish overtones as exemplified in the Essene literature.

3. THE SADDUCEES' RESPONSE

Modern scholarship tends to see the attitude of the Sadducees vis-à-vis Jesus and his disciples in a very different light. Though some priests might have been Pharisees, the majority belonged to a strong Sadducean party, dominated by the aristocratic families from which the High Priest was chosen. They controlled the Temple in Jerusalem, its elaborate ritual as well as its material resources. They were the supreme religious authority, and Jesus had very little chance to become the chosen instrument for the restoration of Israel if they refused to acknowledge his authority. Most of the factors we have described in the attitudes of the people or the Pharisees were also found in the attitudes of the Sadducees toward Jesus, but with them there were other and more serious factors. First, Jesus looked to the Sadducees like a maverick Pharisee. He was one of "them," one of the enemy camp. This was enough to awaken suspicion. If the proclamation of the imminent arrival of the Kingdom of God was not disturbing for the Pharisees, it certainly disturbed the Sadducees, who were most anxious to keep the status quo. Moreover, they were concerned with social stability and had reached a certain MODUS VIVENDI with the power of Rome. Any messianic pretender able to gather a strong following (and some did in the first century) could be a national danger—if he could not prove that he was a true messiah. According to Josephus, as noted earlier, this is the way Herod Antipas looked at John, son of Zechariah, and had him put to death.

The central factor in the attitude of the Sadducees toward Jesus was the latter's attitude vis-à-vis the Temple. Contrary to the Essenes at Qumran, Jesus never spoke against the priesthood as such. When he was in Jerusalem he frequently taught in the Temple. Later his disciples, or at least some of them, would remain faithful Templegoers (Acts 2:46). But in his teaching Jesus seemed to imply that in the new age the present Temple should be transformed or rebuilt. Such a statement was abhorrent to the Sadducees.

Much attention has been paid recently to Jesus' audacious expulsion of the merchants from the Temple. Given the nature of Jewish worship at that time, the selling of animals for the sacrifices in the outer courtyards was a normal and holy activity. In not allowing anyone to carry anything through the Temple (Mark 11:16), Jesus indicated that he did not have in mind an act of purification but was accomplishing a prophetic gesture, proclaiming that the present form of worship with its multiplicity of bloody sacrifices would soon come to an end and the new age would be inaugurated with a new or renewed Temple. If the people were bewildered, the hierarchy of the Temple must have experienced this gesture as a direct attack on their security. Jesus, for his part, knew that he had to challenge the highest authorities of the nation on the validity of his mission and his consequent claim to authority, as had Jeremiah in earlier times. These highest authorities were challenged to respond either yes or no.

The uproar in the Temple probably sealed Jesus' destiny. At his interrogation by the High Priest, the only two points which emerged out of the confusion of testimonies were his attitude toward the Temple and his messianic claims. It is argued by some that Roman security alone was the effective agent of Jesus' arrest. There is little doubt that after his messianic entry into Jerusalem and his brouhaha in the Temple they were keeping a constant eye upon him. It must also be recognized that the Jewish authorities had by then become unable to trust Jesus and in fact refused to give him the minimum of help and protection that national authorities are supposed to give any loyal citizen persecuted by a foreign power. They did not kill Jesus, no, but they did not stop the Romans from killing him, "they" meaning exclusively the reli-

gious establishment controlled by the Sadducees. That a group of Barrabas'
friends clamored for his release rather than Jesus' tells us nothing about the
true feelings of the Jerusalemites. They must have once more felt humiliated
by the shedding of innocent blood.

The tense relationship between Jesus and the Temple authorities is like a
Rorschach test revealing the crucial problem facing the religious establishment when Jesus became a public figure in Israel. "By what authority are you
doing these things? Who gave you this authority to do them?" (Mark 11:28).
The chief priests, the scribes and the elders must have felt that Jesus was not
simply a pious and devoted Jew, or a wise teacher, a HACHAM, or a charismatic rabbi practicing healing and exorcism. Jesus himself had asked, "Who
do people say that I am?" (Mark 8:27). Peter, representing the small circle of
faithful disciples, had answered, "You are the Messiah" (Mark 8:29). The people who already believed that John, son of Zechariah, was a real prophet
(Mark 11:32) must have thought that Jesus, though more enigmatic, resem-
bled a prophet more than anything else. But prophecy had been silent in Israel
for so long, and it was difficult for the religious authorities, accustomed to a
religion of interpretation rather than of revelation, suddenly to accept the
resurgence of the prophetic voice. Earlier, Jesus had asked them to recognize
that John's authority was coming from heaven; they refused to answer, and
Jesus refused to declare himself. Only during the very last days did he give a
hint that he was the Messiah sent by God.

It is a serious mistake in the ongoing Jewish-Christian dialogue to ignore
the witness of the fourth Gospel. The text makes very painful reading indeed
for our Jewish sisters and brothers. Who would be happy to be told, "You are
from your father, the devil" (John 8:44)? Moreover, many Christological texts
have been interpreted in Christian tradition as referring only to the eternal
Word of God without reference to Jesus' humanity. All this cannot be ignored.
The Johannine writings are now dated late first century, and their selection of
memories and sayings reflects the hurts felt by a Christian community recently expelled from the synagogue. There is increasing consensus, however, that
these Johannine writings, when critically analyzed, can be used as an independent source which saved for posterity some otherwise unknown historical
facts. One of them is the centrality of the clash, not between Jesus and the
Pharisees, but between Jesus and the Temple authorities, the strong
Sadducean party.

The fact that the fourth Gospel, for whatever reason, named these religious
authorities "The Jews" turned out to be a tragedy in subsequent history,
because it became a source of lasting anti-Judaism. Jews today are free to
approve or severely condemn the conduct of the Sadducean party at that criti-

cal hour in the history of their people. The impartial historian has to recognize that most Jews at that time, though they respected and acknowledged the authority of the High Priest and his counselors, had very little trust in the actual holders of these offices because of their unholy relations with the occupying powers. According to the fourth Gospel, notwithstanding a protracted controversy, which probably started to become intense at the Feast of the Tabernacles, six months before Jesus' trial, "many in the crowd believed in him" (John 7:31). Though "there was a division in the crowd because of him" (7:43), the Temple police thought, "Never has anyone spoken like this!" (7:46). Later "many believed in him" (8:30, 10:42, 11:45). Some of these texts might be redactional, but the GESTALT which emerges from John's Gospel is that the people were not unfriendly toward Jesus. They were wondering and waiting. "How long will you keep us in suspense? If you are the Messiah, tell us plainly" (10:24). Only a very small group, for reasons of their own, "were looking for an opportunity to kill him" (7:1). Unhappily this very small group was close to the center of the power structure.

The High Priest knew that his own authority came from God, that he was responsible for the well-being and survival of the House of Israel, and that he was surrounded by expert advice. He was suddenly asked to recognize an authority greater than his own. The real question was not which title would best fit Jesus: HACHAM, prophet, or even Messiah, nor the exact meaning of Jesus' quotation of Psalm 110:1, declaring that he would be seated at the right hand of God (Mark 12:35-37). At that moment the real question was: Who is the embodiment of the supreme authority in Israel, the High Priest or Jesus? Judge Haim Cohn, in his TRIAL AND DEATH OF JESUS,[4] suggests that the highest authorities had no real interest in cooperating with the Romans in this case, and that they would have saved Jesus if he had been willing to follow their guidance. "If"! Jesus, who had been so discreet during his public life, giving only some hints of his mission and refusing until the last week to be acclaimed as king-messiah, suddenly proclaimed himself as the one sent by God who had authority to speak in his name. Nothing in the religious life of Israel in 30 C.E. had prepared the High Priest and his entourage to accept such an outrageous claim, presented by a weak man abandoned by all his disciples. The High Priest must have looked at Jesus simply as a rebel who did not even want to be helped. He decided to let Roman justice take its course. He could not possibly trust "that man," notwithstanding his reputation for wisdom and piety among the simple 'AM HA-ARETZ.

Obviously we enter here into the realm of faith, not only faith in God but also faith in his messenger. The Scriptures warn us to be very careful about false prophets. Jesus himself spoke about false Messiahs. Only God can estimate the genuineness of a religious faith (often a social rather than a personal experience). Faith cannot be judged by historians, psychologists or sociologists. We have to respect its mystery. Israel had not always listened to its prophets. In the end the Jews did not receive Jesus of Nazareth as the voice of God. In the same way, centuries later, Jews and Christians would find themselves unable to accept the claim of Mohammed to be the seal of prophecy. In the case of Israel, however, the rejection of Jesus was a slow process which went through many steps. His rejection by the Temple authorities and the surrender of his fate to Roman justice, or rather injustice, were only the first step. Most of the Jewish people were in no way involved in this first step, and probably felt consternation at the tragic end of someone who had reawakened their messianic hope. Those who took on themselves to abandon Jesus remained in power for only a short time. Their influence on the people was probably minimal. They soon lost their role as well as their authority with the destruction of the Temple.

The parting of the ways may have been prefigured in the trial of Jesus. The crucifixion, however, is not the source of the permanent separation. The crucifixion was a tragedy which modern Jewish authors deplore as much as Christians. It is the faith of the disciples, proclaiming that the one who had been condemned and had died a miserable death was truly alive and was the hope of Israel, which started the wrenching process at the grass root level. Jesus of Nazareth, even on the cross, unites Jews and Christians; Jesus the Messiah, however, has separated them for nearly two thousand years.

IV. The Story of a Yes

Jesus of Nazareth encountered his own people not only in the story of a "no," but also in the story of a "yes." This yes was as much a Jewish story as the "no" we have just studied. If Christians are asked to make great efforts to understand all the factors which progressively coalesced into the "no" of the High Priest and his council, the same kind of effort could be asked of Jews interested in a Jewish-Christian dialogue to understand all the factors which entered into the very Jewish "yes" of Jesus' early disciples. It is part of their history, too.

It would be misleading to compare Jesus to a Christian missionary working in the midst of pagans, and inviting his listeners "to turn to God from idols, to serve a living and true God, and to wait for his Son from heaven...who rescues us from the wrath that is coming" (1 Thess 1:9–10). Jesus was addressing himself to his own compatriots who long ago had broken with idolatry, and were expecting the imminent coming of a messianic king to restore the kingdom to Israel. To get rid of the oppressive Roman occupation was their immediate concern. True, there were at that time religious tensions and disputes which weakened the national strength and would ultimately lead to the loss of political autonomy. There was a bitter contrast between the great promises made by God through the mouths of the prophets and the reality of everyday life. The people, however, were not close to despair. They saw themselves as God's people and remained faithful to him by worshiping him alone. In his own good time God would bring to bear on the situation his cleansing and revitalizing powers and would finally establish his Kingdom. Hope was for them an existential reality.

1. THE CALL TO DISCIPLESHIP

The fact that the first disciples of Jesus had been influenced by John, son of Zechariah, was as significant for them as John's baptism had been for

Jesus. It indicated clearly that they were seeking God and were caught in the messianic fever. Simple fishermen of Galilee, they were typical 'AM HA-ARETZ; they would not have gone all the way to the area of the Dead Sea if they had not been anxious to do the will of God, and had not been convinced that John was prophesying the imminent coming of the kingdom. They were not necessarily great sinners who needed to be converted. (Later, such ones as Levi, the tax collector, Mary of Magdala and other public sinners would become disciples.) Spiritually John, Andrew, Peter and James might have been average Jews, but as disciples of John their hearts were turned toward God and they were anxious to meet him at his coming. Given the confusion of the messianic expectations we have described above, it is impossible to guess what exactly they were waiting for. If at the suggestion of John, son of Zechariah, they left him to follow Jesus, they must have seen in the Nazarene someone who was more than a Galilean compatriot, someone more involved in the coming of the kingdom than John himself.

If we can believe the Johannine as well as the synoptic tradition, it was not the works of Jesus, his healings or exorcisms, which attracted the first disciples. They came to him before the wedding in Cana, at a time when Jesus was not yet known as a teacher and a healer. We are led to conclude that the main factor which influenced the early disciples, outside the witness of John, son of Zechariah, must have been Jesus' personality. We use the term here with a psychological rather than theological meaning. Putting in parentheses for the time being the ontological status of Jesus, we take for granted that he could not have been a true man without manifesting unique traits of character and temperament which deeply affected his interpersonal relationships. Some human beings evoke strong emotional reactions, positive or negative, to which none cannot remain indifferent. The fact that these reactions are mostly unconscious in no way diminishes their importance, quite the contrary. Given the literary genre of the Gospels, the human personality of Jesus is implied rather than described. It needs to be discovered and understood.

All who read the Gospels critically, trying to reconstruct the scenes of Jesus' ministry, will recognize in him a strong personality who could awaken in his listeners strong likes or dislikes, and have a lasting influence on those attracted to him. Joseph Klausner has tried to describe this unique personality at the end of his JESUS OF NAZARETH.[1] He found it full of paradoxes and in many ways puzzling. Jesus was open to deeply personal relationships. His desires may have been frustrated again and again, but the insistence with which he called his disciples "friends" at the last supper is a clear indication that he cared for deep mutual sharing with those willing to receive the gift of himself as well as his teaching.

Christians cannot deny that the importance given to the "ego" of Jesus in the Gospels does not accord completely with what we know of his people's expectations vis-à-vis their religious leaders. The dealings of ordinary people with priests and scribes did not call for much warmth and closeness. We can surmise that a more intimate relationship developed occasionally between master and disciple during the formative period of the rabbinic tradition. Respect for the master and care for his needs were certainly requested from any true disciple. Devotion, however, was oriented toward the Law, the word of the living God, rather than toward the interpreter. In the interpretation itself, though there was ample scope for individual opinion, the emphasis was placed on common opinion, the living tradition. Increasingly, Judaism had become allergic to any form of personality cult. The only exception, much criticized by other Jews, will be the unique position of the TZADIQ, the spiritual leader in the 18th century Hasidic movement. Such a position was anticipated centuries earlier in the Jesus movement. Christianity is inconceivable without the cult of Jesus' personality. From the very beginning there was a very special and hard-to-define relationship between some people and Jesus. This relationship transformed simple admirers or sympathizers into true and faithful disciples.

2. THE MASTER'S TEACHING AND HIS EXPECTATIONS

For all that strong personal link between Jesus and his disciples, the most surprising result of their association, which lasted at the most three years, was the extraordinary amount of oral teaching retained by the disciples and later transmitted. Jesus was not a writing or dictating prophet. As in the case of Isaiah, his teaching has come to us through an oral tradition which was not immediately put to writing. If today we study this tradition in its written form with all the tools of modern criticism (text, sources, form, redaction, etc.), we find a teaching in obvious continuity with the teachings of Israel's prophets and sages, presented in the framework of the written Torah. Its originality, however, is clearly apparent. It emphasized an immediate and very personal relation with the living God, together with a great concern for the neighbor. It showed signs of what we could call a non-ascetical radicalism, and at the same time proclaimed again and again the compassion and forgiveness of the living God. It was strongly future-oriented, but also very attentive to the present. Jesus characterized the incoming Kingdom of God in parables, but said very little about its organizational structure. Jesus' teaching was as hard to understand as his personality, being also full of paradoxes. It was seldom presented in a direct manner. Jesus preferred aphorisms and parables—or simply

hints, suggestions and implications. Scholars are still quarreling today about
the exact meaning of many of his sayings. It is not surprising that his disciples, more often than not, did not seem to fully understand their master. The
oldest Gospel, Mark, stressed this lack of comprehension. Jesus sometimes
showed signs of impatience. "Have I been with you all this time, Philip, and
you still do not know me?" (John 14:9). This was said at the end of his life.
The disciples must have had a very great respect for their master if they kept
and repeated words that were fully understood only later, sometimes much
later.

It is unclear to what extent this group of disciples helped Jesus during his
public life. According to Luke, Jesus sent 72 of them ahead of him to the
places he was to visit with the mission of curing the sick and announcing the
imminence of the kingdom (Luke 10:1-12). What was extraordinary for the
time and unheard of was the presence of some women disciples. According to
Mark 15:40–41, and Luke 8:1–3, certain women who had been cured from
evil spirits and ailments, as well as several others, followed Jesus and with
their own resources provided for him and the accompanying disciples. Jesus
was more than a lone preacher going from synagogue to synagogue in
Galilee; he was the initiator of a revival movement characterized by a distinc-
tive messianism. He was interested not simply in transmitting an abstract
teaching which would eventually enlighten many men and women; he wanted
to form, educate and prepare a small group of disciples to become the cata-
lysts of a renewed society in the restored kingdom.

We have mentioned that on a few points Jesus departed from the written
Torah to make it a little more strict. It is regrettable that Jews and Christians
came to look at Torah and Gospel in antithetical terms. The few exceptions
simply confirm the rule. Jesus was teaching the fulfillment of the Mosaic Law
and not a new law. If fulfillment included a few new commandments, essentially it meant that the Mosaic Law would be fully written on the hearts of the
disciples (Jer 31:33). Jesus summarized it in the love of God and neighbor,
which is truly the essence of Judaism. The question could be asked: Who is
my neighbor? Was the non-Jew my neighbor? It was obviously an important
question, but for the disciples, who had only rare social contacts with
Samaritans and foreigners (except the Roman soldiers), it was a secondary
question. The real problem was true conversion, in the sense of a heart turned
toward God in full acceptance of his will. Jesus was not so much teaching
HALACHA as HAGGADAH, seeking a deep renewal of Jewish spirituality.
Though occasionally he might have to answer a critic in HALACHIC terms,
he cared more for the transformation, even the rebirth, of the heart and the
spirit in the framework of covenant and Torah. Modern Christians ought never

to forget that the disciples of Jesus were at first absolutely convinced that no pagan could ever become a disciple if he had not become first a good Jew, a true child of Abraham.

How successful was Jesus in his teaching and in his prophetic proclamation? No sociologist attempting a statistical approach will find the small amount of available data very satisfactory. Jesus at certain moments attracted big crowds, but not always. He evoked more than simple curiosity, possibly some sympathy among the 'AM HA-ARETZ; he might have felt the gratitude of the sick he healed and the possessed he exorcised (sin, sickness and evil spirits were at that time one family); he certainly bound around himself a close group of disciples who remained very faithful—only one of them betrayed him in the end. Everything considered, however, if one limits oneself to the public life of Jesus, one must admit that his endeavors were not very successful. As we noted, the masses remained at a distance. More important, some among the Pharisees became hostile and the Sadducees were definitely antagonistic. How did these varied reactions affect the attitudes of the disciples, given their messianic hopes and their personal relationship with Jesus?

In the earlier, happier period of Jesus' public life, the emphasis of his teaching probably had not been on the eschaton or eternal life, but on the restoration of the kingdom to Israel. Jesus chose among his disciples twelve men to be his companions in preaching and healing. In the coming kingdom they were to sit on twelve thrones to judge the twelve tribes of Israel (Matt 19:28, Luke 22:30), meaning in the old biblical sense of the word that they were to govern the people. This must have been understood by the disciples as a prophecy of a new political order, as well as the future ingathering of the exiles. Rewards were also promised. In this age the disciples were to be repaid a hundred times and in the age to come with eternal life (Mark 10:30). There was a clear distinction between the imminent messianic kingdom in the present age, i.e., the restoration of the kingdom to Israel, and the kingdom beyond history, i.e., eternal life. We know that the disciples were interested in and were arguing about who would be the first among the Twelve (Mark 10:35–37). Jesus had to repeat again and again how he envisioned the exercise of authority in the coming kingdom.

It would be unfair to interpret the devotion of the disciples as being based only on the prospect of a political career. But in Judaism, material blessings need not be separated from spiritual blessings. In this context, the first signs of failure in the Jesus movement must have greatly disturbed the disciples. Three times in various circumstances Jesus tried to prepare them to face the probable outcome of his messianic career: martyrdom. Luke remarks after the third prophecy of the Passion, "But they understood nothing about all these things; in fact, what he said was hidden from them, and they did not grasp what was said" (Luke 18:34). Later, approaching the gates of Jerusalem, "they supposed that the kingdom of God was going to appear immediately" (Luke 19:11). They were to be very disappointed.

3. THE ROAD TO MARTYRDOM

Very early Jesus must have started to suspect that the restoration of the kingdom to Israel might not materialize. He was enjoying friendly receptions in the synagogues of Galilee, but when he went up to Jerusalem at the time of the pilgrimage feasts he was making little headway with the religious establishment. As time passed, the opposition did not decrease but increased. The nature of his mission was changing. "Although he was a Son, he learned obedience through what he suffered" (Heb 5:8). How could he ever make his disciples understand such a total reversal of their expectations? For a few months already they had felt mounting opposition coming from some quarters. When he was teaching them in more intimate conversations, Jesus became more demanding, more radical.

From then on to follow Jesus looked less and less like a way to worldly success. As we already mentioned, the end of the sixth chapter in the Gospel of John indicates very clearly the existence of a serious crisis. Jesus' followers in the synagogue at Capernaum were complaining that Jesus' language was intolerable. "Because of this many of his disciples turned back and no longer went about with him" (John 6:66). Not a few, but many! By contrast, Peter, in the name of the few who remained, said, "Lord, to whom can we go? You have the words of eternal life" (John 6:68). Once more we encounter here the mystery of faith, a faith that remains opaque to purely human understanding. What kept Peter from drifting away with the majority? Who wants to stay faithful to a lost cause?

For Jesus and his close disciples the hour had come to enter into the valley of the shadow of death. Much has been written on the great sufferings of Jesus, physical and spiritual, during his passion. Experiencing the bitterness of complete loneliness he had to entrust his soul totally to the living God. Then...Jesus of Nazareth was dead. For most of his compatriots it was the end of a painful drama and the drowning of a flickering hope. For those who had refused to save him, there was the illusion of a greater security. But for his disciples it was an unbearable scandal.

The disciples did not have to suffer physically. It is significant that they were not bothered by the Roman soldiers, which proves that if Jesus personally was considered potentially dangerous, his disciples did not cause much concern to Roman security. Jesus had never encouraged them to revolt against Rome. It had been different in the past with Judas the Galilean, and later it will be with Theudas and with the Egyptian; many of their followers were massacred by the Romans. Spiritually and mentally, however, the disciples must have entered into a deep agony. Being good Jews, the crucifixion was for them truly a scandal, a spiritual stumbling block, which shook their trust in God. It was not the savagery of the execution which horrified them; they were living in a cruel age. It was not even the ignominy of a holy man crucified between two thieves. Many of the crucified ones, and their number was legion, were true national heroes. What was inconceivable, beyond all imagination, was the brutal fact of a true Messiah abandoned by his God. A true Messiah might have to struggle to reach his goal, but a true Messiah could not possibly fail. Where was the Holy One of Israel during the drama of Calvary, when his beloved Son was executed as a criminal? Centuries later, the same anxious question would arise on the lips of Jesus' brothers and sisters, when they were annihilated like vermin in the gas chambers. This is a supreme test of faith for the human mind, which cannot conceive how a compassionate God lets evil run riot in this world...for a while.

The disciples were not in a mood to seek the consolation of philosophy. Their world was shattered. What had appeared as a brewing storm, which God could dissipate at the proper time, had now become utter destruction. With the King of the Jews, Jesus, dead on a Roman cross, the great vision of the restoration of the kingdom to Israel was utterly destroyed. On the night of the crucifixion Jerusalem was celebrating with great joy the beginning of redemption, the liberation from slavery in Egypt, the great feast of PESACH. The reading of the HAGGADAH reminded each Jew, and taught their children, that again and again in history God's power had saved Israel from mortal peril. Jesus had celebrated PESACH with the twelve one day earlier. He had tried to bring them to the realization that his exodus to God might be the dawn of a new hope. But the atmosphere had remained heavy. They did not dare ask him, "Where are you going?" (John 16:5). They could not imagine being without him. Jesus tried to convince them that after a little while sorrow would turn into joy, but their faith could not pierce the veil of immediacy. They still trusted that Jesus had come from God, but forebodings had taken hold of their hearts, and they followed Jesus in a daze to Gethsemane.

Then it was all over, and it looked final. All around was joy and celebration. The disciples' religious roots were too deep for them not to experience the paradox of the situation. Alas, it was hurting too much! They had to withdraw into nothingness, into the night of the soul where all is darkness and there is no light. How could their complete trust in Jesus of Nazareth ever survive their present agony?

After the first shock of Jesus' death and hasty burial, we can surmise that the disciples could not help turning over in their minds a few unpleasant thoughts. Realizing how much they had been attached to Jesus, they experienced his absence as a great spiritual void. They became uneasy about their own behavior. In Gethsemane, after Jesus' arrest, "All of them deserted him and fled" (Mark 14:50). Peter had boasted of his faithfulness, but he had publicly disavowed his master. Their intimate bond with Jesus had been broken, and their messianic faith could barely survive the complete failure of Jesus' activity among his people. The restoration of the kingdom to Israel might have been a misinterpretation of Jesus' teaching, but dying on a cross as a criminal could not possibly be the choice of God for his Chosen One. Darkness, pain and meaninglessness engulfed their souls.

4. HE IS ALIVE!

When the Sabbath was over, three of the women disciples, having bought some spices, went to the tomb at daybreak to anoint Jesus' body. They found the tomb open and empty. They "went out and fled from the tomb, for terror and amazement had seized them" (Mark 16:8). "But Mary stood weeping outside the tomb" (John 20:11). Suddenly, she saw Jesus standing there, but she did not recognize him, supposing him to be the gardener. Jesus said, "Mary!" Then she knew him and, falling down before him, tried to clasp his feet. Jesus said to her:

> Do not hold on to me, because I have not yet ascended to the Father. But go to my brothers and say to them, "I am ascending to my Father and your Father, to my God and your God." Mary Magdalene went and announced to the disciples, "I have seen the Lord" and she told them that he had said these things to her (John 20:17–18).

In the evening of the same day, with the doors of the house closed where the disciples were meeting, Jesus came, stood among them, and greeted them with SHALOM ALEICHEM. "Then the disciples rejoiced when they saw the Lord" (John 20:19–21). According to Paul, the earliest written witness (1 Cor 15:5–6), Jesus met in Jerusalem with a few individuals or groups. According to John, he met with the disciples in Galilee (John 21:4–14) where they had withdrawn into familiar surroundings. They were trying to make sense of the astounding events in which they had been caught up.

The disciples had many times witnessed the healing activity of Jesus. Now they themselves were in need of his healing. At their meeting in the evening of the first day of the week he had said, "Receive the Holy Spirit. If you forgive the sins of any, they are forgiven them" (John 20:22–23). Obviously their own sin of cowardice had been forgiven. Later, in Galilee, he would ask Peter three times, "Simon son of John, do you love me?" (John 21:17), in order to reaffirm the intimacy of the bond between master and disciple. Only once did he appear again as a rabbi, as a teacher who gives a clear interpretation of some obscure text of the Scriptures, and this was precisely to heal the scandal of the cross. Of the two disciples, discouraged and downhearted, who were on the way to Emmaus, Jesus asked:

"Was it not necessary that the Messiah should suffer these things and then enter into his glory?" Then beginning with Moses and all the prophets, he interpreted to them the things about himself in all the scriptures (Luke 24:26–27).

Jesus must have explained the text of Isaiah 53 on the atoning role of the Suffering Servant, a text which came to play a unique role in the teaching of the early Church, in order to interpret the absurdity of the crucifixion. Most scholars doubt that the concept of a suffering Messiah appeared in Jewish tradition before the revolt of Bar Kochba. For Jesus' disciples, as for their contemporaries, a Messiah was a victor, not a victim. Jesus was inverting all their expectations.

"He is risen from the dead!" is the core of the apostolic preaching, the GOOD NEWS. This statement is intended to be an objective statement; however, it conveys an initial experience in which only a few of Jesus' disciples had been involved. As Peter would say later in Caesarea, "God raised him on the third day and allowed him to appear, not to all the people but to us who were chosen by God as witnesses" (Acts 10:40–41). To convey such an experience, to delineate its content, will be a difficult task for the disciples and the evangelists. Modern exegetes have remarked that Jesus' appearances have been described in some texts as extremely realistic and concrete, in other texts as unfamiliar and strange. Though the presence of Jesus was always experienced as real, it was a reality without precedent, quite foreign to Jewish tradition. It was not a return to present conditions of existence, the way the Pharisees were expecting and conceiving a revitalization of the body, the way Lazarus had come back after four days in the tomb to sit at the family table and enjoy a hearty meal. Jesus' resurrection was an exodus, not a return; he had passed from this world, the world humanity knows so well, to the world to come, the new creation, about which nothing is known. He had become the first-born of this new creation. As such he was not immediately accessible to the natural senses.

The Bible witnesses to the difficult challenge encountered by the great prophets of Israel when they tried to bring their people to the knowledge of the living God, a God who is fully transcendent to the world he creates. All through the centuries there have been sharp discussions about the anthropomorphisms in the Sacred Books. The Bible tells Israel that God is, but not what he is. "You shall not make for yourself an idol, whether in the form of anything that is in heaven above, or that is on the earth beneath, or that is in the water under the earth" (Exod 20:4). Theologians are fond of using various analogies in contrast with the VIA NEGATIVA used by the great mystics. Their quest for understanding contends often with the need to be truthful. The problem is similar with any language or work of art which attempts to describe the resurrection of Jesus. Yet, if the problem is similar, it is not identical. The new creation remains a finite, limited realm of existence face to face with the infinity of the Creator. In relation to this world, Jesus' presence after the resurrection was like the irruption of a transcendent reality into a close world of earthly messianism, as Moses' and Isaiah's visions had been an irruption of a transcendent reality into the closed world of pagan religiosity.

It is not surprising that the disciples were hesitant, and took some time to assimilate what was for them entirely new. They had to overcome the very concrete, carnal concept of resurrection developed by the Pharisees who, given their anthropology, had no other way to conceive of survival after death. Jesus was alive in a way that the disciples could not clearly understand. They must have been caught between the hope of seeing Jesus return to finish his brutally interrupted work, and the fascination of a disturbing newness manifested to them with great immediacy. They hesitated. There was probably more than one doubting Thomas. To quote the anonymous ending of Mark, "[Jesus] upbraided them for their lack of faith and stubbornness, because they had not believed those who saw him after he had risen" (Mark 16:14). Luke describes the disciples at the appearance of Jesus as agitated, with doubts in their hearts. "Their joy was so great that they still could not believe it, and they were dumbfounded" (Luke 24:41). Matthew describes a last meeting in Galilee, "When they saw him they fell down before him, though some hesitated" (Matt 28:17).

Nevertheless, by the time Israel was finishing the counting of the 'OMER, Jesus and his disciples had restored deep bonds of affection. It is implicit in the appendix to the fourth Gospel, which describes the scene on the shore of the Lake of Galilee. Though the disciples experienced in this restored relationship something like a new dimension of existence, their horizon was still limited to an earthly salvation and to the hoped-for restoration of the kingdom to Israel. According to Luke, at the time of their final meeting with Jesus the timing of this restoration was their main question. The answer he gave was evasive:

It is not for you to know times or periods that the Father has set by his own authority. But you will receive power when the Holy Spirit has come upon you; and you will be my witnesses (Acts 1:6–8).

And after reassuring them with this promise, he was taken away from their sight. This new separation, so close to the first one, must have left the disciples somehow sad and apprehensive, but without the bitterness of the first separation. Jesus was alive, this they knew. The lack of a clear orientation toward the future probably troubled them. Yet, they had Jesus' promise, and they could hope that in God's own time the Kingdom would arrive. The fact that they replaced Judas with Matthias to keep the symbol of the twelve tribes indicated that they continued to anticipate the return of the exiles and the restoration of the kingdom to Israel.

5. BAPTISM WITH THE HOLY SPIRIT

Charismatic happenings were frequent in the very first years of Christianity. They make most modern Christians rather uncomfortable, in the same way that HASIDIC enthusiasm made Jews of other persuasions ill at ease. Such charismatic phenomena will not be characteristic of the life of the Christian Churches in the following centuries. The outwardly visible signs of these phenomena are only the chaff which needs to be winnowed to discover the kernel of an original religious experience. As in the case of mysticism, identical external phenomena may hide very different approaches to the sacred. What is important is the content of the disciples' experience on the following celebration of Pentecost, as it can be inferred from the discourse of Peter to a crowd attracted to Mount Zion by strange sounds and lights. The latter were of a very modest character compared to the phenomena surrounding the gift of Torah to Moses, a story much in the mind of the people on that festive day of SHAVUOT.

The disciples did not experience the gift of a new law, but rather the outpouring on them of the Spirit of the living God. Peter recognized in the occurrence the fulfillment of the prophecy of Joel:

I will pour out my spirit on all flesh;
your sons and your daughters shall prophesy,
your old men shall dream dreams,

and your young men shall see visions.
Even on the male and female slaves,
in those days, I will pour out my spirit (Joel 2:28-29).

The disciples were baptized, immersed in the Spirit of God, the Spirit of Holiness. During the last few weeks their attention had been focused on the mysterious appearances of Jesus risen from the dead. Now they were witnessing a theophany, a mysterious manifestation of God's presence, and their attention had to be drawn toward the living God himself and the sanctification of his Name.

In the midst of this new experience, however, the position and function of Jesus were seen in a new light:

> This Jesus God raised up, and of that all of us are witnesses. Being therefore exalted at the right hand of God, and having received from the Father the promise of the Holy Spirit, he has poured out this that you both see and hear (Acts 2:32–33).

The disciples were receiving the Spirit that had been first bestowed on the risen Jesus. Before the Sanhedrin Peter would later proclaim: "God exalted him at his right hand as leader and Savior that he might give repentance to Israel and forgiveness of sins" (Acts 5:31).

It does not matter which title is given to Jesus: leader, Messiah, king, Lord, Savior, prince of life, the just one, etc. They all express the disciples' conviction that Jesus, not only risen but exalted at the right hand of God, was the true shepherd of the House of Israel. In the following months and years, which were so crucial for the formation, in the bosom of Israel, of a new community assembled in his name, Jesus' role would be better understood and more appreciated. But from that time on the disciples would know how true were his last words, "And look, I am with you always; yes, to the end of time" (Matt 28:20).

The outpouring of God's Spirit did not simply enable the disciples to utter prophecies, visions and dreams according to the oracle of Joel; they suddenly were clothed with power from on high (Luke 24:49). The extraordinary transformation of a group of cowards, huddled in fear in an upper room, into courageous witnesses appearing before the Sanhedrin and the Jerusalem crowds, reminds one of the words of Ezekiel:

> A new heart I will give you, and a new spirit I will put within you; and I will remove from your body the heart of stone and give you a heart of flesh. I will put my spirit within you (Ezek 36:26–27).

The meaning of the word "spirit" in the Hebrew Scriptures is elusive. It has a Semitic, and not a Greek meaning. Many exegetes would agree that the most general meaning of "Spirit of God" is the Power of God. The Spirit is God who gets things done. It is not so much a physical as a psychological or spiritual power. In a kind of self-imposed limitation, God always respects human freedom. His Spirit acts by inspiration, not by coercion, bringing any shriveled "ego" curled upon itself to blossom into discovery of and relation with others. The disciples in fact knew an exhilarating experience. To the crowd they looked as if they were drunk, but they were simply going through an expansion of consciousness, deepening the bonds which united them to the living God, to their risen and beloved master, and to each other.

The immediate and visible result of this outpouring of God's Spirit was the formation of a new community. There were at that time various kinds of religious groups in Israel, from the HAVUROT, or loosely structured Pharisaic groups, to the hierarchically structured New Covenanters at Qumran, the Essenes. The characteristics of the group to be known as the Nazarenes (Acts 24:5) are well described by Luke, "They devoted themselves to the apostles' teaching and fellowship, to the breaking of bread and the prayers" (Acts 2:42). This last item, the prayers, might not be characteristic because, like other devout Jews, "day by day they spent much time together in the temple" (Acts 2:46), and from the subsequent history of this community we know how they prided themselves on being "zealous for the law" (Acts 21:20). It is in the other three items that the specific characteristics of the Nazarenes appeared.

6. THE NAZARENES

Being faithful to the teaching of the Apostles must have meant that thanks to the teaching of the Twelve, who had been the whole time with Jesus "beginning from the baptism of John until the day when [Jesus] was taken up from us" (Acts 1:22), the new disciples were listening to the master and absorbing his teaching. At the time when some scribes were diligently remembering and structuring the teaching of past sages, transmitting the traditional oral Law to the next generation, some Nazarene scribes were repeating orally and later transcribing the sayings, parables and deeds of Jesus of Nazareth, most of all the story of his arrest, trial and martyrdom. A Christian oral tradition was thus emerging, parallel to and more authoritative for the disciples than the oral tradition later codified in the MISHNAH. The Holy Scriptures remained: the Law, the Prophets, and the Writings. As the Word of God their status was untouched. Jesus could no longer address the disciples viva voce, but he was alive, and in listening to the Twelve the disciples could enter into immediate contact with his mind and his heart.

Some special form of brotherhood was nothing original in Israel at the time. Still, Luke's description might cause some surprise, "All who believed were together and had all things in common; they would sell their possessions and goods and distribute the proceeds to all, as any had need" (Acts 2:44–45). It was a noble and generous experiment, which seems to have ended in financial disaster; the Church of the saints would need help from outside to survive. The ideal, however, did not die. Later, cenobitic monasticism and some Christian sects will try to revive and maintain it. It presupposes a certain psychological unity, a real solidarity, which goes beyond pragmatic advantages or loyalty to a common way of life. In the Jerusalem community God's Spirit was uniting the first disciples to the risen Jesus and at the same time to each other, making possible genuine interpersonal relations based not on blood, but on a common spirit shaped by the Spirit of God. They not only went to the Temple with one heart, they were starting to live and to act with one heart.

The newest and most important characteristic of the emerging community was the third item, the breaking of bread. As Luke describes their life, "Day by day, as they spent much time together in the temple, they broke bread at home and ate their food with glad and generous hearts, praising God and having the goodwill of all the people" (Acts 2:46–47). Devout Jews always welcome the Sabbath, symbol of the world to come, with the blessing of bread and wine. The disciples, remembering Jesus' blessing at the Last Supper and his command, "Do this in remembrance of me" (1 Cor 11:24), knew that each time they were breaking this bread and sharing this cup they were proclaiming Jesus' death and resurrection. The beloved master had left this world, but he was alive, and it was possible to be perfectly united to him in heart and soul. This simple ceremony became for the disciples worship par excellence, a worship in spirit and in truth. Jesus, the teacher, had become after his exaltation the great intercessor, the eternal priest, the one who could gather together the scattered and sometimes lost sheep of the Lord into a perfect prayer of thanksgiving. With the risen Jesus in this priestly role, the center of gravity of worship was passing from earth to heaven and the disciples were made participants, in faith, of this heavenly liturgy. From now on the perfect holy of holies was the risen humanity of Jesus of Nazareth.

What might seem surprising is the non-messianic style of Luke's description. He was writing after 70 C.E. when the messianic climate had already changed. The oldest Apostolic writings, the letters of Paul, show on the contrary how strongly messianic the primitive community was. In days past, listening to Jesus and witnessing his many healings and exorcisms, the disciples had come to believe that he was the expected one, i.e., the anointed one, the Messiah, who had been sent by God as his lieutenant to restore the kingdom to Israel. His miserable death might have shaken that conviction, but his rising to life had opened new horizons and confirmed his status as the one destined to be the King-Messiah. He had said:

> From the fig tree learn its lesson: as soon as its branch becomes tender and puts forth its leaves, you know that summer is near. So also, when you see these things taking place, you know that he is near, at the very gates. Truly I tell you, this generation will not pass until all these things have taken place. Heaven and earth will pass away, but my words will not pass away. But about that day or hour no one knows, neither the angels in heaven, nor the Son, but only the Father (Mark 13:28–32).

At their last encounter, Jesus had repeated his remark, "It is not for you to know the times or periods that the Father has set by his own authority" (Acts 1:7). Notwithstanding this incertitude, the experience of SHAVUOT had convinced the disciples that the prophecy of Joel was finally realized, that they were living near the end of time, and that the Kingdom of God could not tarry much longer. Exactly what was going to happen was not very clear. In Jerusalem at that time messianic expectations were intense, varied, and offering many possible scenarios. The disciples had no precise scenario of their own to offer. What they knew for certain was that "This Jesus, who has been taken up from you into heaven, will come in the same way as you saw him go into heaven" (Acts 1:11). That he was coming back they were very sure, and they were hoping that it should be very soon. Every prayer meeting was ending with the invocation, "Marana tha!"—Our Lord come! (1 Cor 16:22) or Come, Lord Jesus! (Rev 22:20).

Attitudes that have been nurtured for a long time are slow to die. Some of the disciples seemed to expect that Jesus' first activity after his return would be the restoration of the kingdom to Israel. It would be an earthly messianic kingdom preparatory to a later coming of the heavenly Kingdom of God at the end of days. For others, the mysterious nature of the resurrection and a deep intuition of the impermanence of this world inclined them to look toward the future in more eschatological terms. They were already in "the last days" of history, approaching "the end of time" when Jesus would return as "the Son of Man coming in clouds with great power and glory" (Mark 12:26). His coming would be "the Day of the Lord" announced by the Prophets, blessing for the just and curse for the wicked.

Some might wonder how a community could profess such a strong messianic faith without the object of this faith being clearly defined. Jesus, risen and exalted, was the assurance that there would be a future, a future for Israel and for each one who remained faithful to the covenant between God and his chosen people. In the same way that the Hebrew Scriptures had proclaimed the personal existence of the living God but unveiled little of his mystery, the Apostolic writings proclaimed the reality of the world to come as existing already in the Risen Jesus, but unveiled very little about this new mystery. Once more we enter the realm of faith, in which worldly concerns and pure reason seem to be at a loss.

The coming of the Kingdom was to be a pure gift of God; the present task was to prepare for the Lord a people fit to receive the gift. In the light of Jesus' resurrection something stronger than the voice of John, son of Zechariah, was now available. The teaching of Jesus of Nazareth, the fellowship with him risen and glorified and also with his disciples, as well as the abundant gifts of the Holy Spirit, all were strengthening and deepening the covenantal bonds God had initiated with the children of Israel at Mount Sinai. God had slowly prepared the coming of his Kingdom through a long history. He was now putting the final touch to this preparatory work. True hope was dawning in the House of Israel. Confident, hopeful, joyful and grateful, the little company of disciples, renewed in heart and spirit, was most anxious to proclaim to all their Jewish brothers and sisters that the crucified Jesus was truly Lord and Messiah, and that he would soon return to usher in the long awaited Kingdom of God. Could the House of Israel accept their witness and receive their message?

V. The Story of a No–Part 2

The events which took place on Mount Zion at the Feast of SHAVUOT, probably in the year 30 C.E., caused a slight stir among the population of Jerusalem. In the days following the crucifixion there had been some rumor that the body of Jesus had been stolen, but soon the event of the crucifixion had been forgotten. Jesus' disciples had withdrawn into Galilee, and the dreary life under Roman occupation had continued its course. For those who had not been Jesus' faithful disciples all that remained after fifty days was a vague memory of a rather sad story. Then, suddenly, the Jesus question was back in the news.

1. THE SANHEDRIN'S ATTITUDE

Biblical numbers need to be read with caution. Luke wrote of thousands responding to the calls of Peter and joining the small group of disciples (Acts 2:41, 4:4). Even a large group of priests had become new adherents (Acts 6:7). Whatever the exact number, we are dealing no longer with a small circle of fervent disciples accompanying an itinerant rabbi, but with a new community assembled in the name of Jesus of Nazareth crucified, risen and glorified. Its leaders, though Galileans, were trying to put down roots in Jerusalem in the shadow of the Jewish religious establishment.

Those among the religious leaders who had developed strong antagonistic feelings toward the activity of Jesus (mostly Sadducees in control of the Temple), and especially those who had been involved in his arrest and trial, were far from pleased with the revival of the Jesus question. They thought that it had been ended once and for all, and that they could turn to more important problems. Now, before their eyes, a Nazarene community was in the making. Some of its leaders dared teach in the Temple, in the Portico of Solomon, and were restoring some sick people to health. The Sadducees were particularly annoyed that in proclaiming the resurrection of Jesus, these new

54

disciples were teaching the Pharisaic conception of an afterlife, which they abhorred. Angered by this revival of the Jesus movement, they decided to stop the evil before it could start to grow and become unmanageable. They faced a problem, however, the same one they had faced in the case of John, son of Zechariah, and for a while of Jesus of Nazareth. The disciples of Jesus seemed to be respected by the common people. Luke's expression, "having the good-will of all the people" (Acts 2:47), might be redactional. But the fact that the High Priest and his supporters were satisfied, at first, with a simple admonition indicates that they felt the need to act with circumspection, keeping an eye on the mood of the people.

The second encounter with the Sanhedrin sharpened the positions. The dispute became clearly centered on the death and resurrection of Jesus. The accusation of the High Priest was simple and direct, "You have filled Jerusalem with your teaching and you are determined to bring this man's blood on us" (Acts 5:28). Finding fault with the supreme authority in Israel was like a crime of lèse majesté. Better for the culprit not to stay in Jerusalem, but to retire into the desert like the Qumranites. The answer of Peter was near blasphemy, "We must obey God rather than any human authority" (Acts 5:29). As a principle the saying was above discussion, but the context in which Peter affirmed it implied that in his opinion he, Peter, rather than the High Priest, was expressing the authoritative will of God. His argument was simply that the resurrection of Jesus, being obviously an act of God, authenticated the words and the mission of Jesus. The High Priest and Peter were in two entirely different worlds of perception. The conflict between them reminds one of the conflict between the chief priests and Jesus a few months earlier, "By what authority are you doing these things? Who gave you this authority to do them?" (Mark 11:28). The High Priest was not going to argue about his authority, which he was certain was sanctioned by God. Luke ends the scene with the remark, "When they heard this, they were enraged and wanted to kill them" (Acts 5:33).

There was, however, a great difference between this session and the trial of Jesus. One member of the Sanhedrin, a Pharisee, asked for caution and suggested:

> So in the present case, I tell you, keep away from these men and let them alone; because if this plan or this undertaking is of human origin, it will fail; but if it is of God, you will not be able to overthrow them—in that case you may be found fighting against God! (Acts 5:38–39).

His advice was accepted and they were released. This Pharisee was Gamaliel I, the teacher of Saul of Tarsus (Acts 22:3), the son or grandson of

Hillel and the grandfather of Gamaliel II, who would later expel the Nazarenes from the Synagogue. He and his family were outstanding figures in the creative process which transformed Temple Judaism into Rabbinic Judaism. He was "a teacher of the law, respected by all the people" (Acts 5:34). His intervention allowed the Nazarene community in Jerusalem to survive. It demonstrated that the religious establishment was not of one mind vis-à-vis Jesus and his disciples. Some Sadducees around the High Priest will remain hostile to the end, and will always refuse to recognize that the trial of Jesus had been a mistrial. To please them, King Herod Agrippa will behead James, son of Zebedee, and arrest Peter (Acts 12:1). Later, in 62 C.E., the High Priest, during a vacancy between Procurators, will order James, the brother of Jesus, the highly respected leader of the Nazarene community, to be stoned to death. The Sadducees' "No" was tenacious, and will remain unbending until finally they lose power with the destruction of the Temple.

2. THE COMMON PEOPLE'S ATTITUDE

Notwithstanding this Sadducean opposition, a certain MODUS VIVENDI came into existence in Jerusalem and in Judea. In the first forty years, the Aramaic speaking members of the Nazarene community were rarely molested by their compatriots; only some leaders were occasionally persecuted by the religious authorities. It seems that the Roman power ignored them completely. The reason for this relative tolerance must be found in part in the pluralism displayed by Judaism at that time, but still more in the positive attitude of the 'AM HA-ARETZ, the common people, vis-à-vis the Nazarene community. Their attitude does not seem to have been very different from the attitude they manifested toward Jesus of Nazareth, except that now they were relating not to Jesus, but to the community of his disciples.

The preaching of the Apostles was very similar to the preaching of John, son of Zechariah, and of Jesus himself: Repent, the Kingdom of God is at hand. The coming of the Kingdom, however, was now linked to the return of Jesus, the Galilean sage who had been crucified by Pontius Pilate, but whom God had raised from the dead. Peter, speaking to a crowd assembled in the Temple, said:

> Repent, therefore, and turn to God so that your sins may be wiped out, so that times of refreshing may come from the presence of the Lord, and that he may send the Messiah appointed for you, that is, Jesus, who must remain in heaven until the time of universal restoration that God announced long ago through the holy prophets (Acts 3:19–21).

Peter used two different expressions when he tried to characterize what was to be expected: "times of comfort" and "the universal restoration." These were terms used in the apocalyptic literature. Were they synonymous? Or could times of comfort evoke the restoration of the kingdom to Israel in the "Last Days," whereas universal restoration would evoke the coming of the Son of man in glory at the "End of Days"? Exegetes argue about the exact meaning. We may wonder what the people listening to Peter understood. If their general messianic expectations had been somehow reinforced through Peter's exhortation, they had not been clarified. Most of his listeners were probably looking for a Davidic restoration, as they had been during Jesus' earthly life.

Jesus' disappearance from the scene did not make matters easier. Nobody could now listen to him, see his face, or contemplate his demeanor. The Apostles were proclaiming that he was alive, that they had met with him, that he had been exalted and established in power by God, and that soon he would come back to establish the kingdom he had promised. Such an eschatological faith was asking the simple people, the 'AM HA-ARETZ, to enter into a world quite foreign to their ordinary outlook; they were asked to trust the reports of a few Galilean fishermen who had no status in the House of Israel. As in the case of the previous encounters with the earthly Jesus, they were called to a surrender in faith which seemed to escape any purely psychological or sociological explanation. As this faith was ultimately based on the witness of the Apostles, the religious and moral quality of the community they were representing and leading must have become an important factor in the credibility granted to them. The descriptions given by Luke in the Acts of the Apostles are too brief to allow us to draw a detailed picture of the life of the community. However, we can catch a glimpse of two characteristics, one which might inspire some respect, and another which could engender some uneasiness.

While waiting for the return of Jesus of Nazareth in power, the Nazarenes were exemplary Jews, zealous for the Law and faithful to the prayers in the Temple. They may have shown some similarity with the future Hasidic communities, radiating joy and enthusiasm. The simple fact that they were intensely religious singled them out from the 'AM HA-ARETZ, as had been the case with the Pharisees, the Essenes, and other minor groups. Their total devotion to the sanctification of God's Name and the coming of his Kingdom must have inspired great respect, especially if it was accompanied with occasional gifts of healing and exorcism. However, a psychological distance remained between this attitude of respect and a willingness to become a member of the new community. One needed a deep trust, not only in the living God, but also in the mysterious figure of the risen Jesus and in the community of his disciples.

The spontaneous decision of the Nazarene community, on the morrow of Pentecost, to share goods and resources might have frightened the average Jew, who was easily jealous of his personal autonomy. Communism is not a Jewish tradition, and in modern Israel the saga of the KIBBUTZIM, the collective farms, has been falling on hard times. This first expression of Christian communism may have followed the example of the Essenes at Qumran or been the result of the community's intense eschatological hope for the imminent return of the risen Jesus. If these were the last days before the coming of the Messiah in glory, what was the value of material goods, not to mention projects for the future? Nothing remained important save a spiritual preparation in anticipation of the coming of the Messiah. Though the Nazarenes did not withdraw to the desert as the Essenes did, they may have tended to withdraw from full participation in ordinary social life in order to remain devoted to their religious pursuits. To the extent that their eschatological hope was distancing them from the mainstream of Jewish life, the average Jew may have felt less and less attracted to the Nazarenes' teaching and way of life.

Everything considered, the attitude of the 'AM HA-ARETZ, the people on the street, vis-à-vis the new community and its message was not very different from the attitude we have described toward the person of Jesus of Nazareth. To the extent that the call of the Apostles was a call to repentance, to return to God, to be faithful to all the obligations of the covenant, there could be no objection. They experienced the attraction of this appeal notwithstanding the power of the evil instinct, the YETZER HA-RA', which so often pulled them in another direction. Their messianic hope was intense and remained so until 70 C.E. Those among them who were convinced that Jesus was alive, had been taken into heaven, and was soon to return as King Messiah, were in no way kept from full membership in the Jewish peoplehood. The majority, however, did not experience the same sense of urgency. They adopted an attitude of wait and see. If and when the Messiah came, there would still be time to believe in him and gratefully welcome him. They waited, they waited...until the day of the great catastrophe...and he did not appear.

3. THE PHARISEES' ATTITUDE

The Pharisees were living among the people; they must have shared more or less unconsciously the prevalent attitude toward the new community. Nevertheless, they were "Pharisees," a self-conscious group forming a network of strictly observant people, and intent on the study of the Law and the traditions of the past sages. They must have discussed among themselves the emergence of the Nazarene movement. They had not been able to reach a consensus on the person and work of Jesus of Nazareth, as evidenced by the intervention of Gamaliel I. Some had attacked Jesus bitterly; some had approved him with respect and interest. The problems which had arisen in relation to Jesus' personality or his attitude toward sinners had subsequently ceased to exist. But there were many reasons for remaining suspicious of the Nazarenes and their enthusiasm. The Pharisees were convinced that THEY were the way for Israel, the assured way to regenerate the people and make them ready for welcoming the Messiah. They disliked the fundamentalist Sadducees, the irresponsible Zealots, the clannish Qumranites and other small groups. The emergence of a new party in the Jewish family was not necessarily welcomed. Jesus might have been a popular teacher, but he had failed as a pretended Messiah and was now dead. Charismatic enthusiasm, moreover, was not the way of the Pharisees. It might be expected that they would be still more suspicious toward the Nazarenes than they had been toward Jesus himself.

We have no way of knowing how widely the trial of Jesus had been argued and evaluated among the rank and file of the Pharisees. Even those who were highly critical of the proceedings could not be pleased with the sweeping condemnations pronounced by Peter and by his appeals to repentance. THEY did not feel guilty. Sometimes Peter seemed to accuse all the people without distinction:

This man...you crucified and killed by the hands of those outside the law (Acts 2:23).

Therefore let the entire house of Israel know with certainty that God has made him both Lord and Messiah, this Jesus whom you crucified (Acts 2:36).

But you rejected the Holy and Righteous One and asked to have a murderer given to you, and you killed the Author of life, whom God raised from the dead (Acts 3:14–15).

It is true that Peter later added, "And now, friends, I know that you acted in ignorance, as did also your rulers" (Acts 3:17). Peter might be trying to excuse the crime, but when he was addressing the crowd, he was calling "you" as well as "your rulers" to repentance. Hesitating Pharisees in the crowd had reasons to feel offended.

It has often been said that the main argument between Jesus and the Pharisees concerned matters relevant to the Oral Law. If that were the case, how could we explain that the early chapters of the Acts of the Apostles are completely devoid of any such dispute? Had the Apostles forgotten Jesus' teaching? It is certain that the Nazarenes were and remained zealous upholders of the Law. This must have been pleasing to the Pharisees, and the reason why their attitude at first was not particularly hostile. That does not mean that the new community followed all the prescriptions advocated by the Pharisees, such as the extension to layfolk of the laws of purity required of the priests in the Temple. They probably continued in their daily life as they had done when they were with Jesus. What could potentially become much more serious was the authority attributed to the teaching of Jesus, orally transmitted in the assemblies of the Nazarenes. Jesus was recognized as the ultimate authority in the interpretation of Torah. The ordinary Pharisee who might respect Jesus as a holy man, wise in the tradition of Israel and an inspiring preacher, would be unwilling to give him that paramount position. To single out a human person-ality above all others seemed to impair the awesomeness of God. Face to face with this increasing focus on Jesus Messiah, the ordinary Pharisee—if he was not united in faith with the risen Jesus—must have grown increasingly uncomfortable. His spiritual master could not be a human being. The way of life for him was the Word of God revealed in a legal text, to be properly inter-preted by the labor of countless scribes and sages. The Nazarene community must have appeared to him as a corruption of the pure Jewish religious ideal.

Luke wrote that the disciples daily spent much time together in the Temple. Later James would suggest to Paul that he should take part in a purification ceremony in the Temple (Acts 21:24). Everything in Acts seems to imply that the relation of the Nazarenes to the Temple, at that time the focus of the reli-gion of Israel, was harmonious and beyond question. Then how can we explain that Stephen, in his speech before the Sanhedrin, proclaimed that "the Most High does not dwell in houses made with human hands" (Acts 7:48)? He was implicitly denying the presence of the living God in the Holy of Holies. As had been the case at the trial of Jesus, the central question focused on the sanctity and permanence of the Temple. The Pharisees in the Sanhedrin, though they were embroiled in constant quarrels with the Sadducees, would nevertheless agree with them each time the sanctity of the Temple was questioned. Stephen's remarks must have taken the Pharisees by surprise, as they could see the Nazarenes praying faithfully in the Temple. We might question how representative of the Nazarenes' attitude was Stephen's affirmation. He was not a Hebrew but a Hellenist. The Hellenists had links with the Diaspora and showed a certain openness to Greek culture. They had developed traditions, attitudes and rituals quite different from those of Palestinian Judaism, a situation not unlike the one prevailing today between Ashkenazim and Sephardim. The Hellenists were regularly ascending to Jerusalem in pilgrimage, and some had settled in the Holy City, opening their own synagogues. They seemed to convert more easily to the new way.

Converts among them were sufficiently numerous to cause some strain in the Nazarene community. They received their own leadership under the authority of the twelve. We cannot be sure that the attitude of Stephen represented the sentiments of the original disciples of Jesus. Was his attitude an echo of the tendency of some Hellenists, such as Philo from Alexandria, to spiritualize, even to allegorize, many aspects of Judaism, while at the same time remaining faithful to the letter of the Law?

Rather than being an echo of the Hellenistic tendency to spiritualize matter and history, Stephen's attitude might have resulted from a progressive deepening of the eschatological experience, a deepening which a few years later would find a very articulate expression in the Letter to the Hebrews. Jesus, risen, is experienced as the beginning of the world to come. He is the true and eternal Temple in which "the whole fullness of deity dwells" (Col 2:9). The ritual breaking of bread in homes (Acts 2:46) was participation in this new worship offered by the risen Jesus to the living God. The earthly Temple with its elaborate and at times magnificent worship was not without value. God himself had determined, even in detail, how he wanted to be worshiped. But this ritual was only a figure of things to come, "when the true worshipers will worship the Father in spirit and truth" (John 4:23). It is not impossible that more adventurous spirits like Stephen, when they were worshiping in the Temple, were actually missing the mystical union with the risen Jesus given to them in the ritual breaking of bread. They knew which temple was the true temple of the living God. If faith in the resurrection of Jesus was causing among some Hellenist Nazarenes a spiritual distancing from Temple worship, it would not be surprising that such an attitude, when perceived by some Pharisees, would cause a deep resentment. Though the latter might be personally more involved in synagogal worship and in the study of TORAH, the sacredness and centrality of the Temple was at that time for them unquestioned. It was for the Messiah, when he came, to decide the future of the Temple.

4. THE STATUS OF JEWISH CHRISTIANITY

Given the lack of interest among the majority, the relative hostility of a minority, and the increasing uneasiness of the Pharisees, was the Nazarene community in danger of losing its status as an integral part of the house of Israel? Judaism has known periods of de facto pluralism and periods of great uniformity. In the early centuries of our era what was characteristic of God's people, and gave to the individual Jew his or her sense of identity, was the observance of the written Law, the Mosaic Law. As the essential, central element of the Jewish culture, it was quite concrete and visible. To the extent that the Nazarenes were upholding the observance of all the commandments, they fully belonged to the house of Israel. Neither the belief in the resurrection of Jesus of Nazareth, nor the firm hope of his return as God's Messiah, contradicted the basic doctrines of Judaism. The authority of his teaching was questioned by some, but even the authority of the Oral Law was questioned by the Sadducees and shall be questioned again by the Karaites. Even an unsuccessful messianic claim did not automatically exclude one from the Jewish family. Bar Kochba was and remains a national hero.

After Ezra, at least in theory, the Jewish nation had been essentially an endogamous group. Samaritans and Judeans (like later Karaites and Rabbanites) were intermarrying, until, after a long period of quarreling, such marriages became finally prohibited. Today Cabalists, Hasidim, Reform Jews and secular Zionists all belong to the house of Israel. Nazarenes, on account of their particularities, might not have been "accepted" by the mainstreams of Judaism, but there seems to be no reason why they could not have been "tolerated" as one possible interpretation of Judaism. In fact, they were for a time, but for a time only. History does not stand still. Two new factors entered into and transformed the Nazarene tradition in the making. Early, the community opened itself and received in its bosom a great influx of foreigners. Later, its mystics and theologians presented the mystery of Jesus of Nazareth in a light which seemed blasphemous to any Jew totally devoted to the transcendence and the oneness of the God of Abraham, Isaac and Jacob, the God Jesus had learned to worship in the synagogue of Nazareth. To understand how these two developments brought about a complete break between Judaism and Christianity, we need to leave the nearly self-contained world of Palestinian Judaism, and to follow the disciples of Jesus into the Jewish Diaspora and the world of its many proselytes.

VI. Jews and Gentiles

While the small community of Jesus' disciples was struggling to strengthen and organize its communal life, proclaiming to their Jewish brothers and sisters that the Day of the Messiah was indeed imminent, some non-Jews became attracted to this new hope and begged the Nazarenes to accept them into their community. At first they were few in number, but the influx rapidly gained momentum. Sporadic persecutions favored rather than hindered this process of growth; some of Jesus' disciples, who had to leave Jerusalem for security reasons, spread the new messianic hope in the Diaspora. The Acts of the Apostles describes the various steps of this development, first Samaria, then the coastal plain, and finally Damascus and Antioch.

1. THE JEWISH DIASPORA

The main agents of this expansion were the Hellenistic Jews. The Hebraic Jews in Judea and Galilee were living a national life under foreign occupation; they had limited and unpleasant contacts with foreigners. The Hellenists, on the contrary, were living as a minority in the non-Jewish sections of Palestine, and in all the main cities of the Roman Empire. They lived mostly in Jewish neighborhoods, but their relative separation was no impediment to their becoming aware of the Greek ambience and trying to do business with the Gentiles. Their simple presence awoke a certain amount of curiosity, leading Gentiles to discover and to value the moral standards upheld by the Jewish community, as well as its lofty concept of deity.

A number of synagogues became surrounded by concentric circles of sympathizers. The outer circle comprised those who acknowledged the moral influence radiating from the Jewish community. The intermediary circle was "the God-fearers," the Gentiles who had discovered the living God, were attracted to Jewish worship and the Jewish way of life, but were unwilling to commit themselves to the observance of all the commandments. Finally the inner circle was formed by the proselytes, the real converts, who were taking upon themselves the yoke of the Law, i.e., the full observance of the commandments, and if they were males accepted circumcision.

Without the remarkable efforts of the Diaspora Jews to connect Judaism with its social environment, remaining, nevertheless, faithfully attached to their own religious tradition, Christianity would not have spread so rapidly through the breadth and length of the Empire. The failure of Christianity to penetrate into the antique cultures of Southern and Eastern Asia, all of them bereft of important Jewish colonies, emphasizes the indispensable role played by Judaism in the early Christianization of the West. One of its main instruments was the Greek translation of the Hebrew Scriptures. It was thanks to the Septuagint that the living God could reveal himself to the Gentiles in an intelligible language. With the lessening of Athens' influence, Alexandria had become the intellectual capital of the Empire. Its Jewish minority was strong and vocal. Pioneering spirits like Philo favored and contributed to an encounter between the heritage of the Prophets of Israel and the speculations of the Greek philosophers. These endeavors opened the way to a speculative theology, first in Judaism, and later in Christianity. Though Judaism had not yet overcome the gripping power of paganism on the Gentile mentality, it had made ethical monotheism respectable and had lent to it venerable antiquity. Moses could be presented as the spiritual precursor of Plato.

Not all the social aspects of Judaism were attractive to the Gentiles. Hellenistic culture characterized itself as truly universalistic. Today, because we are aware of the past greatness of Egypt and Babylon, and are in contact with the achievements of various Asian cultures, we know that Hellenistic universalism was in fact quite particularistic. In the first century, the whole world seemed included in the circle of Greek culture, and Jewish particularism appeared to Hellenistic eyes as somehow barbarian. The firm refusal of Jews everywhere to let one's religious tradition be combined with others in a universal syncretism met with strong disapproval among the cosmopolitan population of the big cities. On the Jewish side, how could one hide a deep contempt for idolatry when one had been schooled in the teaching of the great Prophets? The Jews were a unique people, a different kind of people, and the Christians, as long as they were looked on as a Jewish sect, evoked the same feeling of remoteness. In the case of Judaism certain rituals like circumcision, considered by the Greeks as a mutilation, or the dietary laws and Sabbath observances that rendered normal social relations more difficult, if not impossible, were constant reminders that the Jews were "a people living alone, and not reckoning itself among the nations" (Num 23:9).

Jews became convinced during centuries of harsh rule under Christians and

Moslems that they were not, and never had been, a missionary religion, and that converts to Judaism were the exception which confirms the rule. The saying of Jesus in the Gospel according to Matthew (23:15), "For you cross sea and land to make a single convert," seemed to be completely out of place. Modern historiography, however, has put this saying of Jesus back into its proper context. During Temple Judaism there was, among others, one strongly universalistic trend exemplified by Deutero-Trito-Isaiah. God was not simply the God of Israel, but the God of all nations. In the Hebrew Scriptures, if the centrality of Israel as the priestly people is always affirmed, the vocation of the Gentiles to come to Jerusalem to share in the worship of the One and True God is also expressed as an essential component of the messianic hope and vision. Although the posterity of Ezra tended to be very Israel-centered, building a highly protective fence around the Torah, it has been shown that until the Roman wars and the defeat of Bar Kochba many Jewish communities in the Diaspora, less by preaching than by attraction, had been receiving great numbers of proselytes and God-fearers. The high proportion of Jews in the population of the Empire would be difficult to explain if there had not been many converts to Judaism. The Diaspora was not simply a curse; it was also a blessing, allowing the light of TORAH to radiate from Jerusalem.

2. REACHING OUT TO THE GENTILES

Once the witness of Jesus' disciples had made inroads among the pilgrims who ascended to Jerusalem and through them among the Jewish communities of the Diaspora, it was to be expected that, like Judaism, the new way would slowly penetrate into the Gentile world. Whence the extraordinary importance of Antioch, the third city of the Empire; it was to become the main social laboratory for this process. At Antioch the disciples of Jesus, known until then as Nazarenes, came to be called Christians, which means Messianics, probably because of their insistence on the imminent return in glory of Jesus of Nazareth as the Messiah expected to usher in the Kingdom of God. Not only local Hellenist Jews whose families might have been in Antioch for a long time, but proselytes and God-fearers who had come to Judaism from paganism, became awakened to this new messianic hope.

Those proselytes who had already been circumcised could be baptized without raising any further question. Notwithstanding their Gentile origin, they were bona fide Jews who had accepted the yoke of the Law. All they had to do was to put their trust in Jesus of Nazareth as the expected Messiah of Israel, and to faithfully follow his teaching while waiting for his return in glory. The conversion of the God-fearers was a different matter. It presented

an entirely new problem, about which there had been no instruction left by
Jesus. Were they, or not, to commit themselves to the full observance of the
commandments, and if they were males to undergo circumcision?

It is probable that in some cases God-fearers had been accepted into full
membership in the Nazarene community without any change in their status.
Given the charismatic enthusiasm of the early believers, the deep faith of
some God-fearers, their close fellowship with the rest of the Jewish community and their observance of many Mosaic precepts, a request on their part to be
baptized in the name of Jesus, in order to receive the gift of the Holy Spirit,
might have seemed natural and would have been happily granted. When
Barnabas and Saul were sent by the community of Antioch to proclaim Jesus'
message in the synagogues of Cyprus, Pamphylia, Pisidia and Galatia, many
Jews and God-fearers became believers. Luke does not mention any baptismal
ceremony. However, by the time Barnabas and Saul returned to Antioch, some
zealous observers of the Law had come down from Jerusalem to explain to
any baptized but non-circumcised God-fearer that:

> ...unless you are circumcised according to the custom of Moses, you cannot be
> saved. And after Paul and Barnabas had no small dissension and debate with
> them, Paul and Barnabas and some of the others were appointed to go up to
> Jerusalem to discuss this question with the apostles and the elders (Acts
> 15:1–2).

3. STEPS CONDUCIVE TO A GENTILE CHRISTIANITY

We wish for an exact transcript of this passionate debate which gripped the
Antiochene Church. We can only surmise its tenor. It is difficult for us today
to comprehend the acrimony of the dispute, but we must try to understand the
strong resistance offered by the Nazarene community, especially by those
with a Pharisaic background, to such innovation. The theological implications
were shocking. To expect the coming of the Messiah, and to prepare oneself
for his advent, was good and necessary, but in the process the integrity of the
covenant initiated by God with Abraham and sealed through Moses at Sinai
had to be preserved at all costs and in all circumstances. Circumcision was the
symbol chosen by God himself to express the reality of this covenant; the
Mosaic Law was the social structure chosen by God for his own people.
Neither could be touched. Jesus had been sent to bring the covenant to its
final stage by fulfilling the Mosaic Law and opening the door to God's eternal
Kingdom. Could one change God's plans? Could one erect a multi-story
building without building with care its foundations and ground floor? The
covenant had been a process in time: from Abraham to Moses, then to David,

the Prophets, Josiah, Ezra, and finally Jesus of Nazareth. Baptizing in the name of Jesus and ignoring all the constitutive parts of the permanent alliance between God and Israel seemed to be an inner contradiction. To become a Christian without first becoming a Jew in proper and due form was for those who would later be called the Judaizers simply unthinkable.

The real problem was the nature of the Nazarene community. If the baptized God-fearers remained uncircumcised, what would be the future character of the community? Would the community be part and parcel of the Abrahamic covenant, or would it be a community of Jews and Gentiles, i.e., some in the covenant of Abraham and some only in the covenant of Noah? A small minority of Gentiles might not cause much difficulty, but a substantial minority or near majority would change completely the structure of the group. Did the Hellenistic Jews in Antioch know what future they were preparing? They were running the risk of bringing Judaism down to the level of paganism. The Nazarene community could not survive an invasion of uncircumcised who showed no respect for the Mosaic Law. The religious value of Judaism and the survival of God's people were at stake in the activity of Paul and Barnabas—in fact, so were the religion of Jesus and the people of Jesus.

The Nazarene community in Jerusalem, after twenty years of existence, was starting to realize how difficult it was to convince its Jewish brothers and sisters that Jesus of Nazareth was truly risen and would soon return to judge Israel and the nations. A massive gentilization (if a neologism can be allowed) of their community would be like the kiss of death for their witness to the House of Israel. Did Jesus ever intend that his disciples would one day abandon the covenant marked in the flesh of Abraham and in his own flesh, and turn away from the original tradition of the Fathers? This tradition had been so carefully observed by Jesus during his earthly life, that in so doing he had canonized it forever. The signs and wonders worked out by the Holy Spirit among the Gentiles through Paul and Barnabas could not be interpreted as refuting such self-evident truths.

To the surprise of many, the meeting in Jerusalem of the Apostles and the elders, with Peter in the chair, approved the practice inaugurated in Antioch, on the basis of an experience of Peter in Caesarea Maritima. He had witnessed there an outpouring of the Holy Spirit on uncircumcised Gentiles. In a spirit of condescension he asked, "Why are you putting God to the test by placing on the neck of the disciples a yoke that neither our ancestors nor we have been able to bear?" (Acts 15:10). Few realized at the time that a crucial step had been taken, a very small step, but a step which would lead to a deep rift between Jews and Christians lasting down to the present day.

God-fearers accepting Jesus as Lord and Messiah could remain uncircumcised. But what exactly was their relation to the Mosaic Law? Were they excused from all the 613 commandments, including the Decalogue, the sanctification of the Sabbath, all the dietary laws, the rules of endogamy and exogamy, etc.? How could law-abiding and law-breaking Christians live in peace in the same community? Most exegetes would agree that this complex question was not solved, not even discussed in detail, at the meeting in Jerusalem (probably around 50 C.E.). Paul and Barnabas returned to Antioch full of hope. Soon afterward Peter, who from that time on was never mentioned as resident in Jerusalem—he had left the government of the Mother Church to the pastoral care of James, the brother of the Lord—moved to Antioch and started living in a mixed community of Jews and Greeks:

> Until certain people came from James, he used to eat with the Gentiles. But after they came, he drew back and kept himself separate for fear of the circumcision faction. And the other Jews joined him in this hypocrisy, so that even Barnabas was led astray by their hypocrisy (Gal 2:12–13).

Given the severity of the dietary laws at that time, it is not surprising that the most immediate difficulty resulting from the Jerusalem decision was the possibility or impossibility for Christians of Jewish and Gentile origin to sit together at table, not only for ordinary meals, but also for the "Breaking of the Bread" which was still celebrated as part of a regular meal.

Paul opposed Peter "to his face, because he stood self-condemned" (Gal 2:11). For Paul Jews had to adapt themselves to Gentiles and not Gentiles to Jews. The text does not tell us if Paul won his point. The problem of Jewish-Gentile relations was again in the open, and according to recent historical reconstruction the matter was referred once more to the Mother Church in Jerusalem. At a meeting chaired by James, the brother of the Lord, the question was thoroughly discussed and a letter was sent to "the believers of Gentile origin in Antioch, Syria and Cilicia..." telling them merely "to abstain from what has been sacrificed to idols, and from blood, and from what is strangled, and from fornication" (Acts 15:9). Fornication probably meant the rules of conjugal relationships as detailed in Leviticus 18, in order to avoid rendering unlawful a marriage between a Jewish Christian and a Greek Christian. The rule about blood was clearly stated in Leviticus, "The life of the flesh is in the blood....Therefore I have said to the people of Israel: No person among you shall eat blood, nor shall any alien who resides among you eat blood" (Lev 17:11–12). James like Peter showed a spirit of condescension, "We should not trouble the Gentiles who are turning to God" (Acts 15:19). However, great care was taken at the same time to protect the rights of the Jews in the observance of the Law, and to ease relations between Jews and

Gentiles in the community. Greek Christians of Syria and Cilicia were requested to observe some dietary laws.

Many exegetes believe that by the time the letter arrived in Antioch Paul had already left for a well-planned missionary expedition. During his journeys he did not show any awareness of the letter which had been written to Gentile Christians residing in Cilicia and Syria only. Barnabas was back in Cyprus. He had agreed with Paul to baptize the uncircumcised, but there must have been some disagreements between them on the extent to which the Greek converts ought to observe the Mosaic Law. During the incident in Antioch, Barnabas had sided with Peter. Paul decided to start single-handedly a new approach toward the Gentiles. Convinced that he had received a special mission from the risen Jesus himself, he started crisscrossing Asia Minor and Greece, forcing the Jesus movement to leave the bosom of mother Israel and establishing a number of Gentile Churches alongside the Church of the Circumcision. Was such a new missionary activity leading to an absolute break between Jewish Christians and Gentile Christians? Who was this extraordinary man, said by some "to stir up trouble among the Jews the world over" (Acts 24:5)? It is imperative that we seek to understand him, because as long as there is an ongoing Christian-Jewish dialogue, Paul will always stand in the center.

VII. Saul/Paul of Tarsus

Born and raised in the Diaspora, in Tarsus, the capital of Cilicia, a center of culture and education, Saul, whose father was a Roman citizen, had the opportunity in his youth to become acquainted with the ways of the Gentiles. At a later age he moved to Jerusalem and became a pupil of Gamaliel the Elder, the son or grandson of Hillel. From him he learned the love of TORAH and the faithful observance of all the commandments. He styled himself, "a Pharisee and the son of Pharisees" (Acts 23:6). In his Letter to the Galatians he wrote, "I advanced in Judaism beyond many among my people of the same age, for I was more zealous for the traditions of my ancestors" (Gal 1:14). Thanks to this twofold upbringing Saul/Paul was as much at ease among Hebrews as among Hellenists.

Saul must have achieved a certain status among the learned ones because, according to Acts, he was granted some authority.

> Indeed, I myself was convinced that I ought to do many things against the name of Jesus of Nazareth. And that is what I did in Jerusalem; with authority received from the chief priests, I not only locked up many of the saints in prison, but I also cast my vote against them when they were being condemned to death. By punishing them often in all the synagogues I tried to force them to blaspheme; and since I was so furiously enraged at them, I pursued them even to foreign cities (Acts 26:9–11).

We have no way of knowing the charges leveled by Saul against some Nazarenes. We can surmise that they dealt with their attitude toward the Temple, or a less than strict observance of the Mosaic Law. The persecution in Jerusalem, violent (Gal 1:13) or severe (Acts 8:1), was of short duration on account of what happened to the main persecutor. "With the authority and commission of the chief priests" (Acts 26:12) he was on his way to Damascus, intending to arrest a few Nazarenes and bring them bound to

Jerusalem, when unexpectedly he encountered Jesus of Nazareth, that dead man who had been his pet aversion.

Much has been written about Saul's encounter. It was a peak experience of a religious nature that brought about a radical reorientation in the life of Saul. In Christian tradition it is understood as a revelatory act of God. For Paul it was an appearance of the risen Jesus of the same order as the appearances to the disciples immediately after the Resurrection: "Last of all, as to one untimely born, he appeared also to me" (1 Cor 15:8). It was an occurrence, however, not in the subdued manner in which Jesus had appeared to his disciples, but in majesty and glory. It was the first but not to be the sole encounter between Paul and the risen Jesus. In a letter to the Corinthians he refers to visions and revelations, and to that day "when such a person...was caught up into Paradise and heard things that are not to be told, that no mortal is permitted to repeat" (2 Cor 12:4).

On the morrow of such an extraordinary experience, Saul's acquaintances in Damascus, when they met him on the street and started a conversation with him, must have been amazed. He was not the Saul they knew, not even a typical Nazarene, i.e., a devout Jew who was hoping and praying for the imminent return of Jesus of Nazareth as Messiah. Saul had become a profoundly changed man, with a completely new orientation toward past, present and future. He was still very Jewish and very proud to be one of them.

> If anyone else has reason to be confident in the flesh, I have more: circumcised on the eighth day, a member of the people of Israel, of the tribe of Benjamin, a Hebrew born of Hebrews; as to the law, a Pharisee; as to zeal, a persecutor of the Church; as to righteousness under the law, blameless (Phil 3:4-6).

However, his Jewishness had undergone a radical transformation. Was it the product of a sudden enlightenment or the beginning of a process of change? His spiritual pilgrimage during the next fifteen years is unknown to us. Only his mature personality has been revealed in a surprisingly rich literary heritage left to our perusal.

1. THE FUTURE AS GOD'S KINGDOM

When he was persecuting the Nazarenes Saul was very much present-oriented, rather than future-oriented. We have no way to know the nature of his messianic convictions, if he had any. As a Pharisee, son of Pharisees, he was not attracted to the wild speculations of apocalyptic messianism. He must have prayed for the restoration of national sovereignty, with or without a son of David on the throne. His main interest was to ensure the actual fulfillment of

TORAH, the will of God for Israel clearly formulated in the Mosaic Law. Suddenly, the appearance of the risen Jesus took his mind out of his familiar world. Jesus was alive, and in a way hard to conceptualize. He was not like the man from Nazareth whom Saul had seen from afar, or had imagined on hearsay. Jesus had not returned. Rather than coming to Saul, he had taken Saul to himself, into a light brighter than the sun (Acts 26:13), into power and glory. Such an experience did not match Saul's Pharisaic conception of resurrection. The Jesus he had met so suddenly dwelt in an unknown reality, beyond the limits of this world. Paul will always consider the resurrection of Jesus of Nazareth as the beginning of a new creation, forecasting by its appearance the demise of the present world. After his encounter on the way to Damascus Saul has become totally absorbed in the future, "...there is a new creation: everything old has passed away; everything has become new" (2 Cor 5:17).

In this perspective any "earthly" messianism had become irrelevant. Saul's compatriots were conceiving different messianic scenarios, and even the Nazarenes themselves, though confident in the imminent return of their beloved master, were remaining unclear about the kind of kingdom his return would establish. The fact that millenarianism survived during the second century in many Christian Churches and was upheld by writers like Justin, Irenaeus, Tertullian and others (to die only with the establishment of Christianity as the state religion of Rome)—such a fact confirms how strong was the hope for an earthly restoration of the kingdom to Israel among the early Nazarenes. For Paul, on the contrary, the messiahship of Jesus did not belong to this world; it belonged entirely to the world to come, more exactly to the new creation, to the world of the resurrection.

The relationship between the world of the resurrection and this world haunts all of Paul's writings. Were these two different worlds continuous or discontinuous? As long as the risen Jesus had not returned for the final drama of human history, how did the already existing new world impinge on our present old world? Such questions needed an answer. In Paul's classical letters we find the beginning of a response.

In chapter fifteen of the First Letter to the Corinthians Paul states without ambiguity, "If Christ has not been raised, then our proclamation has been in vain and your faith has been in vain" (1 Cor 15:14). This affirmation leads to the natural inquiry, "How are the dead raised? With what kind of body?" (1 Cor 15:35). His answer is coined in a dialectical mood, with a strong emphasis on discontinuity, "Flesh and blood cannot inherit the kingdom of God, nor does the perishable inherit the imperishable" (1 Cor 15:50). Using the contrasting images of a seed and a fully grown life, he writes:

What is sown is perishable, what is raised is imperishable. It is sown in dishon-
or, it is raised in glory. It is sown in weakness, it is raised in power. It is sown a
physical body, it is raised a spiritual body....It is not the spiritual that is first,
but the physical, and then the spiritual (1 Cor 15:42–46).

A "spiritual body" sounds like a contradiction. Paul created the term to
convey his singular experience during his meeting with the risen Jesus. The
Greek concept of a human soul forever "liberated" from the body, i.e., from
evil matter, was totally foreign to Paul. He lived in a biblical world and not in
the world of Greek philosophy. "God saw everything that he had made, and
indeed it was very good" (Gen 1:31). The sole liberation Paul could conceive
of was liberation from "the law of sin and death" (Rom 8:2).

Notwithstanding a sharp discontinuity between what is sown and what is
raised, some continuity could not be ignored. Paul would never conceive of
the risen Jesus as other than Jesus of Nazareth, the son of Miriam, crucified
by order of Pontius Pilate. His perishable body had put on imperishability (cf.
1 Cor 15:50). In a forceful statement Paul affirms that today "we are groaning...so that what is mortal may be swallowed up by life" (2 Cor 5:4).
Continuity is unmistakable, together with a radical discontinuity that renders
the new creation transcendent in regard to the old one. Humanity's ignorance
and sense of mystery face to face with a world which remains in itself beyond
the limits of human experience and knowledge, is a natural consequence of
the transcendental character of the new creation. Once more we are strictly in
the realm of faith.

In his most didactic and carefully crafted letter, Paul affirmed the solidarity
of humanity with its environment, or rather of the natural environment with
humanity. He was well aware that the earth had been cursed by God because
of the sins of the one who originally had received dominion over every living
thing (see Gen 3:17, 1:28–30). Human sufferings are echoing the groaning of
the whole creation in labor pains of a new birth.

For the creation waits with eager longing for the revealing of the children of
God; for the creation was subjected to futility, not of its own will but by the
will of the one who subjected it, in hope that the creation itself will be set free
from its bondage to decay and will obtain the freedom of the glory of the children of God (Rom 8:19–20).

This text is without parallel in the other Pauline letters or in all the New
Testament. Was Paul thinking of pristine nature, in the fashion of a Saint
Francis? As soon as nature becomes cultured or civilized through human cre-
ativity Paul loses all interest. He is no friend of the Greek philosophers and

totally ignores the great achievements of Greek art. In the last hour of a dying world, sex is irrelevant to him as well as economic development.

> I mean, brothers and sisters, the appointed time has grown short; from now on, let even those who have wives be as though they had none...and those who buy as though they had no possessions, and those who deal with the world as though they had no dealings with it. For the present form of this world is passing away (1 Cor 7:29–31).

It would be difficult to classify Paul as a Christian humanist, as humanism is generally conceived, or even as a nature lover. Paul does not condemn or despise anything, except sin and death, but he is not attracted to the exciting beauty of an evanescent world.

Only one aspect of human nature—outside its relation to the living God—captures his attention: the moral integrity of humanity. He remains thus in the most authentic Jewish tradition, aptly defined as ethical monotheism. The struggle in Paul's writings between the flesh and the spirit brings to mind the traditional opposition between the YETZER HA-RA' (the tendency to do evil) and the YETZER HA-TOV (the tendency to do good). In the Jewish tradition the positive inclination tends to be the stronger, but for Paul the negative inclination, "the law of sin and death" (Rom 8:2), tends to predominate. Men and women often choose the way of sin even when their own conscience bears witness against them. But, on his Day, the day of reckoning, God will judge the secret thoughts of all (cf. Rom 2:12–15). Moral behavior is thus for Paul the core of human nature and the aspect in the continuity between this world and the world to come in which he is supremely interested.

Jesus of Nazareth, having achieved victory over sin and death, allowed Paul to catch a glimpse of the new creation. Risen and glorified, Messiah Jesus is a kind of "spiritual prism" through which the awesome and simple activity of God in the present is "refracted" into the multiform splendor of a glorious future—a splendor which is multiform because human activity will be integrated in the glorious future according to its quotient of imperishability.

> Now if anyone builds on the foundation [the Messiah] with gold, silver, precious stones, wood, hay, straw—the work of each builder will become visible, for the Day will disclose it, because it will be revealed with fire, and the fire will test what sort of work each has done. If what has been built on the foundation survives, the builder will receive a reward. If the work is burned up, the builder will suffer loss; the builder will be saved, but only through fire (1 Cor 3:12–15).

The immediate future for the earthlings, however, is not yet "the end of days," i.e., the end of history, but rather "the last days" of the present world, a period of struggle, suffering, wrestling with the powers of evil. The risen Jesus in the glory of the new creation is, as King Messiah, a fighting king. Paul applies to him the first verse of Psalm 110, "Sit at my right hand until I make your enemies your footstool." His disciples on earth do not live in a kingdom of glory, of perfect peace and freedom, but in a community under the shadow of the cross; for only "in hope were we saved" (Rom 8:24). Solely at the Parousia, at the end of history, will the Kingdom of the living God be fully revealed.

> Then comes the end, when [King Messiah] hands over the kingdom to God the Father, after he has destroyed every ruler and every authority and power....When all things are subjected to him, then the Son himself will also be subjected to the one who put all things in subjection to him, so that God may be all in all (1 Cor 15:24, 28).

For the rest of his life Paul will remain fascinated by the splendor of the world to come, peered at through the darkness of faith. His own citizenship is no more on earth, but in heaven (cf. Phil 3:20). He belongs to the Jerusalem above, which is free and symbolized by mother Sarah, no more to the present Jerusalem, still in slavery and symbolized by Hagar, the slave woman (cf. Gal 4:21–28). He belongs to the future, trusting that God who raised Jesus from the dead will give life to his mortal body (cf. Rom 8:9–11). "Forgetting what lies behind and straining forward to what is ahead, I press on toward the goal" (Phil 3:13). Such a strong future-oriented attitude was possible only because the risen Jesus had forever won the heart and mind of Paul:

> Yet whatever gains I had, these I have come to regard as loss because of Christ. More than that, I regard everything as loss because of the surpassing value of knowing Christ Jesus, my Lord. For his sake I have suffered the loss of all things, and I regard them as rubbish in order that I may gain Christ and be found in him (Phil 3:7–8).

For Paul, only an intimate union with Jesus of Nazareth, risen and glorified, was opening a clear path to overcome the caducity of this world and reach in the world to come the true Kingdom where the living God is "all in all."

2. THE PAST AS MESSIAH-CENTERED

The first and fundamental transformation in the personality structure of Saul of Tarsus had been a sudden reorientation toward an eschatological future, toward a real participation in the actual union of the risen Messiah with the living God. Nevertheless, he could not forget his past, nor the past of his own people, because the past is so much part of the present and often survives into the future. To understand the complexity of Saul's personality after his Damascene experience, the best working hypothesis is to suppose that Saul looked backward toward the past through exactly the same medium, the risen and glorious humanity of Jesus of Nazareth, through whom he was perceiving the future. The risen Jesus was still acting like a "spiritual prism" but in reverse. He was not refracting the awesome divine light into a future splendor; he was rather refracting the past, the divine activity during the long history of the chosen people, into the simplicity and the luminosity of one unique, perfectly integrated, Jewish personality, Jesus of Nazareth.

Through this spiritual prism Saul could still contemplate the rich splendor of Israel's past, but he was contemplating it in the context of a new and more brilliant splendor. In this new context the past was perceived in less vivid colors, "What once had glory has lost his glory because of the greater glory" (2 Cor 3:10). This new splendor was obviously the world of the resurrection whose first-born was Messiah Jesus.

Notwithstanding some sharp polemical expressions, there is no trace of "anti-Judaism" in Paul. He was quite aware that TORAH, the heart of Judaism, had come from the living God. "The law is holy, and the commandment is holy and just and good" (Rom 7:12). In chapter nine of the Letter to the Romans he described with pride and devotion all the spiritual richness of the Jewish tradition, "the adoption, the glory, the covenants, the giving of the law, the worship and the promises...the patriarchs...the Messiah..." (Rom 9:4–5). Beautiful and glorious as they were, and still are, these were now the past and "everything old has passed away; see, everything has become new!" (2 Cor 5:17). After the Damascene encounter Paul started to look at everything from an eschatological perspective. The spiritual richness of Israel was to be found whole and complete in Jesus of Nazareth risen and glorified. There was no need to look beyond him.

If everything old has passed away, we may wonder why Paul gave unique visibility and strong emphasis to one particular historical event: the election of Abraham and his response to God. "Abraham believed the Lord and the Lord reckoned it to him as righteousness" (Gen 15:6). God had promised to Abraham descendants as numerous as the stars. Abraham's response was more than an assured confidence that Sarah, though she was sterile, would give birth to a son; it was also a personal commitment to the living God, combining a complete trust in his wisdom and power with a willingness to be guided by him along the way of life. The prophet Micah gave a pithy formulation of such a faith, "to walk humbly with...God."

He has told you, O mortal, what is good; and what does the Lord require of you but to do justice, and to love kindness, and to walk humbly with your God? (Mic 6:8).

To do justice and to love kindness are not sufficient. The human response sought by the living God needs to be a personal, permanent bond between himself and his human creature. We find in Paul a clear priority given to religious values over moral values. Given the extraordinary power of evil tendencies (the flesh), moral tendencies (the spirit) have little chance to flourish if pride of place is not given to genuine religious values, to a confident trust in the living God. Moral behavior left alone, like artistic activity, is susceptible to become an autonomous, self-contained enterprise. Virtuosos and experts can be found in ethics as in the fine arts. They can even stifle any genuine creativity. For Paul, to reduce religious life, consciously or unconsciously, to pure ethics was ultimately to smother and finally choke to death moral life itself.

In the long evolution of humanity Abraham's answer to God had been the first expression of a personal religion according to the heart of God. This made Abraham to be the "ancestor of all who believe" (Rom 4:11), be they circumcised or uncircumcised. The faith of him who is "the father of all of us" (Rom 4:17) was reflected with unique intensity in the total surrender to the living God of the crucified and glorified son of Abraham, the risen Jesus. It provided Paul not only with a basic framework for theological thinking; it afforded him also the possibility of remaining fully conscious of the living continuity with the Jewish identity in which he was born.

All pious Jews know that the essential bond between the living God and Israel was sealed in the Abrahamic covenant. Circumcision on the eighth day is its visible symbol. The Book of Deuteronomy affirms that God set his heart on Israel "because the Lord loved you and kept the oath that he swore to your ancestors" (Deut 7:8). In the "Eighteen Benedictions," the prayer par excellence, which is recited at each of the three services, morning, afternoon and evening, the first benediction invokes God:

Blessed art thou, Lord our God and God of our fathers, God of Abraham, God of Isaac and God of Jacob; great, mighty and revered God, sublime God, who bestowest lovingkindness, and art Master of all things; who rememberest the good deeds of our fathers, and who wilt graciously bring a redeemer to their children's children for the sake of thy name.[1]

God's election and the exclusive spiritual bond which united God and Abraham have always remained vividly conscious in the souls of all pious

Jews, and Paul was one of them. He needed to anchor his new vision of Judaism into its deepest historical roots.

If Paul was so devoted to the Patriarchs, how can one explain that he bare-ly mentions the giving of the Law at Sinai or the role of Moses who trans-formed the family of Abraham into an enduring nation? In fact, Paul passes over in silence most of Israel's history. For him everything old has passed away. It is not the past which explains the future; it is the future which gives account of the past. This paradoxical attitude is not limited to the Hebrew Scriptures. In his letters most of the earthly life of Jesus of Nazareth is passed over in silence. Only his birth, his passion-death-resurrection and the institu-tion of the Eucharist are mentioned. There is no reference to Jesus' parables, sayings, miracles, pilgrimages or prayer life. It is as if his earthly life had no other meaning than his martyrdom, his perfect surrender to the living God. "Even though we once knew Christ from a human point of view we know him no longer in that way" (2 Cor 5:16). Paul could have said as well: Even though we once knew Israel from a human point of view we know it no longer that way. Then the question could be asked: In what way did he know Israel in the light of his Damascene experience?

Except for the history of the Patriarchs, Paul knew Israel only as Jesus of Nazareth, risen and glorified. For him Israel had gone through an eschatologi-cal fire in Jesus' agony on Calvary; on Easter Day it had passed from a reality in the flesh into a reality in the spirit. The risen Jesus had become a spiritual magnet attracting and even absorbing in himself all the spiritual richness and beauty of the Jewish tradition. This unique heritage was now condensed, con-centrated, even constricted, into one single Jew, Jesus of Nazareth, the "Son of God" (Gal 2:20), whose face mirrored the glory of God (cf. 2 Cor 4:6), "born under the law" (Gal 4:4), "descended from David" (Rom 1:3), put for-ward by God as a sacrifice of atonement (cf. Rom 3:25). He had been brought back from the dead to become the great shepherd and the eternal high priest over the House of Israel. In the presence of the living God, Jesus of Nazareth was, is, and always will be Israel personified, the embodiment of the eternal people, the perfect realization of God's great design. God had first chosen Israel among all the nations to be his own people. Then, in a time of favor (Is 49:8), God's own Son was born in its midst, the first-born among many broth-ers and sisters (cf. Rom 8:29). He was the just one, the wise one, the holy one, the fulfillment of the promise made to Abraham.

Only the sudden enlightenment on the way to Damascus and something like an implosion in the person of the risen Jesus of all the religious values God had carefully husbanded among his chosen people for many centuries could explain Paul's puzzling exegesis of God's promise to Abraham. Five times in Genesis God promised to give the land of Canaan to Abraham's SEED forever (12:7, 13:15, 15:18, 17:7–8, 24:7), and after the Binding of Isaac he promised to make Abraham's SEED "as numerous as the stars of heaven and as the sand that is on the seashore" (Gen 22:17). Though the word seed in Hebrew when used in the singular can mean posterity, and even a numerous one, Paul, as some scribes might do, argued from the grammatically singular term as follows:

> Now the promises were made to Abraham and to his offspring; it does not say, "And to offsprings," as of many; but it says, "And to your offspring," that is, to one person, who is Christ (Gal 3:16).

If for Paul the risen Jesus was thus the key to enter into Israel's past and future, what were his status and role in the present, the living present, which had always been the focus of Israel's covenantal life?

3. THE PRESENT AS LIFE IN THE SPIRIT

Paul's inclusive Christocentrism and his radical eschatology were stretching the imagination of his listeners far beyond the proclamation of the Nazarenes. They were altogether an implosion of the past, and an explosion into the future, altering considerably the religious identity of Israel. Such language may have sounded strange to Jewish ears. By focusing all the spiritual richness of the Jewish tradition on one single person, the nature of Israel as a people was fading away. God is One, not many, but human beings, on the contrary, are many and not simply one. Only a people can express all the potentialities of human nature. If God's intention was to establish a permanent bond of love with humanity, he could not reduce this bond to a simple I-Thou relationship.

At the beginning of Sacred History God had established a covenant between himself and Abraham, but with Abraham as the father of a large progeny. At Sinai this Abrahamic covenant became structured into a covenant between God and one nation. In so doing God took account of the essential character of human life, its sociability. The intimate bond between God as Father and Jesus of Nazareth as Son left unanswered the relation of God with all other human beings, and first of all with Israel. Once Paul ceased to focus all his attention on the reality of the world to come, and came to act effectively in this world, the social dimension of human life started to challenge him, requiring an answer in religious terms. The extraordinary experience on the way to Damascus had given him an existential answer in personal but not yet in social terms.

By temperament Paul was not prone to worry about social organization; he was a strong individualist. Webster's definition of individualist, "one that pursues a markedly independent course in thought or action,"[2] is a fair description of Saul/Paul, even as a persecutor of the Church. A few factors contributed to the reinforcement of this individualism. A diligent study of legal or moral cases under the great Gamaliel the Elder did not necessarily deal with the communal aspects of Jewish life. The cases could have been personal or interpersonal matters. More significant was the individualism which was pervading large sections of the Greco-Roman world in which Paul grew up. For the Greeks at that time the religious quest was strongly focused on individual salvation. Moreover, in the first phase of his Christian life, from his first encounter with the risen Jesus to the beginning of his solo apostolate, Paul may not have been completely at ease in the Hellenistic Christian communities of Syria-Cilicia. It was less the typical hardship of any convert becoming socialized into a different religious culture than the divergence of vision concerning community relations with the Gentiles. He could not enter fully into the life of these communities. The spat with Peter at Antioch about KASHRUT and the definite break with Barnabas, who had been his mentor and was an influential member of the Antiochene community, brought into the open the tensions which for quite a while had been simmering in Paul's subconscious. As a strong individualist his willingness to share the life of a particular community had clear limits.

Still, Paul survived fourteen years in conditions which did not correspond to his deepest aspirations. There must have been some latent energy capable of sustaining him during that period of searching. Even with a half-hearted participation in the life of the already established Christian communities, he must have experienced again and again the strong solidarity and warm affection present among their members. He became a witness to, and may himself have been graced by, sudden outpourings of God's Spirit. In the First Letter to the Corinthians he enumerates some of these spiritual gifts: wisdom, knowledge, faith, healing, miracles, prophecy, discernment of spirits, tongues, interpretation of tongues (1 Cor 12:8-11). These visible signs of God's presence were probably more frequent in Gentile Churches, but Luke attests to their occurrence in Nazarene communities. Paul showed a certain uneasiness vis-à-vis some charismata, specially glossolalia. He ends his description by saying that "God is a God not of disorder but of peace" (1 Cor 14:33).

Through the orderly charismata Paul discovered with joy and gratitude the mysterious presence of God's own Spirit, the Spirit of Holiness. These charismata were the sign of the new age, the new aeon, ushered in by the resurrection and glorification of Jesus of Nazareth. The SHECHINAH, the presence of God in the Holy of Holies, the most sacred section of the Jerusalem Temple, was now reaching the new believers at the core of their personality:

God's love has been poured into our hearts through the Holy Spirit that has been given to us (Rom 5:5).

If the Spirit of him [God] who raised Jesus from the dead dwells in you, he who raised Christ from the dead will give life to your mortal bodies also through his Spirit that dwells in you (Rom 8:11).

The gift of the Spirit, at times an extraordinary event, could also be an indwelling presence, as long as that presence was not rejected. This presence in the hearts of the believers, imparting to them some of God's wisdom and power, in no way questioned God's infinite transcendence. Nevertheless, it effected a certain closeness, a real intimacy, "For all who are led by the Spirit of God are children of God....When we cry, 'Abba! Father!' it is that very Spirit bearing witness with our spirit that we are children of God" (Rom 8:14-16). For Paul the immanence in this world of a transcendent God meant the active presence of his Spirit. This allowed him, in the dramatic encounter with the sages of the Areopagus, to affirm, "He [the Living God] is not far from each one of us. For in him we live and move and have our being" (Acts 17:28), an expression akin to pantheism, which was abhorrent to Judaism and evidently to Paul himself. But intimacy is not absorption of one by the other. Divine nature and human nature can never be confused. Paul will always remain a strict monotheist.

The Jewish character of Paul's spirituality could be tested through a comparison with those mystical experiences which are part of the Jewish heritage, such as the mysticism of the MERKAVAH, the Kaballah, and the BAAL SHEM TOV, the spiritual father of Hasidism.[3] God's Spirit was obviously active in Judaism. Paul's mysticism, in comparison with other Jewish mystics, was characterized by a new element, its messianism. In the quoted text of Romans Paul added, "if children, then heirs, heirs of God and joint heirs with Christ" (Rom 8:17). It is by living this joint heritage with Messiah Jesus that Paul's mysticism had become indeed messianic and characteristically unique.

As God's Spirit had been poured in fullness into the human heart of Jesus of Nazareth, now risen and glorified, it was possible for the living God to find in the risen Jesus the perfect human answer to his love. The messianic mystic in seeking unity of mind and heart with the mind and heart of the risen Jesus—a unity pursued through a generous following of the master along the way of the cross—could hopefully participate in the actual union of Jesus with the living God. This could be achieved only by God's Spirit indwelling and creatively working at the same time in the risen Jesus and in the heart of Saul the believer.

God's Spirit, whose presence was so pertinent to the spiritual life of individual believers, played likewise an important role in the social life of the Gentile Christian communities established by Paul during his second and third journeys in Greece and Asia Minor. These new communities were very poor in tradition and social organization. It was the presence of God's Spirit which created a deep sense of fellowship and maintained a living unity in spite of their poor integration. The charismata insured their survival. They helped Paul to overcome his natural individualism, to develop a true appreciation for community life, and to contemplate the Christian community as a diversified unity with the risen Jesus at the head and the disciples as the members fulfilling a variety of functions and services. The union with the risen Jesus in the Spirit was thus a dynamic reality and not simply a quasi-mystical identity.

Later, in the Pastoral letters, be they from Paul or from some of his associates, the classical routinization of charisma appeared, as well as the need of providing the minimal prerequisites for a stable community in a world evanescent but still quite real. The few elements of early Catholicism found in these letters are simply the very first steps in a return toward a Jewish tradition that had been abandoned by the Gentile Churches. This movement will gain some momentum later, but Paul probably did not foresee its future development. He was a practical man, who came to discover that God was not a God of disorder, but a God of SHALOM, a God of peace. In spite of all, we may guess that he died a charismatic at heart, absorbed in Spirit into the intimate union of the risen Jesus with the living God.

4. PAUL'S ATTITUDE TOWARD JUDAISM

When Saul of Tarsus, an enraged persecutor of the Nazarenes, woke up as a committed disciple of Jesus of Nazareth, not only his religious and social environments were utterly different, but his self-image was completely out of focus. He knew he was a Jew, and he felt very deeply his Jewishness, but what did Judaism mean to him in his new predicament? The Judaism of the past was no problem; workmanship of Holy God, it had been holy and conducive to salvation, notwithstanding individual failures. The Judaism of the eschatological future was no problem either; what had been perishable richness had become imperishable, swallowed by life in the resurrection of Messiah Jesus, and fully blossoming in the Jerusalem above. What must have anguished Saul/Paul was the meaning of Jewish life on earth, in the present. He seemed in difficulty trying to bring it into focus.

That all his co-religionists ought to receive Jesus of Nazareth, now that he was risen and glorified, was obvious to Paul. "To the Jews first" was a leitmotiv of his proclamation. The real problem was not the discipleship of individual Jews, but what had happened, or rather ought to happen, to Judaism itself, of which Paul felt himself to be such a part. Was Judaism to continue unchanged until the Parousia, relying for final salvation on the return in glory of Jesus of Nazareth and praying fervently to hasten his return? Or were the Jewish leaders facing a new situation? Realizing that Israel had entered a new age, "the last days" of this world, was God's people to receive and even absorb God's new teaching, together with new blessings coming in the power of the Spirit through the good offices of the risen Jesus? Letters written fifteen years later still convey the feeling of newness, openness, expectation, experienced by Paul during his encounter on the way to Damascus. It was not a feeling of uprootedness, far from it, nor the start of a new life outside Judaism, as if a new seed had fallen from heaven beside it and would now grow on its own. It was rather a sudden expansion, a deep renewal, a great new hope, effected by God's Spirit inside a living Judaism which had been brought into immediate contact with the risen Jesus, with the son of David who had been made the eternal Shepherd of Israel.

The basic framework of Judaism was not changed; it was still the "Sanctification of the Name." This was so self-evident that Paul never argued much about it. He will consecrate the rest of his life to call the Gentile masses "who sit in darkness and in the shadow of death" (Luke 1:79), not knowing the way of peace, "to turn to God from idols, to serve a living and true God" (1 Thess 1:9). All his life Paul shall be a pure monotheist. At the same time he will be a responsible moralist. In his most systematic letter he was indignant "because some people slander us by saying that we say: Let us do evil so that good may come" (Rom 3:8). After a long list of human vices he added, "I am warning you, as I warned you before: those who do such things will not inherit the Kingdom of God" (Gal 5:21). An illuminating remark by E. P. Sanders emphasizes the traditional, but not legalistic, character of Paul's moral teaching:

> Paul considers that what constitutes proper behaviour is self-evident (cf. Gal 5.19; Rom 2.14f.). One may observe that the self-evident proper behaviour, the fruit of the Spirit, coincides materially with the ethical elements of the Old Testament. That is, Paul seems *de facto* to accept the Jewish 'commandments between man and man,' although he does not accept them by virtue of their being commandments.[4]

The commandments between man and God were those questioned by Paul, not in the sense that there was anything wrong with them in the past, but in the sense that they were no more appropriate for an age inaugurated by the resurrection of Jesus of Nazareth and the outpouring of God's Spirit on his disciples. Something new had happened in the life of God's people. From Abraham to Moses, to Solomon and finally to Ezra, the relation of Israel to Almighty God had known important transformations. Now, again, this legacy was going through a new mutation. Here are some examples:

1) The Land promised to Abraham and a numerous posterity was to be their fatherland, their motherland. Paul felt in exile on this land. His citizenship was with the Jerusalem above, symbolized by mother Sarah (Gal 4:21–26).

2) The Law, the Torah given through Moses, was for Paul like a disciplinarian, a teacher of right and wrong (Gal 3:24). Enlightened and strengthened by God's Spirit the disciples could find in the humanity of Messiah Jesus the perfect way to God.

3) In the Temple built by Solomon sacrificial worship was true worship established by God himself. Now, Messiah Jesus is able for all time to save those who approach God through him. "It is Christ Jesus, who died, yes, who was raised, who is at the right hand of God, who indeed intercedes for us" (Rom 8:34).

4) God had chosen one people among all the peoples to be his very own, and Ezra later built a strong fence around it. Messiah Jesus had broken down the dividing wall between Jews and Gentiles. "There is no longer Jew or Greek, there is no longer slave or free, there is no longer male and female; for all of you are one in Christ Jesus" (Gal 3:28).

Given such a change of focus within the traditional frame of reference, Paul felt free to call the present relation of Israel to Almighty God a "new covenant," a term already in usage among the Essenes of Qumran to mean a radical renewal of the covenant on account of an entirely new situation. For Paul this new situation was the appearance of the new creation in the person of Jesus of Nazareth, "declared to be Son of God with power according to the spirit of holiness by resurrection from the dead" (Rom 1:4). The ancient covenant had been renewed in the realism of this novel eschatology. Israel, though still in the flesh, i.e., in the present world, was called by the risen Jesus, through some kind of anticipation in the Spirit, to participate in the already existing reality of the world to come, the Jerusalem above.

This participation was to influence all the Jewish institutions. The martyr Stephen had started along the way. Paul followed with a radical revision of the Jewish way of life. It was to be a Judaism atemporal and universal, without Land, without Law, without Temple and without nationhood. Was it surprising that the Nazarenes, who loved their motherland, were zealous for the Law, prayed in the Temple, and lived apart from the Gentiles, were quite disturbed listening to Paul's proclamation of the new age?

The exact word for describing Paul's outlook on Judaism may be a matter for discussion. His outlook had no exact parallel in the early Church, at least in terms of a sudden and total change of perspective from one extreme to the other. We noted that a comparison between Pauline mysticism and the great Jewish mystics could help to understand Paul better. The same could be said of a comparison between his attitude toward the Pharisaic tradition, soon to become Rabbinic Judaism, and the various movements that at times reacted against it, such as Karaism, early Hasidism, and most of all the nineteenth century Reform Judaism. In the mid-first century A.D., Hellenistic Jewish Christianity was more and more taking the appearance of a reform movement. But it was following an evolutionary process, in the same spirit as the one fostered centuries later by Abraham Geiger, the intellectual father of German Reform. On the contrary, Paul was definitely in favor of a revolutionary approach in the spirit of Samuel Holdheim, the spiritual leader of the radical wing of that movement. Expressions such as the old and the new, the flesh and the spirit, the ministry of death and the ministry of the spirit (2 Cor 3:7–8), the end of the Law (Rom 10:4) versus the law of the Spirit (Rom 8:2), etc., do not allow any doubt that for Paul the new age, and consequently the new Israel, were not to be the fruit of a patient evolution, but rather a sudden leap, a significant mutation.

Paul knew that his encounter with the risen Jesus had been a unique experience. How could he communicate his own certitude to all his brothers and sisters? Once more we are entering into the realm of faith which is beyond social or psychological analysis. Paul knew from his own experience that without becoming disciples of the risen Jesus the religious leaders of his people could only recoil before an atemporal and universal Judaism. When around 50 A.D., twenty years after the resurrection of Jesus of Nazareth, he started his systematic missionary effort toward the Gentiles, he was probably convinced that the time had already passed when one could still hope for a change of attitude on the part of official Judaism. In reading between the lines of his Letter to the Romans one gets the impression that Paul was genuinely heartbroken by this refusal, but at the same time relieved that all the obstacles had been overcome to transmit to the Gentiles a renewed Judaism they could more easily accept without having to become naturalized Jews and to give up their own nationhood.

With such a negative attitude toward the past and a lack of interest for an evolutionary process of change, it is not surprising that Paul kept his distance from Jerusalem. After his encounter with the risen Jesus, he waited three years before ascending to the holy city, and it was only for a very short visit (cf. Gal 1:18). In his letters, there is no sign that he ever expected the Church of the Circumcision in Jerusalem, under the firm leadership of James, the brother of the Lord, to take the initiative in answering the spiritual requirements of the new age. During fourteen years he worked in the area of Syria-Cilicia. The Christian community of Antioch was becoming the mother Church of Hellenistic Jewish Christianity, with numerous Gentiles knocking at the door and asking to be received. Unfortunately, we have no historical documents for this period outside the Acts of the Apostles, and Luke gives very few details. In this fluid situation, with various currents vying for leadership, did Paul see an opportunity for a rapid transformtion of the Nazarenes' tradition among the Christian communities of Syria-Cilicia?

It did not happen. Peter had moved to Antioch and was becoming the rallying point for an evolutionary adaptation to the Gentile world. Paul became convinced that his great vision could materialize only in virgin territory. He literally turned his back to the Church of Antioch, returning only once for a brief visit and never mentioning that Church in his letters. He started to criss-cross Asia Minor and Greece, and to establish Gentile Churches in his own image. "Indeed, in Christ Jesus I became your father through the gospel. I appeal to you, then, be imitators of me" (1 Cor 4:15–16). "Join in imitating me, and observe those who live according to the example you have in us" (Phil 3:17). From then on, he will follow a golden rule:

> Thus I make it my ambition to proclaim the good news, not where Christ has already been named, so that I do not build on someone else's foundation (Rom 15:20).

5. PAUL'S ATTITUDE TOWARD THE GENTILES

As a Pharisee, Saul considered all Gentiles as outsiders, ritually impure, addicted to idolatry and licentiousness, essentially people to be shunned as far as possible. Writing to the Galatians he spontaneously used the old cliché, "We ourselves are Jews by birth and not Gentile sinners" (Gal 2:15). It is to these Gentile sinners that he will be sent by God, through the ministry of the risen Jesus, in order to bring to all of them the good news of the new age, the hope of eternal salvation.

God, who had set me apart before I was born and called me through his grace, was pleased to reveal his Son to me, so that I might proclaim him among the Gentiles (Gal 1:15).

Paul always presented his encounter with the risen Jesus on the way to Damascus to be his empowerment as the Apostle of the Gentiles. "I had been entrusted with the gospel to the uncircumcised, just as Peter had been entrusted with the gospel for the circumcised" (Gal 2:7). Given his state of mind prior to his Damascene experience, one must wonder how such a delicate mission could be entrusted to anyone so unfriendly toward foreigners. For Paul the mission was not his choice, but God's. However, God's chosen ones like Moses, David, Isaiah, Ezra, seemed to have been endowed by nature or by training with a temperamental makeup adapted to their task. How could Saul, steeped in Jewish particularism, suddenly think and feel in universalistic terms? Soon, he will passionately take to heart the cause of the Gentiles and completely identify with them. It is puzzling.

The calls of God to Isaiah and Jeremiah were not pure ecstasies into the presence of the Almighty. They were at the same time an intensified self-awareness. "Woe is me! I am lost, for I am a man of unclean lips" (Isa 6:5). "Ah, Lord God! Truly I do not know how to speak for I am only a boy" (Jer 1:6). Did Saul experience a similar self-revelation in his encounter with the risen Jesus? Such would harmonize with his personal confession, "For I am the least of the apostles, unfit to be called an apostle, because I persecuted the church of God" (1 Cor 15:9). There is no doubt that on the way to Damascus he felt extremely confident, even self-righteous, happy to have been chosen to purify Israel from a new spiritual vermin. Krister Stendahl surprised many exegetes in describing Saul/Paul as a man with a quite robust conscience:

> Nowhere in Paul's writings is there any indication that he had any difficulties in fulfilling what he as a Jew understood to be the requirements of the law. As a Jew he had never been down in the Valley of Despond. He went from glory to glory.[5]

Nevertheless, one question of the risen Jesus was sufficient to break his strong shell of self-sufficiency, "Saul, Saul, why do you persecute me?" (Acts 9:4). He did not know that his hidden sin had been persecution of King Messiah, but when in the power of the Spirit he came to truly "know" him, the risen one, he realized that he, Paul, who was, "as to righteousness under the law, blameless" (Phil 3:6), had been in fact "kicking against the goads" (Acts 26:14).

Face to face with Jesus, the new Adam, the primary source of re-created humanity, Paul experienced in a searing intuition the negativity of his own psyche. In a flash he experienced this negativity as part and parcel of an ubiquitous evil so clearly present in this world. Such an insight, similar to Gautama Buddha's enlightenment, uprooted in him any lingering self-centeredness, but his enlightenment, happening in the framework of a deep Jewish faith, evidenced its own characteristic. It was a sudden awareness not of how ubiquitous is suffering in this world, but rather of how ubiquitous is sinfulness. "All, both Jews and Greeks, are under the power of sin" (Rom 3:9).

With the Day of Retribution appearing on the horizon, Saul became suddenly aware how desperate for salvation were the Gentiles. True, the Gentiles could always be saved by observing the Noahide commandments; but most of them were living, in fact, in idolatry, lust and greed. Saul, experiencing God's mercy toward himself, through the ministry of the risen Jesus, came to realize that in these, the last days, salvation was offered to all. Shaken but forgiven and enlightened, Saul was ready to answer God's call and go to the Gentiles as minister of reconciliation.

> In Christ God was reconciling the world to himself, not counting their trespasses against them, and entrusting the message of reconciliation to us (2 Cor 5:19).

How did Paul envisage the proclamation of this message of reconciliation to the Gentiles? As we have little information on the evolution of his thinking during his Antiochene period, we cannot grasp how he came to formulate his message. Were his Jewish feelings so taken by the glory of the new creation that he was compelled to seek first an eschatological expression for his Judaism before turning his attention to the Gentiles, or was the call of the risen Jesus to save the Gentiles from their spiritual misery the stimulus that forced him to discover a form of Judaism more adaptable to a diversity of cultures and societies? We do not know and probably will never know. The two approaches, however, were complementary and reinforced each other.

Paul at first was in a hurry, he was impatient. The return of the risen Jesus was imminent, and the multitude of Gentiles to be rescued "from the wrath that is coming" (1 Thess 1:10) was enormous. For Paul this was the cogent justification of his solo undertaking. In his earliest letters, the Letters to the Thessalonians, the theme of eschatology is predominant. Paul wants the Greeks to truly worship the Living God, to become aware of his forgiving love and to receive from him the spiritual power which will render them blameless on the Day of the Lord. This was a rather simple message. Some Jews became believers, many more God-fearers did, and also a certain number of Greeks. Individually, they came to believe in Jesus, risen and glorified, as their Savior; jointly, they experienced a deep union with him and among themselves in baptism and the Eucharist. Except for the framework of ethical monotheism, which naturally was the essential, there were few Jewish elements in Paul's early proclamation.

Paul's ethical teaching did not seem to go much beyond self-evident morality, except on a crucial point, his great emphasis on loving each other. This led to the formation of local communities which at first were essentially friendship groups. As noted earlier the active presence of God's Spirit and the gift of various charismata were the source of their cohesion. In time these communities became Christian synagogues which called themselves churches (an equivalent term) to indicate their separateness. Paul was now obliged to face at the same time the problems of social organization, of involvement in this evanescent world, and of relations—not only social but also religious—to the Jewish synagogue next door. The eschatological dimension remained primary, but the sanctification of this world could not be ignored.

The Pauline Churches had had little contact with Temple worship, with TORAH, or with Jewish community organization. They were simply attached to the risen Jesus through Paul's ministry and the works of God's Spirit in their midst. In the course of time they had to create and develop their own tradition. From the Nazarenes Paul had received baptism and Eucharist; they will take the place of circumcision and Sabbath service. A common doctrine proved to be a more difficult and more crucial problem; contentious parties had started to appear in Corinth (1 Cor 1:10–16) and in Galatia (Gal 3:1–5). In his preaching—and only partially in his letters—Paul had the opportunity to expose his "ways in Christ Jesus, as I teach them everywhere in every church" (1 Cor 4:17). He calls his ways: the law of faith (Rom 3:27), the law of Christ (Gal 6:2), the law of the Spirit of life in Christ Jesus (Rom 8:2), or simply God's law (Rom 8:7). Finally the charismatic functions evoked in the First Letter to the Corinthians (12:4-11) will in time become a multiplicity of ministries: apostles, prophets, evangelists, pastors, and teachers, all under the authority given to Paul by the risen Jesus to be "The Apostle of the Gentiles." From simple friendship groups the Pauline communities were becoming organized churches.

The delay of the Parousia and the progressive institutionalization of his charismatic communities brought back to Paul's mind the relative value and the spiritual beauty of his old Jewish roots. When, in the midst of sharp controversies, he wrote a justification of his lifework, his Jewishness overwhelmed him:

I have great sorrow and unceasing anguish in my heart. For I could wish that I

myself were accursed and cut off from Christ for the sake of my own people,
my kindred according to the flesh (Rom 9:2–3).

He had come to realize that all his work among and for the Gentiles was
essentially to graft some of them onto Israel. Comparing Israel to a cultivated
olive tree, he was hoping that the grafted Gentiles (Rom 11:17–24) could be
nourished with the spiritual sap oozing from the rich roots of this olive tree—
through the ministry of the risen Jesus.

What kind of Israel had Paul in mind when he used the metaphor of an
olive tree? A cultivated olive tree is a familiar sight on the hills of Judea. It
conveys a sense of time, even of centuries. Was Paul thinking of historical
Israel, of the teaching of the great Prophets? Wild branches, however, are not
grafted on a root but on a tree. In truth, he had not been grafting his converts
on historical Israel, but simply on the risen Jesus. Paul probably was starting
to wonder and was searching. After emphasizing so strongly the discontinuity
between the new and the old, new circumstances in his life brought to the fore
the opposite element of continuity. However, after such a sharp break with the
past, a real continuity might not be easily recovered! All that could be expected was a partial restoration, the reintegration of some lost elements.

Paul being a realist, and becoming less certain about the time of the
Parousia, finally looked at Judaism in the Land of Israel and at the Church of
the Circumcision in Jerusalem as a continuation of the old ways, which after
all were holy. He knew that Jerusalem is the root and "it is not you [Gentile
churches] that support the root, but the root that supports you" (Rom 11:18).
He wanted the Greek believers, who would never think of sending to
Jerusalem the regular half-shekel for the maintenance of the Temple, to help
the Nazarene community in their needs. He was very happy when the
Corinthians "voluntarily gave according to their means, and even beyond their
means, begging us earnestly for the privilege of sharing in this ministry to the
saints" (2 Cor 8:3–4). Paul also planned for a long visit to Jerusalem which
materialized at the end of his third journey. It was like an act of reconciliation
between Jerusalem and the Gentile Churches. His visit with James, the brother
of the Lord, and the elders of the community may have been a little frosty, but
he lived in Jerusalem like the Jerusalemites, and he agreed to worship in the
Temple with four Nazarenes who, under a vow, needed to go through the rite
of purification.

The return of the risen Jesus seemed at that time to be delayed for
unknown reasons; still he could not tarry too long. Consequently, Paul decided
that there was no need to bother the Jews who insisted on observing all the
traditions of their ancestors.

Circumcision is nothing, and uncircumcision is nothing; but observing the commandments of God is everything. Let each of you remain in the condition in which you were called (1 Cor 7:19–20).

Paul was now considering the Church of the Circumcision and the Church of the Gentiles as two sister-Churches. The Nazarenes, with Jesus as their center, kept the root healthy, but the tree was to expand to all nations and all cultures. With Jerusalem becoming the shrine where the pristine tradition was kept, the a-temporal and universal Judaism that Paul had hoped his people would adopt, together with a firm belief in the risen Jesus, became the endowment of the Gentile Churches born from his tireless efforts and the charismata of God's Spirit. There was only one problem, and a vital one, the negative reaction of the orthodox Jewish synagogues in the Diaspora shocked by Paul's extravagant claims and his unmerited success.

VIII. The Anguish of the Jews

At the time of the Vatican Council, the Rev. Edward H. Flannery published a welcome study on the evils of twenty-three centuries of anti-Semitism. He titled the book, THE ANGUISH OF THE JEWS. When, in the fourth and fifth century, "the imperial government initiated restrictive measures against Jewish privileges and proselytism,"[1] this anguish surfaced in the open. Its roots, however, go back to the painful circumstances surrounding the birth of Christianity in the last days of Temple Judaism. Before taking a definite form as a cultural stereotype, causing a bleeding wound to be reawakened again and again at each persecution, this anguish had been originally experienced as a traumatic shock during the early encounter between Judaism and Christianity. Some rumbles had been heard and a certain uneasiness felt as soon as the "The Twelve" proclaimed the victory of their master over death, announcing his return to usher in the Kingdom of God. However, it was Saul of Tarsus, with his personality, his doctrine and most of all his intense missionary activity, who became the harbinger of the painful breakup between the Synagogue and the Church.

1. SAUL/PAUL AS THE CATALYST OF THE BREAK

Paul was a very proud Jew, as we noted earlier, and remained one until his last breath. He never wanted to harm his own people. Called by the risen Jesus, he consecrated half of his life to bring the Gentiles up to the spiritual level of the Jews. His conviction and his proclamation that such a spiritual fulfillment could be obtained without the Gentiles having to become Jews caused not only a persistent malaise but a deep rift in the life of the early Christian community. The Jewish community in turn was forced to take a second look at the Jesus movement. What they saw led the leaders of the Diaspora Synagogues to completely distance themselves from Paul's reaching out into the Greco-Roman world.

As long as Paul had no part in the leadership of any local Christian community or was holding only a minor position, the acceptance into membership of a few uncircumcised Greeks, mostly God-fearers, had probably attracted little attention. Some of these uncircumcised God-fearers had been in fact so close to the Synagogue that the outsiders had regarded them as Jews. Moreover this type of conversion had happened in the Diaspora and not in Judea. Paul's first journey with Barnabas in Asia Minor was intended as a simple visit to Diaspora synagogues in order to proclaim to Jews and God-fearers alike the new eschatological hope brought by the risen Jesus.

When he found some opportunity to do so, Paul reached beyond the circle of the God-fearers. He was surprised and delighted with the result. From then on he started to advocate a direct missionary approach to the Gentiles. As he did not find much enthusiasm in the Antiochene Christian community for a "Gentile Mission," he finally decided to undertake the task under his own personal responsibility. He was certain of having been sent by Messiah Jesus:

> For I want you to know, brothers and sisters, that the gospel that was proclaimed by me is not of human origin; for I did not receive it from a human source, nor was I taught it, but I received it through a revelation of Jesus Christ (Gal 1:11–12).

Saul/Paul was not the only one to have haunting apocalyptic dreams. Futurists at that time were a minority and not highly thought of, but as long as there were no visible signs of the Messiah's arrival, these visionaries were not disturbing the religious security of observant Jews. If Saul had been merely one of them, he would not have created much tension. What caused much apprehension was his open advocacy of bringing into the family of Israel, without proper socialization, any non-Jew, any GOY who was willing to live a decent life and was sharing Paul's apocalyptic vision. The reaction was immediate and occasionally violent.

In the Diaspora, where the Jewish community was finding itself isolated, surrounded by a certain amount of antisemitism, and under pressure to assimilate culturally, the Synagogue leaders were cautious about the introduction of non-Jewish elements into the religious life of their people. The sudden appearance next door of a group of Messianic Jews, who did not observe the traditions of their ancestors, and in addition accepted without much screening not only God-fearers but all kinds of ex-idolaters, was prone to create, more than grating annoyance, a feeling of spiritual aversion. Nobody is happy with too much competition, but the appearance of a spurious product easily inspires contempt.

Paul did convince some Diaspora Jews to accept his gospel, but the simple fact that he had to establish his own synagogues indicates that the majority did not recognize his spiritual authority. His greatest success was among the God-fearers. Jews were still receiving converts at that time; they could remain God-fearers all their life, if they so desired. Full membership called for full acceptance of the yoke of the Law. Those living in the spirit of Judaism, but finding some specific regulations excessive, would remain God-fearers at the price of experiencing a certain feeling of inferiority. To them Paul was opening new horizons, full and complete participation in the life of God's people without the obligation to submit to all the ritual prescriptions of TORAH.

If Paul had maintained a distinction between circumcised and uncircumcised believers in his synagogues, had specified their respective duties and privileges, and had explained more clearly the difference between Jews and Gentiles (Rom 3:1), the antagonism coming from the Synagogue might have been less severe. Paul in fact accepted a certain distinction between Jews and Gentiles, but only at the socio-cultural level. The Jews remained Jews. The Greeks and the barbarians kept their national characteristics. All, however, were called to share in the spiritual riches of a Judaism transformed by the death and resurrection of Jesus of Nazareth. For Paul national characteristics had no religious value in the perspective of an a-temporal and universal form of Judaism.

What Paul was attempting looked like a true revolution in Jewish tradition. It had been attempted neither by Jesus of Nazareth nor by the Twelve. He was trying to unravel religion and nationhood out of the close-knit fabric of Jewish history. He was differentiating between ISRAEL and THE JEWS, terms at that time nearly identical. Originally Israel was the name given to Jacob by God himself. It will become the name of his progeny. Judah was the name of one of the twelve tribes, the one which survived the destruction of Jerusalem and the exile in Babylon. After the destruction of the Northern Kingdom, the term Israel had come to mean solely the religious, cultural and ancestral characteristics of God's People, whereas Judea, or the Jews, meant the nation in the Middle East which affirmed its identity and its autonomy in the Maccabean revolt. (Today, the cultural-religious meaning of Israel is better conveyed by the term Judaism, and the nation as a political entity is no longer Judea but Israel.)

For Paul's contemporaries the terms "Israel" and "the Jews," even if they would evoke different aspects of the same social reality, could never be isolated one from the other. Jewish religious culture and Jewish society formed a unity incapable of being separated. This unity will remain intact for centuries, until in modern times the emergence of the national states will create new dilemmas. Paul was convinced that a separation was possible, but on his own terms. The religious life of the Jewish nation (Israel in Paul's terminology) had been renewed through the resurrection of Jesus and the gift of God's Spirit, and thus made effectively atemporal and universal. As such it could inform the lives of Greeks or barbarians, while continuing to inform the national life of the Jews. The Jews of the Diaspora, as soon as they saw before their own eyes this new blend of outer-worldly Judaism and alien national elements, felt as though they were being desecrated. Even if the Greco-Roman world was considering the Gentile communities assembled by Paul as some kind of Jewish sect, the Orthodox Jews were looking at them as a fraud. They felt deeply hurt in their own self-identity.

The fact that Jews strongly objected to a new kind of Judaism may not be surprising. What truly seems surprising is the seriousness of the tensions, even the open quarrels among Jesus' early disciples, stirred up by Paul's opening toward the Gentiles. At that time the Nazarenes were still wondering and arguing among themselves about the status of their own community. Had the messianic era already started with the outpouring of God's Spirit, or was it to be inaugurated by Messiah Jesus later at his return? Only the Messiah in person could gather the nations around Jerusalem to worship the true and living God and learn from TORAH. The prophecies were clear on this point. But even then, it would be out of the question for the GOYIM, the nations, to approach the Almighty as equal with Israel. They would be a crown around God's people, like the God-fearers in the Diaspora synagogues. Israel was the holy nation, the priestly nation. Jesus of Nazareth did not come from God to eradicate the privileges of Israel, but to confirm them. The nations were most welcome, but in their proper place!

Luke wrote the Acts of the Apostles in a hagiographic style. He barely mentioned the intensity of the struggle between Paul and some very determined adversaries who thought that in conscience they had to do all they could to stop the transformation of Jesus' community into a Gentile assembly. Paul's letters to the Philippians and the Galatians leave no doubt about the bitterness of the polemic. "Beware of the dogs, beware of the evil workers, beware of those who mutilate the flesh" (Phil 3:2). Reminiscing on his meeting with the acknowledged leaders in Jerusalem concerning his apostolic authority and the problem of circumcision, Paul wrote,

> But because of false believers secretly brought in, who slipped in to spy on the freedom we have in Christ Jesus—we did not submit to them even for a moment, so that the truth of the gospel might always remain with you (Gal 2:4–5).

Such a sharp confrontation was not between Jews and Gentile Christians, but between Jewish Christians and Gentile Christians. It shows how deeply

Jewish were the roots of Christianity in the Church of the Circumcision. The Twelve were caught in the middle. They were contemplating an opening toward the Gentiles, wondering how far to go in untying the bonds of TORAH. Jesus' ministry had been confined to the House of Israel. Only after the resurrection did he call the faithful eleven to "Go therefore and make disciples of all nations" (Matt 28:19). Had he added to this injunction some more specific instructions? It appears that he let his apostles struggle with the many theoretical and practical problems that any opening to the Gentiles would create. The only help promised was the help of God's Spirit.

2. PARTICULARISM NEGATED BY UNIVERSALISM

Why did the prospect of an a-temporal and universal Judaism appear so startling to the Jewish synagogues of the Diaspora as well as to the Church of the Circumcision in Jerusalem? With a sure instinct they knew that once universalism was accepted by the Jewish people as their main orientation, their particular Jewish culture would in no time be divested of its historical uniqueness and their community would be rapidly absorbed by the surrounding milieu. The uniqueness of Israel had its source in the election by the living God of one particular people out of all the nations, an election not out of time and space, but fully inserted in the makeup of this world. Israel was that part of creation which from all eternity God had reserved for himself, to whom he had revealed himself, and whom he had hoped to mold as the prototype of his intimate relationship with humanity. If the function of prototype was going to be restricted to Jesus of Nazareth and if all the Gentile nations were to be included in the election of Israel, the specific role of Israel in salvation history as "the priestly people" (Exod 19:6) would become non-existing, except as a nostalgic memory.

An analogy may help Christians to understand the nature of the problem. When the Reformers in the sixteenth century recalled that Jesus Christ was the only mediator between God and humanity, and that the entire Christian community was a priestly people, they also explicitly denied the existence of any form of ministerial priesthood. The Orthodox and Roman hierarchies were stunned. They knew "they" existed as ministerial priesthood. They could not conceive Christ's Church without finding in her midst the sacramental presence of the risen Jesus in his unique role as shepherd of God's people. In the same way, the Jews listening to Saul of Tarsus knew that they were 'AM NIFRAD, a separate nation by God's choice, called to fulfill a priestly role and a holy function among all the other nations. Paul seemed to be telling them that from now on the chosen nation will be chosen no more, and that only two realities still existed: humanity and Jesus of Nazareth, risen and glorified. It was saying to them: Surely, Christians ought to be grateful to the Jews for giving birth to Jesus, but from now on his kinsfolk have become irrelevant.

With this universalistic view in mind how could Paul write that Israel is the root that supports the Gentile Christians (Rom 11:18)? How could Israel fulfill such a function if its uniqueness and its rootedness in this world were not permanent and somehow related to eschatology and universalism? In his sensibility Paul felt that the Jewish people had a unique role to play. He affirmed that as regards election they are beloved of God because God's gifts and calling are irrevocable (cf. Rom 11:28–29). He suggested that without them the body of Christ is partly disabled. He used a term that no exegete has been able to explain satisfactorily, "what will their acceptance be but life from the dead!" (Rom 11:15). In his feelings Paul was truly experiencing Israel as the existential root of the Christian community, but in his mind Israel as "root" seemed to mean nothing more than a remembrance of the earthly life of Jesus of Nazareth as being a Jewish life. The rest of the Jewish story could be forgotten. In truth, even that earthly Jewish life of Jesus was a kind of past history. And if "everything old has passed away; see, everything has become new!" (2 Cor 5:17), then there is no need for any existential root or foundation other than the death and resurrection of Jesus of Nazareth.

Notwithstanding a deep spiritual need to be rooted in the Judaism of his youth, the past remained for Paul just the past, simply a hopeful promise for the future. The intensity of his eschatological vision did not allow ongoing history to have any deep meaning, except for the development of more moral stamina. Despite the feelings of his heart, in his mind Christianity was eschatological, Judaism was historical, and the twain didn't meet. By giving to the Jewish Christians and to the Synagogue Jews the impression that they had become "antiques," to be cherished but not to be used, Paul was deeply hurting their self-respect, their sense of identity. He was denying the eternal validity of Israel's election as God's own people in the flesh—while at the same time seeming to affirm its existence in reminding the Romans that the gifts and calling of God are irrevocable (Rom 11:29).

Paul never completely harmonized heart and mind. He searched all his life for a concrete way to allow Jews and Gentiles to live together as the Israel of God. History will show that he did not succeed. Nevertheless, he persevered in the darkness of faith, because the risen Jesus had made him understand that being a bona fide member of a Jewish community was not strictly necessary to become a child of God and a brother of Messiah Jesus. His mission was to bring this good news to the Gentiles.

Each time Paul was successful at pulling some Gentiles away from their idols, the Orthodox Jews might have been willing to cheer him up, but when he was pulling some pious God-fearers and even some observant Jews away from the Synagogue, teaching them that Judaism was behind the times and that there was now a better way, they must have been indignant and deeply hurt.

3. THE LAW CHALLENGED BY THE SPIRIT

In Jerusalem, James and the Nazarenes had enemies, but these enemies, even if they were considering the Nazarenes deviant, would not think of them as being outside Judaism. In the Diaspora, on the contrary, when Paul attracted some observant Jews to the new way, he was thought by Orthodox Jews to be leading them outside Judaism. As we noted earlier, the status of circumcised believers in the early Hellenistic-Jewish-Christian communities was in jeopardy. Their obligation to keep all the Mosaic commandments was in conflict with their need to enter fully into the life of a community whose Gentile majority had been declared by Paul free from such an obligation. For example, how could they participate in the community meals, including the Eucharist, without breaking the laws of KASHRUT? If the faithful observance of all the commandments did not create problems for the Church of the Circumcision in Jerusalem, it was at the heart of the relations between Jews and Gentiles in the Churches of the Diaspora. Orthodox Jews were watching, and the attitude of Paul toward the Mosaic Law became the focus of their mutual disagreements.

Israel's election as the chosen people is an abstract concept, and in itself a purely spiritual reality accessible only to the eyes of faith. When accepted and lived by the elect people it will be translated into particular forms of behavior. It is not simply a matter of choosing good and avoiding evil; it is also a complex system of symbolic behavior which reveals and strengthens the permanent relationship with the living God. In the election of Israel, God did not enter into a covenant with individual persons; he covenanted with a people, a nation. Consequently, the resulting covenantal behavior will exhibit a social and even a legal aspect, and, hence, the complexity of the Mosaic Law transmitted during centuries of changing circumstances.

There is a real paradox in Paul of Tarsus. There was nothing more holy in Judaism, after the Temple in Jerusalem, than the Torah, the Mosaic Law. In the Diaspora, far away from Jerusalem, it was the observance of the commandments which characterized the Jews and constituted them as a separate ethnic group. Paul was very attached to Judaism, proud of being one of "them," anxious to expand the spiritual influence of his people. How could he at the same time express clearly negative attitudes toward the Law? To understand such a contradiction we need to unravel two very different strands of thought and feelings in his attitude.

In the mind of Paul there had been from the time of his Damascene experience a clear certitude that the reconciliation God was offering to the Gentiles would never reach the majority of them if they were required to take on themselves the full observance of the Law. Even if to do so would be ideal, it was not realistic or practical. Judaism was held in high esteem by a good number of Gentiles, but the masses looked at the Jews as not belonging to the Greco-Roman world, as being atheists, i.e., not worshiping the gods, as foreigners, etc. They were moral people, but had strange customs, some repugnant like circumcision, some unpractical like not working on the seventh day, others ridiculous like their dietary laws. For Paul, a true worship of the living God, rigorous moral life, and readiness to meet the risen Jesus on the Day of Judgment could exist unencumbered with such a heavy load of ancestral traditions.

As a good Pharisee, Paul did not make any distinction between the Written Law and the Oral Law. He wrote, "Once again I testify to every man who lets himself be circumcised that he is obliged to obey the entire law" (Gal 5:3). James, the brother of the Lord in Jerusalem, agreed with Paul, "For whoever keeps the whole law but fails in one point has become accountable for all of it" (Jas 2:10). Here is the main reason why Paul rejected the Mosaic Law in toto when he taught ethical monotheism to the Gentiles. He did not reject the moral law or laws in general, quite the contrary. He was teaching a strict moral law, even slightly puritanical. He was not entirely clear on the source, the foundation, of this morality. He took it for granted. In his Letter to the Romans he wrote, "When Gentiles, who do not possess the law, do instinctively what the law requires, these, though not having the law, are a law to themselves" (Rom 2:14). Obviously Paul did not object to those moral laws which are enshrined in the Torah, especially the TEN WORDS, but he questioned many of the religious and purely social or communal prescriptions of the Torah. As TORAH, for a good Pharisee, was indivisible, he had no choice and he felt obliged to offer to the Gentiles true ethical monotheism without Torah.

Speaking from the point of view of Gentile Christianity he wrote, "Christ is the end of the law so that there may be righteousness for everyone who believes" (Rom 10:4). If such a statement was welcomed by some Gentiles, it sounded to Jewish ears as if the coming of Christ was the end of Judaism in order that Gentiles who believed in him might become righteous Gentiles. Did the salvation of humanity require the disappearance of Judaism?

There was another reason in the attitude of Paul toward the Law which was not related to his reaching out to the Gentiles. Before his encounter with

the risen Jesus, he had been blameless in the observance of the commandments (Phil 3:6). Did the many interpretations of the Written Law ever appear
to him too complex, too cumbersome? This cannot be proved, but it is not out
of the question either. By nature he was an individualist; he might even not
have been a very tidy person. He enjoyed spontaneity, real creativity, true
freedom. He did not need to have all his activities planned beforehand. With
such a disposition he was more open to the guidance and inspiration of God's
Spirit. For this reason it does not matter which law he was considering:
Mosaic Law, moral law, State law, etc. A law is a law; it will always have a
place in his thinking and organizing, but never a central place. It will simply
be an instrument to show the way when a map is necessary. By itself it has no
power to create.

His main argument with the Mosaic Law was that it made the Israelites
aware of sin, but did not give them the power to overcome the evil in their
hearts. (Writing today he would have to say that the letter of the Gospel alone
could not overcome evil.) The real question was the need to overcome the law
of sin and death, "so that the just requirement of the law might be fulfilled in
us" (Rom 8:4). This emphasis on motivation explains the crucial importance
given by Paul to the presence and the working of God's Spirit in the hearts of
the believers and in the ongoing life of his charismatic communities. For Paul
God's Spirit can fulfill the prophecy of Jeremiah 31:31 and write God's Torah
on the hearts of his new converts. Faithful disciple of Jesus of Nazareth, he
proclaims that on the two commandments, love of God and love of neighbor,
"hang all the law and the prophets" (Matt 22:40).

> Owe no one anything, except to love one another; for the one who loves anoth-
> er has fulfilled the law. The commandments, "You shall not commit adultery,
> You shall not murder, You shall not steal, You shall not covet," and any other
> commandment, are summed up in this word, "Love your neighbor as yourself."
> Love does no wrong to a neighbor; therefore, love is the fulfilling of the law
> (Rom 13:8–10).

4. SPIRITUAL RAGE

Christians wonder why such an elevated spiritual ideal was spurned by the
majority of the Diaspora Jews. Paul was bringing the good news that one of
their own people, Jesus of Nazareth by name, after having been martyred by
the Romans under a false pretext, had been vindicated by Almighty God.
Brought back to life from the dead, he had been glorified and made the eternal
High Priest and Shepherd of the House of Israel and of all humanity. Soon he
would return to judge the living and the dead. This message, simple as it

sounded, was not in harmony with the religious categories of the Diaspora Jews. It was not so much a question of trusting or not trusting Paul's veracity, but of trusting in God's activity made manifest to a very few chosen witnesses (cf. Acts 10:41) and not openly to all the people. Messianic events, by definition, were expected to be public events.

Many Diaspora Jews had been catching the messianic fever that was widespread at the time. Their Jewish messianism, be it national or apocalyptic, was looking for something more than the appearance of a powerful messianic figure. They were looking for a "messianic age" replete with concrete, tangible manifestations. The present world was to be changed in a real, visible manner. In proclaiming the imminence of God's Kingdom, Paul was speaking only of a salvation "in hope." His Jewish listeners were looking for salvation in reality, in the present, in the flesh, not in spirit. Trust in God was the essence of Judaism, but inside this trust Paul was asking for a more specific trust, a messianic trust of a kind, i.e., salvation in hope. Many heard him, but were not convinced. A social scientist, experiencing the unredeemed status of the world he lives in, would also find such a trust puzzling if he did not share the faith of Paul of Tarsus.

What will appear to him intriguing is the difference of attitude manifested by the Jews in Jerusalem vis-à-vis the Nazarenes and the attitude expressed nearly everywhere in the Diaspora with regard to Paul. In Jerusalem the Nazarenes had kept a few tenacious enemies among those Sadducean circles that had been involved in the arrest and condemnation of Jesus of Nazareth. Some Hellenist Jews had been quarreling with Hellenist Nazarenes concerning the Temple. However, the indignation felt by the Jerusalemites at the stoning of James, the highly respected brother of the Lord, in 62 C.E., indicated that the Nazarenes had achieved a certain degree of acceptance in the non-Sadducean circles.[2]

The 'AM HA-ARETZ, the common people, had adopted a wait and see attitude. The reason for such a non-aggressive reaction to the Jesus movement must be found in the zeal shown by the Nazarenes for the observance of the Mosaic Law. If Paul, in proclaiming the imminence of God's Kingdom in the Diaspora, had remained strictly inside the perimeter of traditional Judaism, he would have evoked the same kind of reaction. In that case, he would have converted the Gentiles according to the accepted procedure in force at the time. Those unwilling to take on themselves the yoke of the Law would have been welcomed to the status of permanent God-fearers.

Paul never planned a missionary campaign having in mind the establishment of synagogues for God-fearers only. In coming to a new city, Paul always asked permission from the elders at the Shabbat services to address the local community. When the opposition of the leaders was such that he had to leave and start his own synagogue, there were always, at least at the beginning, a small number of circumcised believers who made the first nucleus of the new synagogue. When Paul in his Letter to the Romans wrote that the Gentiles were grafted on the cultivated olive tree which is Israel, he was translating an historical fact into a theological statement.

Paul's Judaism, as we tried to describe it, was not this-worldly and national, but a-temporal and universal. For Paul this interpretation was the normal outcome of the arrival of a new age, the messianic age announced by the Prophets. It was a transformation of Judaism in the power of God's Spirit under the guidance of the risen Jesus. Paul felt that through Jesus of Nazareth's fulfilling the promise made to Abraham, a true continuity with the tradition of his ancestors was maintained. In the eyes of the synagogue from which he was departing, however, he was starting an unorthodox movement. He was a sham. He intended to bring Gentiles into Israel, God's chosen people, and at the same time he was rejecting the social structure God had carefully and clearly laid out for his people. Like the God-fearers, Paul's Gentile converts may have absorbed important spiritual values transmitted by the Jewish tradition, but they did not participate in the life of the nation, did not accept the burden of national duties and consequently could not enjoy its privileges

Very quickly it was not so much the nature of the messianic proclamation as the strict observance of the Mosaic Law which became the focus of the quarrel. Paul never pretended that the Gentiles he received in his synagogues had to become Jews; quite the contrary, they were not under the Mosaic Law, but had become members of the true Israel, the Israel of God. Observance of the Mosaic Law was maintained only by those who were circumcised. And even for them this observance was in abeyance during community functions. The uncircumcised, however, after baptism in the name of Jesus, were received as equals. The HALACHAH, the religious observance of these synagogues, was liberal enough to allow for a real community life among the circumcised and uncircumcised members. In the eyes of the Orthodox Jews, Paul might have been forgiven some strange apocalyptic expectations, but deliberate transgressions of God's explicit commandments in the Torah turned him into a public dissenter to be completely avoided.

Matters grew much worse when observant Jews heard of some expressions used by Paul in preaching or writing that were disparaging the word of God, the sacred Torah: "The ministry of death, chiseled in letters on stone tablets" (2 Cor 3:7); "For all who rely on the works of the Law are under a curse" (Gal 3:10); "No human being will be justified in the sight of God by deeds prescribed by the Law" (cf. Rom 3:20); "The Law brings wrath" (Rom 4:15).

The non-observance of some commandments was one thing, for there have always been some sinners in the midst of God's people, but contempt for the Law was entirely different. It was blasphemy! It brought to the fore a strong emotional reaction as the religious security of the Orthodox Jew was based on the authority of the Law. Paul may have said that the Law was holy and spiritual (Rom 7:12, 14), that there was glory in the ministry of the Law (cf. 2 Cor 3:9); such positive statements were ignored and the negative ones were carefully reported because from now on there was a climate of dispute leading to increased misunderstanding.

The break did not happen in one day; it probably occurred sometime during the second journey of Paul and became apparent during his third journey. On one side there was Paul, fighting for the Gentile believers to be freed from the Law; on the other side were the leaders of the Synagogues in the Diaspora of Asia and Greece, together with those Nazarenes called by Paul the false believers (Gal 2:4) and later called the Judaizers. The two camps suddenly entered into a spirited spiritual contest for the loyalty of the Diaspora Jews and the conversion of the Gentiles to true ethical monotheism. The spiritual animosity was fed by mutual hurts. The Jews felt that Paul was in revolt against the living God and his living word in TORAH. Paul felt that by their refusal to accept the word of Jesus of Nazareth they were disobedient to God and had become broken branches cut from the cultivated olive tree, the true Israel.

Paul wanted, planned and finally tried a reconciliation with the moderates among the Nazarenes. He found himself able to live with those who insisted on maintaining a strict observance of the Law in the Land of Israel, but agreed on a liberalized HALACHAH for the uncircumcised Christians. The problem of the Jewish Christians in the Diaspora remained a bone of contention and was not really solved. With the Synagogue on the other hand the conflict was never healed. For the Jewish leaders Jesus of Nazareth was to be subservient to TORAH, the word of God; for Paul TORAH was only a first sketch of God's plan which had been finalized in Jesus of Nazareth, risen and glorified. It was a clash of ultimate loyalties.

In the long history of Judaism there have been many quarrels, various interpretations, many factions, schools, trends, etc. trying to answer the difficult questions: Who is a Jew? What is Judaism? The fact that Paul's answer caused a very bitter disagreement is not enough to explain the absolute rejection of each other which characterized the last years of Paul. Each side had a great need for spiritual security. They wanted to be sure that "they" were the true Israel, the people of God. They felt that the other side was denying their spiritual identity; more than that, their own survival was suddenly threatened.

The Gentile Christians wanted to be accepted not as Jews but as Israelites, as spiritual children of Abraham, beneficiaries of the promise made to the father of many nations. The Synagogue's answer was a resounding NO. For the Synagogue, there was not supposed to be any distinction between Jew and Israelite. Nobody could be a real Israelite and at the same time reject the Law of Moses. It was the same as rejecting the covenant. The rabbis later will assign all the Gentile Christians to the universal covenant of Noah. Their Christian identity was totally denied. They were simply human beings who might be among the just ones of all the nations.

Paul appeared to the leaders of the Diaspora Synagogues not only as an apocalyptic dreamer, a scoffer deriding God and his Torah, but as the destroyer of God's people. Paul seemed completely blind to the specific character of Israel's election, the election of a nation as God's chosen nation, and not an election of individual Gentiles in need of salvation. He was so much absorbed in the glory of the world to come that the reality of this world seemed to escape him. The Jews felt, and have felt ever since, that the way Paul presented Christianity meant their disappearance as God's chosen people, their priestly function as a nation having become useless. If they followed Paul, they themselves might remain Jews, because the imprint in their souls was so deeply marked, but their children would be systematically dejudaized, and the next generations completely assimilated to Gentile Christianity. If they fought back, building around themselves a still stronger protective wall, they would be told that they were not supposed to be around. Any time the Christians would be in power, their existence as Jews would be threatened.

At the time of Paul the Jews had already learned to survive. They thought that the Jesus Movement had no future. The few Pauline Synagogues were so small, so unimportant! They tried to arrest the movement before it was too late. This explains the systematic opposition and occasional persecution which followed Paul at every step of his journeys until his final arrest in the Temple in Jerusalem. Paul who was so Jewish in temperament, and so deeply attached to and so proud of his own people, was asking them to accept religious extinction, a kind of "final solution" to a glorious history whose main actor had been Almighty God. The Jewish people simply said NO. They did not want to die. Seeing no reason to encourage a movement which was going to bring their own destruction, when they had the opportunity to do so, they tried to stop it.

In the years to come, from deep in the collective mind of the Jewish people where archetypes are formed, feelings of contempt, a sense of desecration, a subdued rage and a gripping fear will surge at the simple mention of Pauline Christianity. These will create a dark cloud rendering completely opaque the image of Jesus of Nazareth, and endangering the course of any Jewish-Christian dialogue.

5. THE LAST YEARS OF A SPIRITUAL WARRIOR

A medieval writer would have chronicled Saul/Paul of Tarsus as a man of God who blossomed during the years 48 to 58 C.E. He was probably in his late forties, early fifties. These were his most active, most creative and most productive years. He focused on the depth and sharpened the contours of his vision. He wrote very personal letters that all the critics recognize as his, letters to the Corinthians, the Galatians and the Romans. Most of all, he spread the message, converting Gentiles to the living God and to his Messiah, organizing God's assemblies which he called churches rather than synagogues, though they looked so much alike. He was a dreamer, but proved to be an amazing doer. For this achievement he paid a very heavy price. There were not only the great difficulties inherent to such an enterprise, there was also the constant, and sometimes bitter, conflict with his Jewish brothers, and most painful of all the conflict with his own, those who were for him false believers, the Judaizers. All these contradictions made of his life an unceasing struggle and a very harsh test of his loyalty to the risen Jesus. Once, when his authority was contested by many in Corinth, he burst into a protest:

Are they ministers of Christ? I am talking like a madman—I am a better one: with far greater labors, far more imprisonments, with countless floggings, and often near death. Five times I have received from the Jews the forty lashes minus one. Three times I was beaten with rods. Once I received a stoning. Three times I was shipwrecked; for a night and a day I was adrift at sea; on frequent journeys, in danger from rivers, danger from bandits, danger from my own people, danger from Gentiles, danger in the city, danger in the wilderness, danger at sea, danger from false brothers and sisters; in toil and hardship, through many a sleepless night, hungry, and thirsty, often without food, cold and naked. And besides other things, I am under daily pressure because of my anxieties for all the churches (2 Cor 11:25–28).

This apology was written in the middle 50's. The details from Paul's own pen indicate that Luke's descriptions in the Acts are very sketchy and give only a small part of the story. Luke, however, was in Jerusalem at the time of Paul's arrest in the Temple. He is able to describe the scene and the following trials with many details. The accusations against Paul were precise. From the mouth of James, the brother of the Lord, we learn that the Nazarenes "have been told about you [Paul] that you teach all the Jews among the Gentiles to forsake Moses, and that you tell them not to circumcise their children or observe the customs" (Acts 21:21). When Paul, accompanying four men under a vow, was going through the seven days' rite of purification in the Temple, he was recognized and arrested by Jews from Asia who shouted, "Fellow Israelites, help! This is the man who is teaching everyone against our people, our law and this place; more than that, he has actually brought Greeks into the Temple and has defiled this holy place" (Acts 21:27–28). This last accusation was false, but Paul's popular image, though a caricature, gave the reasons why his personality had become so objectionable. He was dejudaizing the Jews of the Diaspora and was accepting the Gentiles as religiously equal to Jews.

During his four years of captivity in Caesarea and Rome Paul was allowed to maintain contacts with the outside. His life style became different and he had plenty of time for personal prayer and meditation. The captivity letters, i.e., the letters to the Colossians and to the Ephesians, as well as the pastoral letters, are dated by many exegetes after 70 C.E. and would not have been written by Paul himself. Do they project an echo of Paul's spiritual evolution during the last years of his earthly life? Those who placed these letters in the Pauline corpus thought so.

By then Paul must have realized that the Parousia of the risen Jesus was not imminent. In the cultural and social context of the Greco-Roman world his Churches did not appear too different from the neighboring Synagogues, except that they were increasingly Gentile and their HALACHAH was more liberal. In everyday life it was difficult to maintain a strong messianic expectation and to look at this world as evanescent! Paul must have realized that Church organization, Scriptures, i.e., Hebrew Scriptures, worship, care of the sick and the poor, all needed to be lived for their own sake, sanctifying the Name of God in the present, but in the light of a true and strong eschatological hope.

If the role of God's Spirit and the shepherding of Gentile converts were experienced by Paul in a more earthly manner, his conceptions of the risen Jesus and of life everlasting were on the contrary becoming much less earthly and less involved in apocalyptic imagery or scenarios. During his long captivity Paul had time to read and to study the Scriptures. Already very aware of the indwelling presence of God's Spirit, he may have given much more attention to the mystery of God's Wisdom.

> Before the ages, in the beginning, he created me,
> and for all the ages I shall not cease to be....
> All this is the book of the covenant of the Most High God,
> the law that Moses commanded us as an inheritance
> (Wisdom of Jesus Ben Sirach 24:9, 23).

If for Jesus Ben Sirach the Law of Moses, the Torah, was pre-existing in the Wisdom of God, it would not be surprising that Paul started to speculate on some kind of pre-existence for Jesus of Nazareth. For example, in the Wisdom of God, he would be the seminal idea of the whole creation, which holds together the entire cosmos in harmonious unity. In his concrete existence as the risen Jesus he was the only mediator between God and humanity, but he was now perceived closer to God than to humanity. Paul had such a tremendous love for the risen Jesus that he may have experienced at times the mystery of the Almighty God—whom Jesus had called Father—as simply the background to the powerful figure of Jesus of Nazareth, crucified and risen, the focus of all his attention. Jesus was like the Son turned toward Paul rather than the Son turned toward the Father. To what extent the Jews and their leaders became aware of an evolution in the piety and theology of Paul cannot be known. The existence of texts like Col 1:15-20 and Eph 1:3-14 in the corpus of Pauline letters gave apostolic authority to a new emphasis on Jesus of Nazareth as the only Son of God and the Lord of all creation.

There is general agreement that Paul was beheaded in Rome during the 60's. He may have lived until the beginning of the war of Rome against Judea in 66 A.D. If the 50's had been glorious years, though difficult ones, the 60's seem to have been truly arduous ones. Nobody will read the Second Letter to Timothy, which echoes for us the last words of Paul, without becoming aware of the poignancy of his situation. Many of Paul's great dreams had had only a humble beginning. In this hour of grief his only hope and joy was the presence in his heart of the vision he had experienced on the way to Damascus.

We may wonder what were the reactions of his many friends and foes when they received the news of his martyrdom. The Gentile Christians lamented the passing away of their father in messianic faith, fully aware that without his incessant labor they may have never known Jesus of Nazareth, risen and glorified. His Jewish sisters and brothers who had been unable to share his messianic faith were convinced that, sincere as he might have been, he had lost his Jewish soul and had endangered their survival. Deep in their hearts they were greatly hurt.

IX. Sequel to the Catastrophe

The horrors of the First Jewish Revolt against Rome (66-74 C.E.), and the destruction of the Temple in Jerusalem by the legions of Titus (70 C.E.), were experienced by Jews and Christians alike as a searing trauma, a meaningless catastrophe. The protracted conflict contributed to unforeseen transformations in Judaism and infant Christianity. These transformations, in turn, were to have significant consequences for the unfolding of their mutual relations. History is a continuous flow. No date is a dividing partition neatly separating two periods into before and after. Nevertheless, particular events have occasionally brought a clear reorientation of the life of a nation. Such was the burning and utter destruction of the Holy Temple. Suddenly, Judaism was deprived of the mysterious presence of the living God in the Holy of Holies, of a physical center in which to conduct its worship, and of the seat of its supreme religious and national authority. How it survived, and found new life, is an amazing feat in history; it remains barely intelligible in terms of natural causes.

1. REBIRTH OF JUDAISM

At the birth of Temple Judaism Ezra had played the role of catalyst. A similar role was played by Yohanan Ben Zakkai at the birth of Rabbinic Judaism. Though the Romans were in the midst of a bitter political conflict with the Jewish nation, they never intended, as did Antiochus Epiphanes, to convert the Jews to pagan worship. They always respected the singular privileges granted by the Roman Senate to the Maccabees, privileges which recognized Judaism as a RELIGIO LICITA, and exempted the Jews from participation in the Imperial cult. As soon as the conflict with Rome had started, some elders and sages realized that their nation was deprived of sufficient resources to overcome the power of Rome. Soon the rash deeds and the fanaticism of the Zealots who had taken control of the Holy City destroyed any hope of a settlement. Yohanan Ben Zakkai, a highly respected scholar, with the formal or more probably tacit consent of the Roman commander, the future Emperor Vespasian, left the besieged city and established an academy of learning in Yavneh (Jamnia). Yavneh and Jaffa were the only two towns on the coastal plain with a Jewish majority.

Yohanan Ben Zakkai was able to gather around himself some surviving sages. They formed a college, perhaps of seventy-one elders, who were willing to face the countless problems arising from the new situation. It will take some time for its moral authority to be acknowledged by the surviving Jewish communities, but by the end of the century this "Yavneh Academy" will become the recognized center of the religious as well as the national life of the Jewish people.

The brutal fact the Yavneh Academy had to face was the destruction of the Temple. No one looked at that horrible situation as permanent. There had been only one precedent, and it had lasted but 50 years (from 587 to 537 B.C.E.). Still, the nation had to survive, and to do so without the celebration of Temple worship. How could sins be forgiven without the offering of sacrifices? Yavneh was able to replace this liturgical vacuum with strengthened synagogal services. For nearly two centuries, under the leadership of the Pharisees, a synagogal piety had developed as a powerful religious experience complementary to the more ritualistic cult of the Temple. On the basis of that experience, Yavneh affirmed that communal prayer could take the place of sacrifices, and sins could be expiated by prayers and acts of charity. Though the local synagogues were poor and unassuming in comparison with the magnificence of the Temple, their smallness favored the existence of small communities in which interpersonal relations and loyalty to the group could flourish more easily.

In faithfulness to the Deuteronomic reform initiated by King Josiah, nascent Judaism had maintained the uniqueness of Temple worship: one God, one Temple, one people. The multiplicity of small synagogues might eventually loosen the unity and the integrity of Israel. Moreover, after the destruction of the Temple, all the traditional forms of religious/national authority had disappeared. There was no ruler in Israel, no judge, no king, no prince, nor any kind of central authority. The voice of prophecy had not been heard for a long time. Some priests were still alive and transmitting their priestly prerogatives to their male children, but they had become unable to exercise their priestly functions. Like any organ incapable of functioning they were rapidly becoming wasted. The authority of the High Priest and the Jerusalem Sanhedrin had died in the burnt ashes of the Temple.

In the Yavneh Academy and through its work a new authority figure was emerging. It was an original creation in the history of God's people. The scribe, the technician of the Law, became vested with religious authority, and his social position became clearly recognized through the institution of a rite of ordination. The scholarly scribe, now entitled rabbi, was not a priest, but a layperson. He was not a prophet, not being the voice of God, but only the interpreter of the Law given once and for all to Moses on Mount Sinai. He was not a king, as the local Jewish communities—each autonomous—were generally governed by a council of elders. But he was more than a delegate of the community; his ordination had been performed, not by the community, but by other rabbis on the basis of academic achievement. He became the judge speaking the law, as well as a spiritual leader for the community.

2. CENTRALITY OF TORAH

The status and role of the rabbi is incomprehensible without taking into account the respect and deep attachment to TORAH which rose from the ashes of the Temple. From Ezra on, there had been a long tradition that focused on an exact transmission and a correct interpretation of God's words. Suddenly, TORAH was the only sanctity left to Israel. Israel had no national authority, no Temple, no priesthood, no voice from heaven to comfort and sustain a people reduced to extreme poverty and constantly humiliated by the arrogance of a colonial power; it had nothing, absolutely nothing, except TORAH and a flickering messianic hope which at that time was painfully tested. The people caught hold of TORAH as a drowning man seizes a life buoy. Some surviving Pharisees, sages or scholars, knowing that their hour had come, put all their energy into presenting TORAH to the people as the only hope of national salvation. As the word of God it was a source of strength and joy that called the people to answer with deep devotion and faithful observance. The rabbi, as the official interpreter of TORAH in rendering legal decisions or in teaching the meaning of God's word, became vested with the spiritual aura arising from TORAH itself. It was the TORAH rather than the rabbinate which took the place of the Temple: one God, one Law, one people. During the centuries of dispersion and in the midst of the many crises Israel had to endure, TORAH alone maintained the unity and integrity of God's people, because it became the organizational principle of its social, cultural and religious life, all at the same time.

An unexpected but dangerous consequence of the destruction of the Temple was the physical separation of Israel not only from the Temple but also from the Holy City and potientially from the land. Ezra had foreseen the possibility of a national life without full national autonomy. Yavneh did nothing to separate the religious and national aspects which are always inseparable in the life of Israel, but in creatively transforming the national structure, he saved the national spirit. From earlier times, when the elders of Israel complained to Samuel that they ought to have a king as the other nations did (1 Sam 8:5), there had remained in the subconscious of the people a strong desire to be like the others. Consequently, it was not an easy task for Yavneh to recreate a national unity in a shape and form unlike that of the other nations. Yavneh succeeded in such a renewal by bringing disconnected local communities to share consciously the same religious and cultural traditions in all essential matters. With complete trust in God and total loyalty to God's Word, the Torah, Israel remained a people dwelling apart, aware of its unique identity, but not limited to a specific territory or a particular political organization. This original creation was so strong that it endured for centuries, in good and bad fortune, as long as the people's faith in TORAH remained unshaken.

3. THE PARTING OF THE WAYS

How did the bitter national defeat affect the messianic expectations which had been so intense on the eve of the Great War among most of the people, among Pharisees as well as Nazarenes? Those who recently had to live through the great ordeal of the Holocaust may have some insight into the progressive feelings of dejection and abandonment experienced by the inhabitants of Galilee and Judea as they witnessed the various stages in the destruction of their national life. The Lord of Hosts, the Shield of Israel, had totally ignored his chosen people. The Romans had enjoyed a free hand, slowed down only by pockets of unwavering Zealots. Instead of the Kingdom of God, the kingdom of Rome was now firmly established in the land given by God to Abraham and his descendants forever.

Face to face with this catastrophe, some remained unshaken in their messianic faith. For them the burning of the Temple was a time of great distress preceding the coming of the Messiah. The battle just lost could not be the last one. Resistance had to continue in secret and preparations had to be made for the victorious battle which would crush the arrogance of Rome. The existence of such a current of opinion explains how, sixty years later, in answer to Emperor Hadrian's decision to prohibit circumcision and erase Jerusalem, building over its remains a splendid pagan city called AELIA CAPITOLINA, Bar Kochba could call to arms a large number of Judeans and be proclaimed Messiah by none other than the saintly Rabbi Akiva. This gallant gesture will be the last gasp of a strong movement which for years had been expecting the imminent restoration of the kingdom to Israel.

A more important trend of opinion was at work, influenced by the original

vision of Yohanan Ben Zakkai. God would deliver his people; but the
Messiah would come, neither in the immediate future, nor in the power of
arms, solely through divine intervention. The present task did not call for
meaningless preparations toward the imminent coming of a Messiah, but for
helping the people to survive by sanctifying the Name of God, by accepting
faithfully and gratefully the yoke of the Law, and by using all the resources of
the Oral Law in order to restore the life of the nation in the context of the present circumstances. The Zealots, far from saving Israel, had brought her to
utter destruction, and the dreams of the apocalyptists had been blown away,
showing how unsubstantial they were. Pious men and learned rabbis ought
not to speculate about times and dates, but leave the future to the wisdom and
the power of God.

There was in Yohanan Ben Zakkai and his disciples a down to earth, very
pragmatic, approach to the survival of Israel. It looked more toward the past,
toward Sinai, than toward the future. It was focusing entirely on the present
needs of Israel. It did not show much hatred toward foreigners, but felt toward
them little sympathy, rather indifference. It was confident that God would
never abandon his people as long as they remained faithful to the observance
of the laws of his covenant. Such a liturgical messianism, limiting itself to an
incessant prayer for the redemption of Israel, must have created endless
debates in the Yavneh Academy, which counted among its members some par-
tisans of an active political messianism. But on the morrow of the Second
Jewish Revolt led by Bar Kochba (132-135 C.E.), what remained of two centuries of messianic fever was solely the vision of Yohanan Ben Zakkai. That
vision sustained the hopes of Israel for centuries.

Rabbinic Judaism proved to be the expression and the efflorescence of
Pharisaism, previously a minority trend. It suddenly blossomed when an
entirely new social and political context began to threaten the survival of
Israel. Jewish pluralism had expired in the flames of the Catastrophe. The
Pharisees won by default. The Sadducees had lost power and prestige with the
utter destruction of the Temple. The Zealots had been pitilessly pursued and
annihilated by the Roman legions. Qumran, the spiritual center of the Essenes
on the shore of the Dead Sea, had been completely destroyed, with the exception of the library cleverly hidden in caves. The Nazarenes had their own
story, but they proved unable to match the quiet and powerful dynamism
unlatched by Yohanan Ben Zakkai.

These Nazarenes, the Church of the Circumcision in Jerusalem, had experienced some relatively peaceful and spiritually uplifting years under the strong
leadership of James, the brother of the Lord. This was from 50 to 62 C.E.
From Josephus and Hegesippus we learn, if not the exact details of James'

martyrdom at the hands of an unworthy high priest, at least the surprising fact that James had acquired the reputation among the Jerusalemites of being a TZADIQ, a just one, a man of God.[1] How can we explain that a man inspiring such religious respect convinced so few of the validity of his message? Why did the Nazarenes have so little influence on the rebirth of Judaism?

Yohanan Ben Zakkai had been a teacher in Galilee for fourteen years. He must have been aware of the Jesus movement. He was present in Jerusalem in the sixties. If he did not know James personally, he certainly knew his reputation. There is no sign that he ever showed antagonism vis-à-vis the Nazarenes, as his successor at Yavneh will. In the mid-sixties, on the eve of the First Revolt, the Pharisees were not yet of one mind on the Jesus question; a number of them had joined the Church of the Circumcision. However, when Yohanan Ben Zakkai secretly left the besieged city to start a new school, he must have been convinced that the Jesus movement was not the way to bring about the regeneration of Israel. A return to TORAH was the only hope of salvation.

Two factors probably influenced Yohanan Ben Zakkai in forming such an attitude unfavorable to the Nazarenes' own efforts at renewal. The most important was the Nazarenes' strong messianic orientation. Yohanan Ben Zakkai was not simply, like many others, taking an attitude of wait and see. The great emphasis of the Nazarenes on the return of Jesus of Nazareth as King Messiah left him skeptical. During the sixties, the cruelty of the Zealots and the unleashed imagination of many apocalyptists had repelled him. He could not see any sign whatsoever of the imminent coming of King Messiah. When the Revolt against Rome started, he looked at the situation in terms of power politics. Like Jeremiah on the eve of the destruction of the first Temple, he said publicly that resistance to the oppressor was not an act of God. Because of his attitude, a deep distrust of messianism, and even of any political activity initiated by human intervention, entered into the texture of Rabbinic Judaism. Only a liturgical messianism imploring a divine intervention at God's discretion was encouraged—though the presence of messianic aspirations in the depth of the Jewish soul remained unabated. Jewish history, in fact, is witness to many messianic eruptions.

The second factor is more difficult to circumscribe. Essentially, it was the reaching out of some Hellenistic-Jewish-Christians toward the uncircumcised, and especially the activities of Saul of Tarsus. There was a certain tension between Palestinian Judaism, speaking Aramaic, and Hellenistic Judaism, speaking Greek, because their relations to the predominant Greco-Roman culture were different. Among the Jewish Christians an analogous tension existed between the Hebrews and the Hellenists. To what extent the broad-mindedness exemplified by some Hellenistic-Jewish-Christians in Antioch struck the

Jerusalemites as just one more case of the strange Hellenist ways is hard to ascertain. Saul's behavior, however, was beyond the limits of tolerance. After the tumultuous scene in the Sanhedrin subsequent to his arrest, everyone in the city knew that Saul, the Hasid turned disciple of Jesus of Nazareth, had unexpectedly become a national risk. Were the Pharisees linking the saintly James and the local Nazarenes with his missionary activities? James had just received Paul as a brother. They had had, and still had, serious disagreements on tactics, but they could not disagree on the basic strategy of bringing the Gentiles to turn away from idols toward the living God and to find in Jesus of Nazareth the way to salvation. In the eyes of Yohanan Ben Zakkai the Nazarenes must have looked hopelessly compromised by their non-rejection of Saul's unorthodox efforts.

Was Yohanan Ben Zakkai's attitude a deliberate answer to Saul? Not necessarily! But their ways were clearly divergent. Saul was strongly oriented toward the future; Ben Zakkai was immersed in the present. Saul wanted to reduce the Mosaic Law to basic morality; Ben Zakkai was upholding the fullness of TORAH, written and oral. Saul wanted the nations to share in the spiritual privileges of Israel; Ben Zakkai wanted to strengthen the fence built around Israel by Ezra and was turning his back on the GOYIM. Each was facing and worshiping the same holy God, the God of Abraham, and was intensely committed to do his will and to obey his commandments, but they were listening to God's words, one through the Torah given to Moses at Sinai, the other through Jesus of Nazareth crucified and glorified. By consciously and deliberately choosing one way and completely ignoring the other, they were starting a divorce procedure whose first casualty will be the Church of the Circumcision, the mother of all Churches.

4. THE DEMISE OF JEWISH CHRISTIANITY

There were disciples of Jesus of Nazareth, Nazarenes in Jerusalem and Christians in Antioch, who neither desired nor intended to confront God's TORAH, and all the spiritual richness of the Israelite heritage, with the messiahship of their beloved Master, the risen Jesus. For them TORAH and Jesus Messiah were not incongruous, still less incompatible, but truly complementary. The Catastrophe was for them likewise a traumatic experience. How did they react to the event?

Many exegetes believe that the writing of Mark's Gospel was contemporary with the First Revolt and the events leading to the destruction of the Temple. Mark is a somber Gospel, emphasizing the fact that the Christian way is the way of the Cross. Its description of the future capture of God's City, together with the sudden apparition of the Son of Man in the midst of frightening cosmic upheavals, forms a unique, awe-inspiring scenario. The Gospel seems to echo the messianic fever, the great eschatological expectations, characteristic of the infant Church at that time. These expectations must have led many of Jesus' disciples to wait for his immediate return as soon as the military events in Judea took the appearance of a catastrophe.

God's City was now destroyed, the Temple burnt to the ground, and nature had stood still; the Son of Man had not appeared with great power and glory to gather his elect from the four winds (cf. Mark 13:26). The Nazarenes had always placed the return of Jesus of Nazareth in glory at the heart of their messianic vision; the absence of the risen Jesus and the total silence of God in the midst of these astounding events must have been stunning for them. Not only were they deprived of their earthly Temple, their messianic vision was suddenly darkened and restructured into an uncertain future.

> Truly I tell you, this generation will not pass away until all these things have taken place. Heaven and earth will pass away, but my words will not pass away (Mark 13:31).

Catastrophic events had in fact taken place in the last days of "this generation," but the expected Parousia of the Messiah had not been enacted by God. God's ways seemed increasingly mysterious. The destruction of the Temple was for all the Jews an acute crisis of faith, but for the Nazarenes it was becoming also a crisis of hope.

History has not recorded the name of any inspiring leader who would have accomplished among the Nazarenes a program of reconstruction similar and parallel to the work of Yohanan Ben Zakkai. Life must have continued as before the war, short of participation in the Temple liturgy. The house-churches of the Nazarenes looked very much like the small synagogues existing already in Judea before the destruction of the Temple. In these Nazarene assemblies the in-group feeling must certainly have been heightened; nevertheless, as late as the end of the first century, some Nazarenes were still taking part in synagogal worship. What is certain is that the Nazarenes remained staunch observers of the written Law. Their subsequent history of increasing separation from the Gentile churches evidences the strength of their own tradition.

To follow the survival, the evolution and the lack of expansion of the Church of the Circumcision after the martyrdom of James in 62 C.E., we are bereft of any important historical document. Around 180 C.E., Hegesippus, a Jewish Christian, wrote many details about the life of the Jerusalem Church in the five volumes of his MEMOIRS, but, unhappily, they have been lost. Only a few fragments have survived in Eusebius' CHURCH HISTORY, written in the fourth century.

After the martyrdom of James, the brother of the Lord, one of his cousins, the son of Clopas, Simeon by name, was elected to the leadership of the Nazarenes. He lived into old age and was crucified under Trajan, having been accused by Christian heretics before the Roman authorities of being a descendant of David. Under Trajan the Jews had once more become restless; a serious revolt was exploding in Cyrenaica, and Rome was searching for potential leaders.[2] Nothing would lead us to believe that Simeon showed strong qualities of leadership, but he was able to maintain the cohesion of the Nazarene community in trying circumstances.

As early as 66 C.E., the elders of the Church of the Circumcision correctly read the signs of the times; they organized an exodus to Pella, a Gentile city, in the Decapolis, southeast of Lake Kinneret. How many went with the leadership and how many remained in Jerusalem is unclear. In the eyes of these Jews who did not abandon the Holy City the Nazarenes must have appeared unwilling to fight for its survival. After the Catastrophe, however, they were accepted again in the Jewish family as were Yohanan Ben Zakkai and the Yavneh Academy. Seven years after they had left, Simeon and some Nazarenes returned to the ruins of Jerusalem. They decided not to follow the example of Yohanan Ben Zakkai, nor to establish a new center elsewhere; for them it was important to resuscitate the Jerusalemite community.

Were they hoping that the Church of Jerusalem would remain the spiritual mother of all the Christian Churches? If so, they were disappointed; the past could not be retrieved. On one hand the rapid decline of all messianic expectations in Palestinian Judaism undermined the spiritual appeal of the Jesus movement among the Rabbinic Jews. The most common vision had ceased to be a brilliant future; it was rather a return to the past and to an authentic Jewish tradition. The Nazarenes could not pretend to be more Jewish than the Yavneh Academy.

On the other hand, the seven-year exodus to Pella had brought the Christian communities of the Diaspora to downgrade their relations with the center of the Church. During that period the Gentile Christians found themselves pulled in opposite directions by the political conflict between Judea and Rome. With the exception of John, son of Zebedee, the Twelve and their prestigious authority had passed away. The local Churches withdrew unto themselves, governed like the Synagogues of the Diaspora by a board of elders. The Jesus movement was passing through a period of extreme decentralization, and the Church of Jerusalem, on the morrow of the Catastrophe, became one local Church among many local Churches. Of the Nazarenes who had remained in Jerusalem many must have been killed or sold into slavery. Those who returned were in small number because livelihood in a devastated city had become problematic. After the Catastrophe, the Church of the Circumcision was in fact reduced to many small communities, mostly in Transjordan and Syria.

At the beginning of the post-war period, the Nazarenes were still part of the Jewish family. How long could they stay bona fide members? Jewish pluralism was rapidly dying out. The Nazarenes may have been the only organized group in the Land of Israel which was not joining the movement of Jewish reintegration under the Yavneh leadership. There is no reason to doubt a priori that they were following the efforts of Yohanan Ben Zakkai with interest and sympathy. They were still hoping that someday the Yavneh Academy would receive Jesus of Nazareth, risen and glorified, as the true way to the living God. In the course of time, however, substantial differences appeared in matters of worship, HALACHAH and spirituality. Slowly, these differences alienated the surviving Nazarenes from the Yavneh leadership.

The bond of common worship in the Temple had been broken. Before Yavneh had the opportunity to institutionalize a renewed synagogal worship, the Nazarenes had already started to crystallize their own tradition, emphasizing the actual priesthood of the risen Jesus and giving to the Breaking of Bread pride of place in communal devotion. Sooner or later the Church of the Circumcision was going to have to receive or to reject the legal interpretations and decisions of the Yavneh Academy. It was now the Nazarenes who were asking: Who gave you authority to interpret the Law? At that time there were already circulating one or more gospels in Aramaic recording some of the words and deeds of Jesus of Nazareth. For the Nazarenes Jesus was the supreme rabbinic authority and his sayings were overruling any other interpretation.

Serious as such developments were, the most dividing element in their respective visions was the title Messiah given to Jesus by the Nazarenes. For Yohanan Ben Zakkai and the majority of the rabbis, Jesus of Nazareth was obviously not the Messiah. The present situation of Israel was completely bereft of messianic blessings; it had become the worst it had ever been. Messianism had suddenly lost the strong popular appeal it had enjoyed before the war. The task of the hour for Judaism was to rediscover itself, to return to Mount Sinai and to rejuvenate the spirit of Ezra.

The Nazarenes, for their part, were aware of the need to refocus their messianic vision. Any hope of seeing the restoration of a Davidic kingdom, or even the full sovereignty over the Land of Israel, seemed in the new circumstances like a misinterpretation of the messiahship of Jesus of Nazareth.

Messianism was to be understood as an eschatological, even an apocalyptic event. The time of the Parousia, however, ought not to be postponed to an indefinite future. Jesus, definitely, would return as Son of Man to judge the living and the dead. Apocalyptic literature became very popular among the Nazarenes who had become convinced that the risen Jesus would appear at a moment when he was not expected.

Meanwhile, preparing themselves for the Day of the Lord, the Nazarenes remained staunch observers of the Law. Their strong faith in the future coming of Messiah Jesus did not by itself take them out of the main Jewish tradition, but it certainly was taking them away from the increasingly successful reintegration of all the Jewish traditional forces around the Yavneh Academy. For a moment each movement was hoping to absorb the other; finally, after a brief lapse of time, Yavneh alone remained as the living expression of Judaism for many centuries.

X. The Birth of Gentile Christianity

When the dust started to settle after the protracted war between Rome and Judea, a war that lasted from 66 to 73 or 74 C.E., it became clear that the Jesus Movement was surviving, but showing signs of slowly becoming a Gentile religion. Its extension through the Jewish Diaspora into the Greco-Roman world had been diverse. As previously noted, after 70 C.E. it entered into a period of extreme decentralization. The various local Churches could be classified into three different groups, each upholding its own spiritual and communal tradition. Two groups are easily characterized: James' Church of the Circumcision in Jerusalem, living in the traditional framework of Palestinian Judaism, and Paul's Greek Churches around the Aegean sea, living in the charismatic framework of a transformed Judaism, a Judaism a-temporal and universal. Between these two relatively well defined groups a considerable number of local Churches of mixed Jewish and Gentile membership lived in the traditional framework of Hellenistic Judaism, the religious Judaism most common in the Western Jewish Diaspora. The majority of these Churches were in Syria, with an important community in Antioch playing a leading role, but some were in Rome, Egypt, and elsewhere.

It is important to reconstruct the life of these Hellenistic-Jewish-Christian communities, because it is these Churches, and not the Church of the Circumcision in the Land of Israel, which became the fountainhead of Gentile Christianity. James in Jerusalem and Paul in Greece, with the traditions of their respective communities, influenced significantly the early evolution of the Jesus Movement, but their influence survived only to the extent it became integrated into the more general and more amorphous tradition of Hellenistic-Jewish-Christianity.

1. A QUEST FOR A MIDDLE POSITION

Christianity in Syria, struggling between a purely Jewish Christianity in the Land of Israel and a Christianity liberated from the Law in Ephesus and

Corinth, was favoring a middle-of-the-road attitude toward Jewish tradition, somewhere between James and Paul. Any effort at reconstruction will encounter specific obstacles. We know much less about Hellenistic Judaism— the matrix of this development—than we do about Judaism in the Land of Israel. The latter was rejuvenated by and survived in Rabbinic Judaism, whereas the former completely disappeared from the scene during the third century C.E., when Hebrew was reintroduced in the synagogal services. The Judaism of Philo of Alexandria, a contemporary of Jesus of Nazareth, is well known today. How representative was it of the Hellenistic Judaism flourishing in the Synagogues of Antioch, Rome or even Alexandria? Popular Hellenistic Judaism, with its liturgy in Greek and its Septuagint version of the Scriptures, left few traces in the Mishnah and the Talmud. Outside the writings of Philo preserved by some Christians, very few literary documents allow us to enter fully into the spiritual life and the ritual observances of this strand of Judaism.

Another obstacle to our efforts is the lack of historical documents concerning the Christian Churches. During the nearly forty years that elapsed between Paul's arrival in Rome in 61 C.E. and the First Letter of Clement to the Corinthians at the end of the century, we have no description of current events in the life of the Churches. Forty years is a long time; it means total silence during an entire generation at a most crucial moment in the life of the Church. Recently, the ingenuity of many great exegetes, working with the tools of source criticism and redaction criticism, has led to satisfactory conjectures about the approximate date of most of the New Testament's writings. These texts, gospels and all, were written at various times in the second half of the first century. To the extent that modern exegetes have been able to pinpoint the time and the place of each writing, something has become known about the life of the communities in whose midst and for whom they were written. Obviously much of this reconstruction is tentative. Nevertheless, it allows us to sketch the evolution of the Jesus Movement in its infancy, at a time when it was trying to define itself in contrast to the nascent Rabbinic Judaism.

The most interesting document for a sociologist is the Gospel of Matthew, written around 80 C.E., in and for a Greek-speaking community of mixed Jewish and Gentile Christians. Caesarea Maritima, and more probably Antioch, are favored as possible places of origin. It is clearly a document from the Diaspora. The writer/compiler writing in the shadow of a strong Jewish community, and in relative closeness to Jerusalem and the semitic world, was very sensitive to the relations between the Synagogue and the Church. Aware of a variety of trends, attitudes and traditions in his own community, his work offers a view of Hellenistic-Jewish-Christianity as it stood after the destruction of the Temple and the eclipse of the Jerusalem Church.

The author may have been surrounded by a group of Christian scribes whose task was different from but parallel to the efforts of the learned rabbis working at the Yavneh Academy.

2. A FADE-OUT IN MESSIANISM

Before the Catastrophe, messianism, understood as the imminent coming of God's Kingdom, had been the hallmark of the Jesus Movement. The exact date of Jesus' return and the exact nature of the kingdom he was to establish had not been revealed to the disciples. Nevertheless, they had been living in intensive hope, closing their prayer meetings with a fervent "Marana Tha," Our Lord, come! Paul of Tarsus was convinced at first that he would witness the Parousia of the risen Jesus in his own lifetime.

As the years passed and the problems of everyday life solicited the attention of the Church leaders, such strong eschatological expectations became more subdued. In an early tradition recorded by Mark, edited by Matthew, but corrected by Luke, the return of the risen Jesus was thought to coincide with a future destruction of Jerusalem and the end of this world. The protracted Jewish Revolt, and the final victory not of God but of Rome, without any sign of Jesus' return, brought about a severe challenge to the early messianic expectations. In the case of the Nazarenes, as noted earlier, a frozen vision emerged. In consonance with those rabbis who in disaccord with Yohanan Ben Zakkai were still preparing a new revolt against Rome, the Nazarenes reacted to the burning of the Temple with a keen interest in apocalyptic literature and a firm conviction that Jesus' return was postponed for a short while only. The Hellenist Christians, on the contrary, showed little interest in Armageddon. Except for the Book of Revelation and a few chapters in the synoptic Gospels, the various writers in the second half of the first century, while remaining mindful of the past and the future, were mostly concerned with the present way of life of their community.

The Hellenistic-Jewish Churches in the Diaspora had not been directly involved in the horrors of the First Jewish Revolt. They had lived the war at a distance. Obviously the "triumph" of Vespasian and Titus, entering Rome with the spoils of the Jerusalem Temple, and the transfer of the half-sheckel tax to the Roman temple of Jupiter Capitolinus, were for them a deep humiliation. Their own world, however, had remained unchanged. This stability may account for the dearth of apocalyptic literature among the Gentile Christian communities in the Diaspora. For them the end of history had ceased to loom on the immediate horizon of everyday life, and messianism, as the imminent coming of the Kingdom of God, had lost its centrality. The Jewish title

Messiah, in Greek Christos, had already become too traditional to be changed; it was by then the proper name of Jesus of Nazareth: Jesus-Christ. In the Greek Church it came to mean, not the expected King Messiah, but the Savior who brings life to the world.

Before World War II, a famous controversy arose between the supporters of A. Schweitzer and those of C.H. Dodd concerning the meaning of the expression "Kingdom of God" in the synoptic Gospels. Schweitzer, tired of hearing liberal exegetes present Jesus of Nazareth as nothing more than a humanistic moral teacher, pictured him as an heroic figure who was proclaiming the end of time in apocalyptic images. He referred to this interpretation as "thoroughgoing eschatology," and understood the Kingdom of God as essentially an imminent but future reality. C.H. Dodd, through an analysis of Jesus' parables and John's Gospel, answered that, on the contrary, the Kingdom was already realized in the earthly Jesus, and consequently was experienced by his disciples as a present reality. Nothing new was to be expected in the future. Christ was supposed to confront each individual in the present, and this confrontation meant the Day of Judgment. Dodd referred to this interpretation as "realized eschatology."

Neither Schweitzer nor Dodd was doing justice to the manifoldness of Jesus' teaching and to the clear distinction in Jewish thought between this world and the world to come. However, their contrast between a thoroughgoing eschatology and a realized eschatology is like an echo of the radical change brought about by the Catastrophe of 70 C.E. in the spiritual outlook of the Hellenistic-Jewish-Christians. Before the Catastrophe they were expecting a prompt return of the risen Jesus, but after the Catastrophe this return receded to the unknown horizon of human history, and the present became all-important. Such a contrast was akin to the change from political messianism in late Temple Judaism to liturgical messianism in early Rabbinic Judaism.

On the morrow of the Catastrophe a common trend could be found in revitalized Judaism and nascent Christianity; their respective leaders were trying to conceptualize what exactly was the will of God concerning the everyday life of their own people. Recent exegesis, as for example the classical work of Dom Jacques Dupont on the redaction of the Beatitudes in the Gospels of Matthew and Luke, offers a good confirmation of this important shift in the attitude of the early Church toward the ESCHATON.[1]

Exegetes had always been puzzled by Matthew's redaction of the Beatitudes. In the introduction to the Sermon on the Mount, he attributes to Jesus of Nazareth seven or eight long blessings (Matt 5:1-12), when Luke mentions only four short ones, followed by four corresponding curses (Luke 6:20-26). Not only are the literary forms different, but also the contents. It is generally agreed that Luke remains closer to the early tradition, retains the original number of blessings, but gives his own interpretation through the addition of the corresponding curses. On the lips of Jesus of Nazareth the four original blessings must have meant a clear eschatological pronouncement: Blessed are the poor, the sorrowing, the hungry, the persecuted; they will know complete happiness in the coming Kingdom. There was no reference to their inner motivation; only their present physical or social misery was intended. The Beatitudes proclaimed that the misfortunes of the present age were to be transformed soon into the blessings of the age to come.

Writing in the eighties, Matthew changed poor into "poor in spirit," and hungry into "hungry and thirsty for justice." He was passing from existential social reality to the realm of religious and ethical values. From the Psalms, or from other sayings of Jesus, he introduced new blessings for the meek, the merciful, the pure in heart and the peacemaker. To all of these an intimate union with the living God was promised in the world to come. If we compare Matthew's understanding with the earlier tradition, a clear change of focus becomes obvious. In the context of a much delayed Parousia, the need was felt to emphasize the existential link between the moral life of the disciples and God's gift of his Kingdom. Many parables and sayings of the Master had stressed the importance of this link, and the Sermon on the Mount was nothing else but the setting forth of true righteousness in this world. Matthew was not losing sight of the future—the Parousia was for him the Day of Judgment—he was focusing his attention on the present. He felt the need to answer the question: What is the Christian HALACHAH, what is the path along which the disciples of Jesus of Nazareth were supposed to "walk" in this world on the way to the world to come?

Matthew's framework was essentially Jewish. He brought back the messianic hope, "Thy Kingdom come," into the basic framework of Judaism, i.e., the sanctification of the Name, "Hallowed be thy Name." However, in this traditional framework, the introduction of a new element became the source of a profound transformation. The teacher of the way, the teacher of righteousness, was not Moses or one of the Prophets, it was first and foremost Jesus of Nazareth, now risen and glorified. All through his work Matthew will emphasize how unique was the relation of Jesus of Nazareth to the living God. He did not speak like the scribes, but on his own authority. He did not simply confirm or explain the Torah; he occasionally modified some commandment or gave a stricter interpretation of others. He constantly stressed the importance for the disciples of receiving God's words with truly obedient hearts and not solely with obedient lips. For Matthew, Jesus was the most authoritative teacher Israel had ever had and ever would have. He was obviously the supreme rabbinic authority.

Though he gave such a unique and quite extraordinary position to Jesus of Nazareth, Matthew was careful not to separate him from his people or their religious tradition. Jesus confessed, "I was sent only to the lost sheep of the house of Israel" (Matt 15:24). It is only during his farewell to his disciples that he commanded them to go to the Gentiles (Matt 28:19). On two points he may have scandalized some devout souls: he associated with sinners and argued about arguable points of the Oral Law. Such behavior, however, was intentional and part of his teaching endeavor. Jesus and his family—if his brother James was typical—were observant Jews. Jesus' spirituality was very close to the spirituality of the ANAWIM which flourished in late Temple Judaism, a spirituality inspired by the Psalms and Deutero Isaiah. These marks of oneness with his people in no way canceled the originality of his teaching, but he was totally immersed in the life of his people, even when confronting them. By introducing in the text nearly fifty quotations of the Hebrew Scriptures, Matthew and his school of Christian scribes wanted to prove the continuity of the life and teaching of Jesus with the structure of the Mosaic covenant and the religious life of biblical Israel.

Though by the time the Matthean Gospel was published, around 80 C.E., the messianic fever had already subsided among Jews and Gentile Christians alike, the early apocalyptic tradition was kept by Matthew as a minor theme. The Day of the Lord, foreknown by the great Prophets, will be the Day of the Son of Man, the Day of Judgment. Matthew was absolutely sure that the Kingdom of God would come. The time for the harvest, however, was still in the future. The present was not yet "the end of days," but rather "the last days" of this world. In spite of the delay of the Parousia the present was important as a time of spiritual growth, of maturation, of immediate preparation for the inauguration of God's Kingdom.

3. WHICH TORAH?

By bringing the Sanctification of the Name to center-stage, the fade-out in messianism rendered the Christian communities more self-conscious of their own identity, for they had become externally less different from the other Jewish communities, and easily an object of comparison with the revitalized Judaism achieved at the Yavneh Academy. The Matthean community knew that the Church of the Circumcision had very little prospect of expanding beyond the borders of the Land of Israel. On the other hand Paul's rupture with Judaism was going against the grain. Though Paul's Letters and

Matthew's Gospel shared a common frame of reference in ethical monotheism and gave to Jesus of Nazareth a unique role in the inauguration of God's Kingdom, concerning the interconnectedness between Judaism and nascent Christianity, they were expressing antithetical conceptions.

Paul had conceived of the relation between the Israel of his youth and "the Israel of the new age" in terms of origin and promise only. For him, the new Israel was a mysterious eschatological reality, newly created in the power of God's Spirit, and totally centered on the risen Jesus. Matthew, on the contrary, conceived of his own Hellenistic-Jewish-Christian community in the present as the old Israel fulfilled thanks to the authoritative teaching handed down to his disciples by Messiah Jesus. While Paul was thinking in terms of a new covenant more glorious than the old, Matthew thought in terms of the old covenant achieving maturity through the teaching and activity of Jesus of Nazareth, in preparation for the eternal feast in the Kingdom of Heaven.

Paul had not been interested in preparation, but in entering through the gate opened wide by the death and resurrection of Jesus of Nazareth. Practically ignoring the long history of the Covenant, except for the initial promise made to Abraham, he overlooked the rich spirituality created by God in the past through the ministry of Prophets, Sages and Psalmists. By contrast Matthew was anxious to find the life and teaching of the same Jesus announced and prefigured in the Hebrew Scriptures in order to contemplate in him the perfection of the covenant, and not its dismissal.

The most significant contrast was to be found in their respective attitudes toward the observance of the Mosaic Law. For Paul the Mosaic Law was by nature transitory and had lost its legal status with the coming of the Messiah. Its observance was forbidden to Paul's uncircumcised disciples and only tolerated as a form of devotion for the circumcised. For Matthew, on the other hand, the Mosaic Law had lost none of its obligatory character.

> For truly I tell you, until heaven and earth pass away, not one letter, not one stroke of a letter will pass from the law until all is accomplished (Matt 5:18).

Consequently, as long as heaven and earth had not passed away—and obviously they had not passed away at the time of Matthew—all the prescriptions of the Mosaic Law had to be fulfilled.

How could Matthew's community remain faithful to this teaching of the Master and at the same time follow the rulings enacted by mother Church in Jerusalem, according to which the Gentile converts were exempted from circumcision and strict KASHRUT? Matthew probably shared the rabbis' conviction that the Law, written and oral, had been given to Moses by God on

Mount Sinai (Matt 23:2). For him as a Jew, as for Paul or for James, the observance of the commandments did not suffer any exception in principle. In reality, the rabbis were making a distinction between the Law and the fence around the Law. Many details of the Oral Law, even some interpretations of the Written Law, had been passionately argued among the Scribes and the Pharisees, and were again argued among rabbis at the Yavneh Academy. Moreover, the exact observance of the commandments in the Hellenistic Synagogues of the Diaspora is not fully known to us. The Synagogues of the Diaspora did not necessarily follow the Pharisaic interpretation of the Oral Law. In the eighties the Hellenistic-Jewish-Christian communities may have in fact enjoyed a modest area of freedom in creating their own life-style. It allowed them to insert into the framework of traditional Judaism the specific commandments given by Jesus of Nazareth to his disciples.

If there was a modest area of flexibility, the core of the Mosaic Law, however, was revered as the word of God; it was sacred and immutable. All Jews, even the sinners, would consider circumcision and the basic observance of Sabbath and KASHRUT as belonging to that immutable core. Consequently, any baptized Gentile still uncircumcised, though a sincere disciple of Jesus of Nazareth, even a true God-fearer, one to be counted among the just in this world and in the world to come, would remain forever a simple associate and not a full member of God's people. If so, would Matthew's community accept to be a two-tiered community, as is the case in Buddhism, with monks and laymen, the monks alone being full members? If not, and if the community allowed the circumcised and the uncircumcised to live in perfect equality, how was the Hellenistic Jewish Church able to square its behavior with the words of the Master? The election of Israel, circumcision as the mark of the covenant in the flesh, and the clear separation between Jews and Gentiles had never been questioned by Jesus of Nazareth.

It could be argued that the decisions taken to facilitate the reception of Gentiles had been taken by staunch observers of the Law in Jerusalem in a spirit of leniency, and that the Master himself had used his authority in such a spirit. However, he did so only in matters of Oral Law, such as Shabbat restrictions or ritual purity. Jesus never canceled the prescriptions of the written Law. When he pronounced halachic rulings, as he did in the Sermon on the Mount, it was to offer a stricter interpretation than the one current among the scribes. He showed leniency only in less important matters, those concerning the fence around the Law. In weighty ones, the core of the Law, he showed increased severity. Observant Jews who had some sympathy for the Jesus movement must have been startled by the ease with which his disciples were tampering with the Written Law, the word of God.

Matthew presents in his Gospel an implicit rationale for the halachic observance of his community. At his farewell to his disciples Jesus had said, "All
authority in heaven and on earth has been given to me. Go therefore and make
disciples of all nations" (Matt 28:19). The disciples had recognized Jesus of
Nazareth as the supreme legal authority, even when he was tightening the
Mosaic law on divorce (Matt 5:32), or declaring himself master of the
Sabbath (Matt 12:8). Consequently, the word "therefore" pronounced in such
a context may have been understood as the handing down by Jesus to his disciples of a share of his own authority. Once, he had told them, "Whatever you
bind on earth will be bound in heaven, and whatever you loose on earth will
be loosed in heaven" (Matt 18:18). This power had been given especially to
Peter with the keys of the Kingdom (Matt 16:19). Matthew is the only one
among the Synoptic Gospels who explicitly mentions Peter's appointment.
These texts indicate that the disciples of Jesus were convinced that halachic
decisions taken by the community under the guidance of God's Spirit could
validly interpret TORAH in answer to crying spiritual needs.

From a Jewish point of view such decisions had no halachic validity. No
human authority could justify such acts of disobedience. Only a deep faith in
Jesus of Nazareth as God's Messiah could explain the withholding of a behavior clearly prescribed in TORAH.

Once some radical exemption or interpretation had been accepted in good
conscience, it was easy to foresee the future. More of the same would follow,
especially if the number of Gentiles interested in joining the community was
steadily increasing. For quite a while the Hellenistic Jews would be the majority of the community, but the time would come when the majority of the
members would be uncircumcised. Though the traditions, the spirituality and
the ritual, not to mention the Holy Scriptures, would be strongly Jewish, the
community as such would have ceased to be Jewish. It would in fact be
Hellenistic-Gentile-Christian. In no way could it still claim to be part of God's
own chosen people. The community spirit might be quite different from the
one prevailing in the Pauline Churches; in Jewish eyes, such a community
would have become, exactly like Paul's Churches, a foreign body, devoid of
any ritual purity, a goyish religion.

Any serious student of Matthew will always be surprised by the contrast
between the very positive attitude of the evangelist toward Judaism and his
bitter attacks against the Pharisees. In chapter 23, Matthew collected all the
sayings he could find that disparaged those who had been contending with
Jesus of Nazareth. In the Gospel these were called scribes and Pharisees, but
Matthew had in mind the rabbis of Yavneh who at that time were criticizing
the halachic behavior of his community. This Yavneh criticism was disturbing

to those who had perceived their Christian HALACHAH as an authentic continuation of the Jewish religious tradition. Matthew, anxious as he was to uphold this tradition, nevertheless remembered the saying of Jesus, "Unless your righteousness exceeds that of the scribes and the Pharisees, you will never enter the kingdom of heaven" (Matt 5:20). His devotion to the Mosaic Law in no way lessened his devotion to the teaching of Jesus of Nazareth. "Every scribe who has been trained for the kingdom of heaven is like the master of a household who brings out of his treasure what is new and what is old" (Matt 13:52). Given the presence of a new element in the formulation of the Christian HALACHAH, controversies were unavoidable with those who accepted solely the boundaries established by Hillel and Shammai for the interpretation of the Law.

By the time of Matthew, the allegiance to the word of God through TORAH, or through the risen Jesus, had ceased to coincide completely. Jews of different persuasions could accuse each other bitterly of spurning the observance of certain commandments. The presence of some Gentiles in the Hellenistic-Jewish-Christian communities did not make matters easier. It was not surprising that each community was deeply convinced of its spiritual superiority and considered itself alone to be the authentic and true Israel. What was at stake in the ongoing controversy was nothing else than the authority to interpret TORAH, the word of God.

4. WHICH MESSIAH?

If the non-appearance of a Son of Man or any other messianic figure at the time of the Catastrophe had considerably cooled the messianic fever among Jews and Christians alike, such a significant change in spiritual attitude will have a special impact on the Christians' self-image. How could Christians, i.e., Messianics, live without messianism? Since their raison d'être as a distinct brand of Judaism was the messiahship of Jesus of Nazareth, how could they justify their existence to the YAVNEH Academy? The disappearance from liturgical worship of the final appeal MARANA THA, Come, O Lord, must have created some spiritual unrest. Those born in Judaism or long time God-fearers may have wondered about the meaning of their new way if finally their Church was not very different from the neighboring Synagogue, except for a more liberal interpretation of the Mosaic Law.

Questions would naturally arise. In what sense is the risen Jesus still the Christ, i.e., the Messiah? What is his present status and role in the life of the Christian community? Could Gentiles be truly interested in a Jewish Messiah? Travelers visiting various Churches were aware of a certain pluralism in the Christian attitude, not toward the living God, but toward Jesus of Nazareth risen and glorified. There was an obvious need for a Christian theology which would give a clear meaning to the word Messiah, a word which had become a component of the personal name Jesus Christ.

In Matthew's Gospel Jesus of Nazareth is presented as the Master, as a teacher, a pedagogue, the one who trains disciples who will in turn teach the people of God in preparation for the Day of Judgment. Now raised and glorified, Jesus functions like the supreme rabbi in the House of Israel, as the master of God's household who through the teaching of his disciples "brings out of his treasure what is new and what is old" (Matt 13:52). Heir to the great Prophets, he imparts to those willing to receive his teaching the final word of the living God.

Paul, who devoted all his life to the proclamation of the Good News among the Gentiles, had been less interested in teaching. For him the role of pedagogue was to deal with immaturity. Paul did not like his disciples to be children, but rather grown-up, fully mature people (see Gal 3:24). It was in a spirit of resignation that he wrote to the Corinthians,

> I could not speak to you as spiritual people, but rather as people of the flesh, as infants in Christ. I fed you with milk, not solid food, for you were not ready for solid food (1 Cor 3:1–2).

Paul was aware that among his disciples spiritual learning may be deficient, but he seldom focused his attention on spiritual development.

From the moment of his encounter with Jesus of Nazareth on the way to Damascus Paul had been completely absorbed in the content of this extraordinary experience. His approach to Jesus then and there had been instantaneous, without any learning process. His letters show little sympathy or understanding for the long, tortuous, painful approach to the living God attempted by higher religious cultures or by searching individuals. For Paul, nature is all around us, proclaiming the glory of the living God, and the Good News, i.e., the victory of Jesus of Nazareth over death, is now proclaimed to all in the power of God's Spirit. He expects an immediate and total surrender to the leadership of the risen Jesus.

Paul was living in Jesus' presence not as a disciple sitting attentively at the feet of a master, eager to be enlightened by his teaching, but rather as an athlete running toward Messiah Jesus, a Messiah who had learned in his own flesh to overcome the pain and suffering of a deathly struggle with the forces of evil and had already been welcomed into the promised land. Jesus of Nazareth, risen and glorified, was for Paul the actual King Messiah, the leader not only of Israel but of all humanity in its struggle against the powers of darkness. "For he must reign until he has put all his enemies under his feet" (1 Cor 15:25).

A most interesting text, a kind of first essay in systematic theology, brings to light how a new attitude developed toward Messiah Jesus. This untitled text became known as "The Letter to the Hebrews" and is found at the end of the Pauline corpus. Though Matthew was the most read Gospel in the Gentile Churches during the second century, a number of quotations taken from this anonymous text have been found in various writings. It betrays a Pauline eschatological mood...with a special twist given to it.

There is a general consensus that such a text could not have been written by Paul. It shows affinity with the Hellenistic Judaism of Alexandria. The exact date of its writing remains uncertain—probably very soon before or after the burning of the Temple. The thesis of the author is obvious: the Temple in Jerusalem and its magnificent liturgy have become obsolete—an echo of Stephen's speech before the Sanhedrin, and a translation in liturgical terms of the Pauline attitude toward the old after the new had appeared. In the new age, Jesus of Nazareth, risen and glorified, has been constituted the eternal High Priest of Israel.

> When Christ came as a high priest of the good things that have come, then through the greater and perfect tent (not made with hands, that is, not of this creation), he entered once for all into the Holy Place, not with the blood of goats and calves, but with his own blood, thus obtaining eternal redemption (Heb 9:11–12).

The liturgy of the Jerusalem Temple was holy, but only as a shadow of the heavenly liturgy. Its sacramental value was proleptic, anticipating the complete and perfect worship to be rendered to the living God by the risen Jesus. Now, after the destruction of the Temple and the lowering of the messianic fever, the role of Jesus as High Priest is taking precedence over his expected role as the Son of Man, the one to come at the end of days to usher in the eternal Kingdom of God.

This change of perspective was significant, because it indicated an important change of attitude. Instead of being attentive to the future, looking for the restoration of the kingdom to Israel, or hoping eschatologically for a new heaven and a new earth, the disciples of Jesus became more attentive to the present. They connected the present directly with eternity without reference to history, by relating creation, which is transitory, to the living God, who is eternal. It was a change from a horizontal to a vertical dimension, from looking ahead to looking above. In so doing they returned to the traditional Jewish pride of place given to the sanctification of the Name. For them, however, this relation with the living God was not immediate, person to person, as was the case in nascent Rabbinic Judaism. The relation was through, with and in Jesus of Nazareth, risen and glorified, "the one mediator between God and humanity" (1 Tim 2:5).

From these three examples: Matthew, Paul, and Hebrews, it is obvious that the early Gentile Christians were relating to Jesus of Nazareth, the Jewish Messiah, in more than one way. All through the second century these apostolic writings will circulate among the Gentile Churches and start a process of cross-fertilization. It is only 150 years after the death and resurrection of Jesus of Nazareth, in the writings of Irenaeus who, born in Asia Minor, had become the shepherd of a Greek community in Southern Gaul, that a harmonious presentation will be found of the manifold aspects present in Jesus' messianic activity. By then the Church was starting to theologize in the framework of Greek thinking.

In the early days, immediately after Pentecost, the risen Jesus had been given the title Messiah to signify that he was the "anointed one" whom God would send in the near future to inaugurate the Kingdom, a Davidic kingdom or an apocalyptic kingdom, the disciples were not sure. The delay in his return, the limited success of the Apostles' ministry among the House of Israel, and the influx of Gentile proselytes, brought a progressive change of perspective.

Still proclaiming Jesus' basic role as the Son of Man who will judge the living and the dead at "the end of time," the disciples saw him fulfilling a different role in the present, in "the last days" of this world. God's Kingdom, i.e., eternal life or eternal bliss, was only to be inaugurated at the Parousia, at the end of history. Meanwhile the resurrection and ascension of Jesus of Nazareth had meant his enthronement by God as King Messiah. The messianic kingdom was to last until the Parousia when Jesus as King Messiah would hand over his kingdom to God "so that God may be all in all" (see 1 Cor 15:20-28). Meanwhile, the messianic kingdom was the realization of Jesus' answer to Pilate, "My kingdom is not of this world" (John 18:36). The kingship of the risen Jesus was transcending any earthly kingdom and different from any messianic scenario popular in Israel at the time.

As a king could he reign alone, without loyal subjects? Within the Scriptures we have a few hints. When Jesus expired on the cross, the earth shook and "The tombs also were opened, and many bodies of saints who had fallen asleep were raised" (Matt 27:52). The Creed of the Apostles and the Athanasian Creed are witnesses to an old tradition according to which Jesus descended to Hades between death and resurrection in order to liberate and take with him all those who had lived in holiness and justice (1 Pet 3:19). The

Seer of Revelation, speaking of the martyrs, saw those who had not worshiped the beast, come to life and reign with Christ (Rev 20:4-6). Early the
Church prayed for the dead and rejoiced with the saints in glory. The time
before the Parousia, the messianic time, is the time during which the heavenly
Jerusalem is "prepared as a bride adorned for her husband" (Rev. 21:2), the
time of preparation but for which there would be no heavenly Jerusalem..

As long as our present transitory world was still in existence, the messianic kingdom in heaven and the Christian community on earth would exist
concurrently. In this new perspective how would the Christian community
define its own status? It had been told by Jesus on the eve of his departure
that "they are in the world" but "they do not belong to the world" (John
17:11, 14). They were no more Israel the chosen nation, not yet the
Kingdom of God, and not exactly God's messianic kingdom as the King
Messiah was not resident in their midst. On the other hand they were not
simply praying, working and living in the power of God's Spirit; they were
experiencing a quasi-mystical union with Jesus Messiah who had assured
them at his departure, "I am with you always to the end of the age" (Matt
28:20). United to him, though still in this world, they were in communion
with the heavenly Jerusalem. But, according to Paul, they were saved in
hope only, groaning in the Spirit toward a fulfillment still in the future. If in
faith and charity they were united to and strengthened by Messiah Jesus, in
hope they were yet waiting for him. In that sense they were still expectant
Messianics.

It is in such a context that were brought into unity the various traditions
remembering or contemplating the risen Jesus. In the power of God's Spirit,
the risen Jesus was able to perform among his earthly disciples the various
functions which God had progressively established in order to structure the
Sinaitic Covenant and which in the later days had fallen in abeyance:
Kingship, Priesthood and Prophecy. For the early Christians Messiah Jesus
became their Shepherd, their High Priest and their Pedagogue or Master, acting invisibly in the secret of the heart or visibly, in word and sacrament,
through his delegates, those he had sent, his apostles.

In the eighties and nineties, the Gentile Christian communities returned to
Judaism in the sense that they lived more in the present than the future; they
upheld some form of HALACHAH and defined some kind of authority in
order to structure their communities; they maintained the sanctity of family
life in the home and worried about religious education for children, etc. At the
same time, they departed from Judaism, because the center of gravity of their
worship, the core of their religious and ethical ideal, the community they truly
belonged to, were not on earth, but in the kingdom of Messiah Jesus. In this

unique situation, the disciples rarely called themselves Israel or the Kingdom of God, but rather the Assembly of God's people, the Church of God. In common with Israel they were still in pilgrimage toward the heavenly Jerusalem, but in the darkness of faith they were glancing now and then at its radiance.

5. WHICH GOD?

What Paul, the writer of the Letter to the Hebrews, Matthew and many others had been exploring, was the messianic role of Jesus of Nazareth. As the first generation was leaving this world "to be with Christ" (Phil 1:23) the memory of a vivid, intimate, personal relationship between master and disciple was slowly fading out. Could the next generations still relate to him personally, rather than in the framework of various messianic functions? Who was he? Was he still Jesus of Nazareth and were his disciples still his sisters and brothers? What was "his" relation to the living God?

Certain expressions in the Letter to the Hebrews, such as the risen Jesus entered through the greater and perfect tent, "not made with hands, that is, not of this creation" (Heb 9:11), could be read as a departure not only from this world but from his human condition and a sudden irruption into the divine sphere. Such an interpretation would destroy the lofty concept of divine transcendence which Israel had achieved through centuries of spiritual struggle. It could only evoke deep feelings of spiritual revulsion in a Jewish soul.

The covenant made at Sinai had established a permanent bond between God and his chosen people. It implied mutual knowledge, mutual devotion, and even mutual cooperation, but never a cooperation between equals. God had delineated precise limits to Israel's activity. If Israel trespassed these limits, the covenant was temporarily in abeyance, and divine justice would take its course. One limit carefully respected after the exile in Babylon was the separation between the sacred and the profane, between God and everything in creation. Nothing created was sacred by itself, and in fact Israel would slowly demythologize every aspect of nature. Objects, places, times or persons could be sacred only through a consecration by God himself. There was a kind of natural "redline" between God and everything in the cosmos, between the infinite and the finite, between the one who creates out of nothing and the objects of his creative activity. Religiously, this redline was experienced as a clear separation between the sacred and the profane. It was vividly evident in Ezekiel and in Deutero-Isaiah. It was to become the soul of Jewish worship and spirituality.

Bodily resurrection in this context was not perceived as a transgression of the redline. Even the concept of Ascension which we find in the apocalyptic literature—Ascension of Enoch, Ascension of Moses, Ascension of Elijah, Ascension of Isaiah—did not infringe on God's transcendence. But the imagery used by the writer of the Letter to the Hebrews was unclear. It could convey the impression that Jesus of Nazareth, as High Priest of Israel, had entered permanently BEYOND the veil of creation into the sphere of the Transcendent. Even to a devout Jewish mystic, hoping to be granted a glimpse of the divine mysteries, such a thought must have seemed audacious. The Nazarenes had never conceived the glorification of Jesus of Nazareth as transgressing the redline. Were the Hellenist Christians—Jews or Gentiles—willing to erase it and reverse the fundamental trend of Jewish spirituality toward an increased awareness of God's transcendence? The Johannine writings which witness to a transition from Palestinian Judaism to Hellenistic Judaism seem even more ambiguous about the existence or non-existence of a redline.

The Fourth Gospel mentions a mysterious figure, "the disciple whom Jesus loved." At the last supper he was reclining next to Jesus, and on Calvary Jesus, seeing his mother standing near the cross, told him, "Here is your mother" (John 19:27). Afterward, she will live in the home of this disciple on Mount Zion for an unknown number of years. A unanimous tradition has recognized in this disciple John, the son of Zebedee. Some modern exegetes argue about this attribution. There was, however, a disciple whom Jesus loved, who had a close personal relationship with him and later with his mother. He seems to have been the spiritual ancestor of a Jewish Christian tradition which grew beside the mainstream of the Nazarenes, and gave birth to a community with a very particular history.[2]

This Jewish Christian community moved first to Syria and later to Ephesus, which had been Pauline territory. After a while its membership opened to Gentiles, but it had first received proselytes from Essenism, from Samaria and from Hellenistic Judaism. Clear traces of its doctrinal evolution are apparent in the redaction of the Fourth Gospel and in the Johannine letters, that are generally dated around 90 C.E. The evolution of ritual observances in the community is unknown. One of the serious mistakes of early higher criticism had been to explain the Johannine tradition as an acceptance of Hellenistic Gnosticism and/or mystery cults into Christian theology. The discovery of the Dead Sea Scrolls came as a surprise; it proved without a doubt that the Johannine tradition had its roots in Palestinian Judaism.

All the Johannine writings have a peculiar characteristic: Jesus of Nazareth manifests in them a close, even intimate, union with the living God. He does not seem to keep that distance which is proper for anyone born of a woman in relation to his or her Creator. Such an attitude may have been perceived only by his close friends or those contradictors who were carefully scrutinizing his behavior. Jesus being a just man, a religious man, speaking about God with reverence, was looked at by the crowds as a prophet. Occasionally he did not use the common expression Our Father, calling God "my Father." Some listeners were indignant, "because he was not only breaking the Sabbath, but was also calling God his own Father, thereby making himself equal to God" (John 5:18). He was not making himself God, but by making himself "equal" to God, he, a Jew, was certainly in their eyes showing great presumption. He was crossing the redline and acting with insolence toward God.

Still more serious from a Jewish point of view was the impression given by some other sayings that it was not Jesus of Nazareth who was transgressing the redline, but God himself who was the transgressor. The Johannine Jesus is conscious not only that he has been sent by God as all the great Prophets were, but that he "is from God" (John 6:46, 7:29), "I am from above...I am not of this world" (8:23), "Before Abraham was, I am" (8:58). He styles himself the bread of life, "The bread of God is that which comes down from heaven and gives life to the world" (6:33). John, son of Zechariah, testified that "the one who comes from above is over all" (3:31). Probably referring to those mystic souls who were trying to pierce the divine mysteries, Jesus disclosed himself:

> Very truly, I tell you, we speak of what we know and testify to what we have seen...No one has ascended into heaven except the one who descended from heaven...(John 3:11–13).

The Community of the Beloved Disciple, thanks to the living memory of its founder who had been so close to the Master, and through a loving scrutiny of some of Jesus' sayings, came to understand that Jesus of Nazareth had been from the beginning with God; he was the Wisdom of God spoken to the world, not by the mouth of a Prophet, but through a unique act of HESED, of lovingkindness, on the part of God. "For God so loved the world that he gave his only Son, so that everyone who believes in him...may have eternal life" (John 3:16). "The Word became flesh and lived among us..." (John 1:14). God himself in Jesus of Nazareth had crossed the redline. He did not simply visit, or dwell among his creatures. He did more; he acquired a human identity and experienced our joys and pains, acting out all essential human activities.

God had frequently shown lovingkindness toward Israel, but had also forcefully upheld his holiness. For any sensitive Jewish mind, not sharing John's paradoxical faith in God's self-abasement, such a transgression of the redline, such a confusion of the above and the below, must have appeared a real sacrilege, a desecration of God's Name. In a sense it was. Paul dared to write, "For our sake God made him to be sin who knew no sin" (2 Cor 5:21). Could there be any rationale for such incomprehensible behavior? The early Christians experienced in this mystery the supreme expression of God's love for Israel and through Israel for all humanity, the crowning achievement of all creation.

Some members of the Community of the Beloved Disciple felt quite uneasy about this unfolding of an incarnational theology.

> They went out from us, but they did not belong to us; for if they had belonged to us, they would have remained with us. But by going out they made it plain that none of them belongs to us (1 John 2:19).

Their theological qualms did not arise from the profanation of God's Name through the deification of a human being, but rather the opposite, through the humiliation of the transcendent God of Israel made a prisoner of matter. They could not accept that the Word of God had become a tiny part of humanity. They knew that Jesus was from above, was God's Word, Wisdom, Life, Light, infinite in majesty. He could not be a man, living even for a time in a mortal body. For them, God had manifested himself in and through a bodily appearance, as he did when he was walking with Adam and Eve in the Garden, or visiting Abraham accompanied by two Angels, or speaking to Moses in a burning bush and to the Prophet Elijah in a whispering murmur. It was possible to conceive God acting "in" this world, but not "from" this world. From then on, Docetism will challenge Christianity, denying that the Word of God had become flesh and proclaiming that it was through bodily appearance that God's Word had visited his people to enlighten and save them.

The community of the Beloved Disciple let the dissenters go their own way. It drew nearer to the surviving Pauline communities in west Asia Minor, and possibly to the Church in Antioch. In the second century the Johannine writings will be progressively received and admired among Gentile Churches. Through them it became well understood that, rather than a deification of the human, the Church was contemplating in Jesus of Nazareth, risen and glorified, the humanization of God, in order to bring the Covenant to its absolute perfection.

Once all is said, however, the Gentile Christians started from then on to relate to the risen Jesus more and more as one who is with the living God, away from this world. His humanity became a transparent icon of his divinity or a practical instrument of his divine activity. His mediatorship as teacher, priest and leader was not to be denied, but often was de-emphasized, and for the faithful Christian the humble carpenter of Nazareth was simply, "My Lord and my God" (John 20:28).

To the extent that the risen Jesus was considered in worship and devotion exclusively above the redline, and his humanity ignored or at least poorly understood, he became totally separated from his own people. No longer a Jew, he was the rootless, universal and abstract humanity of God's Word.

XI. Mistrust and Animosity

During the thirty years following the destruction of Jerusalem and the burning of the Temple, from 70 to 100 C.E., Rabbinic Judaism and Apostolic Christianity emerged from a rich spiritual tradition with contradictory self-images. However, to any social scientist they would have looked very much alike.

1. SOCIO-CULTURAL SIBLINGS

Around 90 C.E., people on the street as well as Roman authorities, all across the Empire, had no clear idea of what differentiated Christians from Jews. Thanks to a well-known privilege granted by the Roman Senate to the Jews at the time of the Maccabees, the two groups were abstaining from any kind of participation in the official cults of the city or the Empire. Each group was clannish, tending to associate among themselves. Few of them were patrons of the theater or the circus. Their family life and their public morality were respectable. They all suffered from a latent antisemitism brought about by their aloofness in religious matters. Separation between public life and religious life was at that time an unknown concept.

Religiously they had so much in common! They were strict monotheists, despised the idols and their temples. Their forms of worship were similar. After the burning of the Temple every kind of sacrifice had ceased. They were reading the same Scriptures with great reverence and were singing psalms, hymns and spiritual songs to God. They were breaking bread and blessing a cup of wine, the Jews in their homes on Sabbath eve, the Christians in their Sabbath assembly.

Each group was argumentative. Judaism was not yet monolithic, and various trends were still vying against each other. The situation was similar in nascent Christianity; Paul had to contend with various factions in Corinth: "I belong to Paul," or "I belong to Apollos," or "I belong to Cephas," or "I belong to Christ" (1 Cor 1:12). Occasionally Jews and Christians argued with each other. The pagans not understanding the reason for these disagreements were bewildered. Jews, in general, belonged to better social strata than the Christians. In this period, in the aftermath of the First Jewish Revolt, some Diaspora Jews preferred to keep a low social profile. Only in the second half of the second century will they recover an advantageous position. The Christians for a long time will remain at the bottom of the totem pole.

The political situation after the Catastrophe may have encouraged some Gentile Christians to make themselves known in Greco-Roman society or to the imperial authorities as a religious group distinct from the Jews. Personal security would discourage them to do so. Such a recognition would immediately deprive them of their status as members of a RELIGIO LICITA, and their refusal to participate in the imperial cult would then expose them to being thrown to the wild beasts. The day the Christians felt that in conscience they could not declare themselves to be Jews, or ceased to be recognized by the Jews as belonging to the circumcised People of God, their legal protection was lost. From mid-second century on the Christian Church endured a number of systematic persecutions at the hands of the Roman authorities. The Jewish character of Christianity was not an academic question. In some instances it was a matter of life or death.

Though socially and culturally the Diaspora's Synagogues and Churches looked so much alike, and though spiritually they shared a common basic framework of ethical monotheism, nevertheless, by reason of their disagreement on the person and the role of Jesus of Nazareth they became estranged from each other. The nature and the speed of this process of alienation were different in the various regions of the Empire, but some basic factors were at work everywhere in the Diaspora.

2. LOYALTY TO THE COVENANT

In the tension which arose after the destruction of the Temple between Jews and Christians, the Jesus Movement was the challenger. Before the Catastrophe, the Nazarenes had claimed legitimacy in Jewish eyes as a new and more authentic strand in the interpretation of Torah. They were not alone to do so. The Essenes and others were seriously questioning the religious establishment's interpretations and policies. After the Catastrophe, once the Yavneh Academy started to integrate all the surviving forces of Temple Judaism into a loosely structured but culturally coherent institution, well adapted to the new conditions in the Land of Israel, the Nazarenes at home and the Christians in the Diaspora had to take a clear position vis-à-vis Rabbinic Judaism and the emerging authority of Yavneh.

On the ground of Jewish tradition Yavneh had a claim to authenticity. It upheld and even reinforced a deep devotion to the only surviving sanctity, the Torah. The others, i.e., Prophecy, Temple, Priesthood, Kingship, Sovereignty over the Land, all had vanished; solely remaining was the word of God, calling his people to a sincere renewal. In contrast with this zeal for the Law, the Nazarenes and the Christians were arguing about TORAH, unable to agree on its validity and its fulfillment. Indeed, they worshiped the God of Israel and kept the Ten Commandments, but their worship, their community life, and their hope were structured around the crucified Jesus of Nazareth whom they proclaimed alive and Messiah of Israel. They seemed to be more attached to a heavenly Israel than an earthly one. The sages at Yavneh, spiritually wounded by the destruction of God's Temple, were in no mood to recognize any kind of messianic authority which was not sustained by clear, public and successful messianic deeds. They recognized only the authority of TORAH, the word of God. For them the messianism of the Nazarenes and their Gentile followers, far from alleviating the difficult task of renewing Israel's life, was making it more burdensome by distracting them from the common endeavor.

Fifty years after the tragic events under Pontius Pilate, the figure of the historical Jesus was already disappearing from Jewish consciousness. He was not even remembered as a national hero martyred by the Romans. During his public life he had attracted the Galilean masses; they became disappointed when they saw no sign of an imminent liberation from Roman occupation. After his miserable death on a Roman cross, his disciples had tried to convince the Jerusalemites and others that, now risen and glorified, he would soon return to restore the kingdom to Israel; the opposite came to pass, the loss of everything. False messiahs are not necessarily evil figures in Jewish tradition. Bar Kochba is seen today as a national hero. Jesus of Nazareth appeared as a man of God, but failed in his promise of national liberation. His name had to be added to the long list of false messiahs.

The strong conviction of Jesus' disciples that he was still alive was the basic reason for their challenge to Yavneh, as well as their increasing separation from the TORAH movement. The disciples who were scattered in the Diaspora had been profoundly shocked by the humiliation of Jerusalem at the hands of Rome, and disoriented by the burning of the Temple and the non-appearance of the Kingdom. But their radiant faith in the resurrection of Jesus led them to scrutinize some of his sayings to which they had paid little attention, for example "My Kingdom is not of this world" (John 18:36). Their daily life became suffused with an eschatological hope. They felt that

Yavneh's efforts were focused on secondary matters, missing the central aspect of God's revelation, the life, death, resurrection, and future return of Jesus of Nazareth.

The sages at Yavneh looked at this new Christian vision as one apocalyptic scenario that had little chance to be actualized. Such a vision was distracting the attention of the suffering people from the difficult task of reconstruction. As expected in such circumstances, the rabbis showed signs of annoyance, even of irritation, at the bravado of the Nazarenes. Occasionally they entered into forceful arguments with them.

Was Yavneh hurt by the survival of the Jesus movement? In the Land of Israel it was a nuisance rather than a real object of concern. It could be dismissed without further ado. Yavneh in fact was ignoring all the strands in Judaism which did not harmonize with the Pharisaic tradition of the House of Hillel. Ultimately it succeeded.

The situation in the Diaspora, however, was quite different. Christianity had made more inroads into Hellenistic Judaism than it ever did into Palestinian Judaism. Moreover, the God-fearers and those attracted to the moral standard of Jewish family life tended to congregate around Christian Synagogues, because the latter were less standoffish from the Greek socio-cultural world. A missionary rivalry was born which would last until late in the second century. Each group was convinced that its own tradition was the true Israel. They were starting to define their own self-identity in contrast with each other, like Protestants and Catholics in the sixteenth century.

Paul had correctly guessed from the beginning that the main bone of contention between traditionalist Jews and the disciples of Jesus of Nazareth would be loyalty to the Mosaic Law. Rabbis and disciples of Jesus were working in the same frame of reference of ethical monotheism, but the only sanctity they could share was the Hebrew Scriptures and the practices regulated by them. These will naturally become the locus of arguments and controversies. In the eyes of the rabbis the allegation of the Christians that they were still a part of God's chosen people, and consequently legitimate sons and daughters of the Covenant, could be proved only by complete loyalty to the Torah.

On the authority of Mother Church in Jerusalem the Greek proselytes had been excused from a number of important commandments such as circumcision, strict Sabbath observance, some dietary laws and possibly others. In the eyes of Yavneh these Gentile Christians, obviously unwilling to accept the yoke of the Law, baptism notwithstanding, remained Gentiles and in no way sons or daughters of the Covenant as they claimed to be.

In the Pauline Churches the question would not even cause a ruffle since there were no Greeks, no Jews, no males, no females, only one people, the

Israel of God. Jesus, risen and glorified, was the termination of the Law. In other Hellenistic-Jewish-Christian Synagogues, in which a real continuity with historical Israel was maintained, the question must have been asked: Were the new sisters and brothers still "Gentiles"? What was their relation to Israel? Could they be considered by the Jewish people as "New Jews"? This was out of the question because Jewishness meant unity of religion and nationhood and their national status was still "Gentile." The outcome was the birth of a "third kind" of peoplehood: henceforth in the communities of the new way the circumcised as well as the uncircumcised members will cease to be Jews or Gentiles; all will be called "Christians." They will understand themselves as the true people of God (see 1 Pet 2:9–10, quoting Exod 19:5–6).

The soul-searching of the Hellenistic-Jewish-Christian communities of mixed membership brought to light the basic religious problem arising between the Synagogue and the Church. James and the Church of the Circumcision in Jerusalem had a vibrant faith in the resurrection of Jesus of Nazareth and his Messiahship. Because they were staunch observers of the Law, they considered themselves, and were considered, members of the House of Israel. Paul's Gentile Christians who were uncircumcised and rejected Mosaic observances were outsiders, GOYIM, unconnected with the House of Israel. But the uncircumcised Christians in Antioch at the end of the century, who studied the Law and the Prophets, maintained the prayer ritual of the Diaspora Synagogues, worshiped the same God, and upheld the same moral ideal, were also considered "Gentiles." It was not by reason of their belief in Jesus of Nazareth, risen and glorified, but on account of their non-observance of some prescriptions of the written or oral Law that had been established to sanctify the Jewish nation and protect her from the pernicious influence of all other nations.

Such separation may appear to modern Christians unreasonable, a question of pride, of selfishness, of ethnocentrism, of a lack of generosity or what not. Was it truly arrogance? To all Jews the Mosaic Law meant a social expression of the Covenant God made with Abraham, the basic constitution of their nationhood, and the structure of their daily life. Its ultimate meaning and value were to be found in the nature of the covenant itself. It singled out one particular nation among all others for a unique relation with the living God and for a special function in his plan for human history. It was not a covenant made separately with a number of single individuals, but a covenant between God and A NATION AS NATION.

The covenantal integration of religion and nationhood has been a constant source of misunderstandings between Jews and Christians. Incorporation in the Jewish nation and in the Sinaitic Covenant are one and the same process.

Every aspect of national life is included in the covenant—religion, family life, land, art, economics and politics, international relations, even war. The Mosaic ideal is a theocratic society, separated from all others, in which everything except sin can be sanctified and consecrated to God, some persons, places and objects being reserved exclusively for his service, and the rest consecrated for proper usage by the people. Such a spirit of holiness, concentrated in a tiny part of creation, will lead Rabbinic Judaism to extend the application of the Law to more and more aspects of Jewish social life.

Christianity is not a covenant between God and a nation, but a covenant between God and a group of individual believers united by their personal relationship to the risen Jesus. Christians form a religious community in the midst of other religious communities, not a chosen nation among the other nations. One could be a baptized Christian and remain Greek, Roman or Barbarian. The seed was planted for the future development of two independent societies, with a clear distinction between Pope and Emperor, Church and State. In the Sinaitic Covenant, God's people could never be divided into a sacred society and a secular society. The priest was naturally a sacred person, but so was the King, the anointed of the Lord. Every aspect of Israel as a nation was God's own possession.

On the morrow of Jesus' resurrection, through the sudden outpouring of God's Spirit, a small fraction of this chosen nation had been transformed into an eschatological community, still "in" this world, but no more "of" this world, as Israel was. It was held together from above and enjoyed a foretaste and anticipation of the world to come. From then on, any extension of this small group would come through a personal commitment to the risen Jesus by some Jew or non-Jew who through baptism would then be grafted onto him and become a member of this eschatological Jewish community. As Paul saw clearly, the eschatological transformation had not united the whole nation with the risen Jesus, but solely a remnant. Only when the full number of the Gentiles will have come in, "will all Israel be saved" (Rom 11:26). In this statement Paul was not thinking of individual conversions, but of the national salvation of the House of Israel at the grand finale of human history.

The path to membership clearly illustrates the difference between Judaism and Christianity. The baptism of children has always been an intricate question in theological discussions because baptism is to be received in faith. The contrast is striking between the social membership of a child born to a Jewish mother and that of a Gentile child. It is birth, not circumcision, which makes a boy a son of the Covenant, forever a Jew. An uncircumcised daughter is as Jewish as her brother and a true daughter of the Covenant. Adult conversion is possible, but only as a lengthy process of social birth. The offspring of a

Jewish mother is always a Jew or a Jewess; a non-Jew, on the contrary, is born a pagan, and can become a Christian only through baptism.

The transformation of the Sinaitic Covenant into an eschatological covenant, through the resurrection of Christ and the active presence of God's Spirit, explains why the differences between Rabbinic Judaism and nascent Christianity became progressively more apparent. Without going to the extremes of Paul who saw no value left to human history, the early Christians dealt carefully and selectively with the values of this world. Martyrdom and virginity were looked at as true discipleship of the crucified Jesus. The anchor of religious life moved from this world into the world to come. However, in heaven, no babies are born nor are personalities growing to maturity. This world had to retain for Christians a profound religious value as preparation for eternal life.

The relative freedom from this world made the nascent Church more adaptable to a variety of human societies. There was a tendency not to transplant most of the socio-cultural requirements of the Covenant into Gentile Christianity, but only its strictly religious and moral prerequisites. As we noticed in the study of Matthew those leaders who succeeded the Twelve were confident that they had the authority to do so. Notwithstanding its particularistic debut the Jesus Movement experienced in itself a dynamic power to reach all nations, to become universalistic, to bring to existence the messianic vision of the Prophets who had seen all the nations surging toward Jerusalem to worship with Israel. The opening of an angle at its point of origin may be quite small, but if the two lines extend from this point to great length, the distance between them may become incredibly great. Yavneh and Christian Antioch were not going in opposite directions, nor along parallel ways either, but starting from the same point they were becoming increasingly different, like two siblings on the way to becoming estranged from one another.

Very rapidly the Christians came to consider Judaism in their own image, i.e., as a religious community and not as a nation. The destruction of Jerusalem, the ruin of national sovereignty and the preservation of Jewish nationhood through a religious framework, the success of the Yavneh revival along synagogal lines, and other factors, may have convinced a good number of Christians that the Sinaitic covenant as a socio-political covenant had come to an end in the burning of the Temple. In their eyes Judaism was simply a religious community, somehow old-fashioned, with a narrow legalistic outlook. The warmth and depth of Jewish piety had become hidden beyond a nascent wall of prejudice.

The break between the two communities had been heralded by Paul, but it really occurred only some time after the Catastrophe, when the Yavneh

Academy affirmed its leadership and some non-Pauline Hellenistic-Jewish-Christian Synagogues, after receiving a large number of Gentile converts, found themselves with an uncircumcised majority. These Churches were still Jewish in spirit, at least in all matters concerning their religious life, and they continued to look at themselves as the true Israel, but they considered the Yavneh Academy as a group of traditionalists who had been unable to read the signs of the times.

The Nazarenes in the Land of Israel had accepted to exempt adult Greek neophytes from the obligation of circumcision and certain laws of KASHRUT. The progressive dejudaization of the Jesus movement in the Diaspora must have caused them great anxiety. Relations became strained between the Church of the Circumcision and the Hellenistic Churches that had become non-Jewish. Until late in the second century some individual Jewish Christians in the Diaspora will continue to observe the ritual commandments of the Torah and encourage other Christians to do the same. As time passed, they were less and less successful. The Nazarenes, the Ebionites and other small Jewish Christian groups were finally considered heretics by the Greek Churches.

The traditionalists in Yavneh, on their part, did not consider the Gentile Churches a secessionist group like the Samaritans, or later the Karaites. For them they were strangers, goyish groups belonging to the covenant of Noah. They had no right to claim membership in the covenant of Abraham, notwithstanding their own affirmation. They may have been devout God-fearers, but in no way could they be part and parcel of the national community of Israel.

Jewish tradition, nevertheless, will never feel completely comfortable in styling the Christian nations as GOYIM. They were looking like a strange species; they had so much Jewishness in them!

3. MONOTHEISM IN JEOPARDY

As renewed Judaism and nascent Christianity started to face each other in the Jewish Diaspora, their incipient antagonism was not purely social, as in the case of an intellectual disagreement, a rivalry in popularity, or an improper mixture of social categories. There was in their feelings and social attitudes the beginning of a real religious indignation.

Jews felt that the Christians in the Diaspora, Jews or Gentiles, despised TORAH, the word of the Almighty, his greatest gift to Israel, the organizing principle of its religious and social life. These Messianics placed themselves above TORAH, picked and chose what they liked, discarded anything they felt inconvenient. They falsified the nature of the Israel they pretended to be and misled the Gentiles attracted to their false ways. In dishonoring God's beloved people, they were disgracing his Name.

Christians, on their part, felt that the Rabbinic Jews despised Jesus of Nazareth, the word of the Almighty, his greatest gift to Israel, the anointed sent to enlighten them and lead them to God's eternal Kingdom. Rather than accepting to be judged by him, they were putting him in judgment, him, his teaching and his activity. Not only did they refuse to receive God's salvation through him, they hindered his disciples who were trying to gather the nations into the service of the living God. In dishonoring his faithful servant, they were disgracing the God of Israel.

This mutual exclusion, even if it was in part conditioned by socio-cultural factors, was essentially a religious conflict resulting from two different faith structures. (To describe these faith structures the social scientist needs some empathy with the subjective conviction which sustains them, even if he does not share such a conviction.) Though Jews and Christians were thinking and acting in the same framework of strict ethical monotheism, one faith was crystalized around TORAH, which had been given to Moses at Sinai in order to transform one nation into God's own people, the other was crystalized around Jesus of Nazareth crucified and glorified, who had been sent to lead Israel and the nations into the life of the world to come, the true and eternal life.

Up to this point it seems that the basic frame of reference of ethical monotheism remained intact. The parting of the ways was caused by a different apprehension of God's activity toward his creation. There was no blasphemy, no impugning the holiness of God, no trespassing the redline of divine transcendence. The conflict was about the nature of the true Israel. It was only indirectly about God himself.

Some time after the Catastrophe of 70 C.E., a configuration of religious factors among the Hellenistic Christians started to question the framework of ethical monotheism as it was understood by the Rabbinic Jews at Yavneh and the surviving Nazarenes in Jerusalem. In the Land of Israel there had never been any temptation to deify Jesus of Nazareth, to make him a god. When he was remembered, it was as a prophet-like figure or a martyr dying on a cross or the chosen Son of God among God's chosen people. Even for his disciples his resurrection was still mysterious; they were mostly awaiting his return.

In the Diaspora's Synagogues the Jews and the God-fearers had been attracted to Jesus of Nazareth as God's Messiah, but the converts from among the Gentiles had been placing their hopes in him as the Savior of their immortal souls. As pagans they were accustomed to worship divine saviors and deified human beings, gods in human form. Jewish life in the Diaspora had been a long struggle to maintain and uphold pure monotheism in the midst of all these spiritual perversions. Was the proclamation of Jesus of Nazareth, not only as Messiah but as "Lord," some surreptitious effort by Gentile Christians to deify Jesus and paganize Judaism?

The background of the question, and the source of later confusion, was the choice made by the Jewish translators of the Septuagint to render the proper name of God into Greek. Already at the beginning of the third century B.C.E., in the Land of Israel, the proper name of God was not pronounced anymore, but read ADONAI—meaning my lords, a plural of majesty like ELOHIM. The translators chose KURIOS in the singular rather than using a plural of majesty. It was a secular word meaning a person with authority; the antonym was DOULOS, a servant, a slave. They kept this word KURIOS, Lord, for the tetragrammaton and they used the Greek word for god, THEOS, for ELO-HIM. In faithfulness to the original the two different Greek words kept the distinction between the two different Hebrew names used in the Hebrew Scriptures for the One God.

During the public life of Jesus of Nazareth it is most probable that his disciples called him in Aramaic MARI, my lord, and spoke about him as MARAN, our lord. The term MAR in Aramaic or ADON in Hebrew is equivalent to "Sir" in English. Those sent by Jesus to fetch a colt were to say: "the Lord needs it and will send it back" (see Mark 11:3). The disciples seldom called the master RABBI, my teacher. After the resurrection they continued to refer to him as our lord, but enlightened by the theophany of Pentecost they gave him the title Messiah, and referred to him as our lord the Messiah.

As the Aramaic MAR was habitually translated into Greek as KURIOS, lord, this term KURIOS in Christian parlance came to mean at the same time the proper name of God (ADONAI) and the name of the risen Jesus (MARAN or ADONEINU). This had an important consequence. When in the Scriptures, for example in the Psalms, the term KURIOS was read, it could be understood to refer to the living God or to the risen Jesus. Paul must have been aware of the problem because he is careful to use the term THEOS for God and KURIOS for the risen Jesus. He wrote:

We know that "no idol in the world really exists," and that "there is no God but one." Indeed, even though there may be so-called gods in heaven or on earth—as in fact there are many gods and many lords—yet for us there is one God, the Father, from whom are all things and for whom we exist, and one Lord, Jesus Christ, through whom are all things and through whom we exist (1 Cor 8:4–6).

Probably quoting a Hellenistic Christian hymn, he wrote about the title Kurios, "Therefore God also highly exalted [Jesus] and gave him the name that is above every name, so that at the name of Jesus every knee should bend" (Phil 2:9–10). Jesus of Nazareth, risen and glorified, occupies the supreme rank in creation. It is through him that God exercises his sovereignty over all the world. He has been established by God not only as the lord of humanity but as the lord of creation.

After the Catastrophe of 70 C.E., the letters of Paul were collected into a corpus and started to circulate among the Greek Churches. Paul's concept of Jesus' lordship—a translation of his experience on the way to Damascus—became the catalyst of an incipient Christology. Paul was not saying that Jesus of Nazareth was God, but was affirming that he had been taken by God into his own sphere of existence. When the rabbis at the Yavneh Academy became aware of the teaching of Paul's disciples they were shocked. The seniors among them had known this son of a carpenter, now said to be reigning at the right hand of Almighty God. Such an incredible exaltation could be understood only as a deification of Jesus of Nazareth. Any deification of a human being was for the rabbis the equivalent of erasing the redline separating creatureliness from transcendence, the redline which guaranteed the pure monotheism of the Torah.

When in the late first century the Johannine writings made their appearance, the rabbis' uneasiness of mind was not only confirmed but much aggravated. The concept of God with us, Emmanuel, was in the pure Jewish tradition. The living God, though completely transcendent in his godhead, interfered again and again in the history of Israel; he spoke through the Prophets and was dwelling in the Holy of Holies in Jerusalem. The rabbis after the Catastrophe developed the concept of SHECHINAH, of God's special presence in the midst of his people Israel. God's indwelling in the risen Jesus was not inconceivable. However, Emmanuel conceived as an incarnation of the God of Abraham, Isaac and Jacob, meaning that he had become completely identified with an ordinary Jew, even one from Nazareth, was not only inconceivable, it was sacrilegious. In the hearts of many rabbis, such a concept could only awaken a feeling of spiritual revulsion.

In the early second century the Johannine writings started to be accepted progressively by all the apostolic Churches. Around 112 C.E., the great Bishop of Antioch, Ignatius Martyr, writing to the Ephesians, calls the risen Jesus: our God (Eph 1:1). About the same time, Pliny the Younger wrote from Bithynia to the Emperor Trajan about the Christians, a crude superstition, who sing hymns to Christ as to a god (Epistle 10). Not only the living God is worshiped through the risen Jesus and remains so in the official worship of the Church, but instances of private prayer from the second century on indicate that the Lord Jesus himself can be the direct addressee of the worshiper.[1]

It will take the Christian Church until the third Council of Constantinople in 681 C.E. to craft a final satisfactory expression of Jesus of Nazareth's true humanity and his unique relation to the living God. It has been upheld unchanged until today by the Greek and Latin Churches. It is not surprising that the first essays in Christology were confusing.

Often the rabbis were puzzled. They suspected idolatry. Nevertheless, they were aware that the Christians were professing a belief in the God of Abraham, Isaac and Jacob. All the Christian creeds will start with "We believe in one God." On the other hand, the rest of the text will not sound to Jewish ears like pure monotheism. During the second century the opinion prevailed among the rabbis that the Christians were in fact worshiping two Gods, a Father and a Son; moreover the Son was an unacceptable mixture of the divine and the human. Christian belief was not as bad as pagan idolatry; nevertheless, it seemed to be a radical distortion of Jewish monotheism. The parting of the ways was becoming unavoidable.

4. THE ANXIETY OF THE CHRISTIANS

The flamboyant proclamation of Paul of Tarsus that Torah Judaism was obsolete, that the time had come to let its historical shell be cracked open by God's Spirit to let Messianic Judaism emerge in glory, had awakened a feeling of anguish in the hearts of the Diaspora Jews. On the other hand, the subtle but strong reaffirmation by the Yavneh Academy of the perennial presence of Torah Judaism awoke in the hearts of the Gentile Christians a deep feeling of anxiety, but of quite a different and more unconscious nature.

For the Gentile proselytes, the progressive transformation of Judaism into Christianity was supposed to be a light to reveal God to the Gentiles and a manifestation of the glory prepared by God for his people Israel (see Luke 2:32). Given the lavishness of God's gifts to Israel, the Rabbinic Judaism's strong disapproval of the new way was rather puzzling. God was supposed to have patiently prepared his people during centuries for the coming of the Messiah. The Jews had the privilege of being present where and when it all happened. They were his own people, his family. If they were unable to believe, how could Gentiles believe? They had not seen the risen Jesus. They had to rely entirely on the witness of his Jewish disciples. Faith and doubt are the two sides of the same experience. They started wondering how secure was their security blanket. It was hard enough for their faith to overcome the world; must they also have to overcome Jewish indifference? At certain moments a feeling of resentment against those who had been expected to be the trail blazers of the new way crept into their minds and found its way to nest in their subconscious.

There was another anxiety, more spiritual. Though still Gentiles, they had learned to identify to some extent with Judaism itself. They were worried that the Yavneh Academy was not giving to God a proper answer to the tragedy of the Catastrophe. Could Judaism live a healthy life without Temple and sacrifices? More than ever the ministry of the risen Jesus was needed. Obviously such an anxiety made sense only in the framework of a deep Christian faith. To those living in this faith, who had not yet acquired negative feelings toward Judaism, the Yavneh renewal was causing a real anxiety.

It was not only the spiritual welfare of Israel which seemed to be in jeopardy. The new Gentile Christians could hear the clamor for enlightenment coming from their blood brothers and sisters. If history had been different, if Israel had welcomed Jesus of Nazareth and had given him a chance to become like a second Ezra, bringing the vision of Deutero-Isaiah to existence, it would have been so much easier to bring the Gentiles to worship the God of Israel in Jerusalem. Why had God allowed the Romans to crucify Jesus and to burn the Temple?

Resentment crept in also because the Jews not only disdained the Messiah sent to them by God, but were constantly creating obstacles to those bringing the good news of salvation to those Gentiles who were willing to receive it with joy. This was a natural kind of anxiety, the fear of failure experienced by activists of a new religious movement who find themselves limited in their activity by powerful rival forces. We must not project into the first century stereotypes valid in other historical periods. The Jews had always been respected for their antiquity. Notwithstanding the tensions brought about by the First Jewish Revolt, the Judaism of the Diaspora was still an impressive religious establishment compared with young Christianity. As we noticed earlier Diaspora Judaism will remain missionary-minded until late in the second century. To join a Jewish synagogue was to accept a stricter HALACHAH, but it was also to receive the protection of a RELIGIO LICITA.

Today, many Jews and Christians are surprised to discover that for nearly 300 years the disciples of Jesus of Nazareth, whether Nazarenes in the Land of Israel or Messianics in the Diaspora, were real underdogs—underdogs in the Synagogue and underdogs in Greco-Roman society. Only some God-fearers may have experienced a higher status when after baptism they were received as equal by their Jewish brothers and sisters. With so little human succor it is understandable that the early Gentile converts welcomed with joy the charismatic gifts bountifully provided by God's Spirit. By the end of the first century, however, even these were starting to subside!

In the period between the First and the Second Jewish Revolt, from 70 to 130 C.E., there was not only the religious rivalry between Jews and Christians, which Paul had welcomed as a spiritual "jealousy" (Rom 11:11, 14), there were also altercations, quarrels, even violence. Given the deep religious animosity engendered by their mutual disenfranchisement, some fanatics may have been led to fratricide, or at least to various processes of oppression.

We know the painful stories of all the measures taken by Byzantine emperors, Visigoth kings, Roman popes, Luther's disciples, Orthodox princes... finally by Hitler trying to achieve a final solution. The list of Jewish martyrs at the hands of Christians, or nominal Christians, is very long indeed. This repetitive harassment is not well known in Christendom and seldom acknowledged. It transformed a religious quarrel into a deep social conflict which is still with us.

There is another persecution which seems to have disappeared from the collective memory of Jews and Christians alike. What really happened between the two communities in the first century of their confrontation has passed into oblivion. When the Christians started to become differentiated from Judaism, they had nothing, absolutely nothing, except their faith. They were censured by the Yavneh Academy and deprived of the respectable position enjoyed by the Jews in the Roman society; ceasing to be Jews, they automatically became a RELIGIO ILLICITA, criminals who could be persecuted at any time by the Roman magistrates. Indeed they were often persecuted.

Notwithstanding their deep faith, they could not avoid acquiring the mentality of the persecuted. No one seemed to care for them, to want them, not even their spiritual mother Israel. They were the ANAWIM, the poor ones. Tertullian around 200 C.E. wrote these harsh words, "The synagogues of the Jews were the sources of the persecutions" (ON THE SCORPION'S BITE, 10). His polemical style echoes the complaint expressed by most Christian writers in the second century. Marcel Simon has challenged this statement and James Parkes, in studying the authentic Acts of the Martyrs, has found few cases of Jewish intervention.

It might be necessary to differentiate more clearly the periods before and after the Bar Kochba revolt. In the early period Rome had barely discovered the existence of Christianity as a religion distinct from Judaism. Jewish authorities in Palestine enjoyed the use of some coercive power, and the synagogues in the Diaspora, except under Hadrian, had the benefit of religious freedom. In these circumstances a number of Christians were persecuted by Jews: Stephen the first martyr; James, son of Zebedee; James, the brother of the Lord; Paul, who five times had 39 lashes from the Jews (2 Cor 11:24); the martyrs under Bar Kochba in Judea, and others unknown to us. The Johannine Gospel, compiled toward the end of the century, attributes to Jesus these prophetic words,

They will expel you from the synagogues
and indeed the hour is coming when anyone who kills you
will think he is doing a holy duty for God (John 15:2).

In the first 100 years of Christianity, there were Jewish authorities who occasionally tried to stop by force the birth of what appeared to them pseudo-Judaism. The disciples of Jesus, already greatly disappointed by Jewish unbelief, acquired their persecution complex under the shadow of the Synagogue, before they realized that their real persecutor was Rome.

After the Bar Kochba revolt the situation changed. Synagogue and Church disengaged from each other. Judaism progressively withdrew into a defensive position. It developed toward Christianity an attitude of serene indifference. Hostile activity of Jews toward Christians was only a matter of personal grudges in local situations. Still, personal relations were sometimes friendly, and even Tertullian admits that some Christians were saved by Jews in time of persecution. Christians must never forget that in those dark hours there were "Righteous Jews."

5. THE FIRST OFFICIAL SKIRMISH

It is not the hesitant steps of an early Christology which caused the break between the Synagogue and the Church, nor the occasional persecution the Christians encountered. It was, on one hand, the refusal of the Church to recognize that the Sinaitic Covenant, with its formal structure engraved in the Mosaic Law, will remain valid for the Jews as long as this world will endure, "until heaven and earth pass away" (Matt 5:18). God always remains faithful to his promises—even if all his children are sinners and he has to punish them—and the Sinaitic covenant is not a covenant with individual believers, but a covenant with a particular nation which God had chosen as his own.

On the other hand, the refusal of Yavneh—soon to be sanctioned by all Diaspora Synagogues—to recognize the messiahship of the risen Jesus made the break equally inevitable. The Rabbinic sages denied any authoritative value to Jesus' teaching and were unwilling to recognize the need of new halachic interpretations to fulfill God's promises to the Gentiles.

The parting of the ways between the two siblings was a slow process, subsequent to a progressive awareness of their reciprocal exclusion. The fact that the Christian devotion to the risen Jesus was endangering the transcendence and perfect oneness of the God of Israel played a part, but a minor part, in the rupture. Obedience or disobedience to the word of God was the real problem for each sibling. The possibility that the Christians were worshiping two Gods gave to the critical attitude of the Jews a greater religious depth. It strengthened an animosity which originally sprang from their loyalty to the Covenant.

Two historical events "symbolically" mark the point of no return in the estrangement between the two siblings. They took place around 90 C.E. One was the addition to the Eighteen Benedictions of a curse against the MINIM, i.e., the heretics. The Eighteen Benedictions, the 'AMIDA, was and still is the central prayer of the synagogal service. Many scholars are of the opinion that the new benediction was aimed primarily but not exclusively at the Nazarenes. The other event was the publication on the Christian side of the Gospel according to John, in which "The Jews" were condemned as the enemies of Jesus on account of their unbelief and their attempts at his life. It took some time for the curse and the condemnation to spread everywhere among Jews and Christians. They implied a final repudiation of each other.

The Yavneh Academy had at that time a very strong leader at its head, Gamaliel II of the House of Hillel. He was the grandson of Gamaliel I who had defended the freedom of the Nazarenes when Peter and John had to appear before the Sanhedrin. Gamaliel II succeeded in having the title of NASI (translated President, sometimes Patriarch), and his authority in non-criminal matters, recognized by the Romans. He was a community builder. He streamlined the liturgy, encouraged some writing of the Oral Law, upheld the canonization of the Scriptures, and in short institutionalized Rabbinic Judaism. Though Judaism was an orthopraxy much more than an orthodoxy, Gamaliel II fought all those who did not represent the authentic Pharisaic tradition. There were still many alive at the time. He fought all of them, but it seems that his pet aversion was the Nazarenes, who earlier had been respected by Yohanan Ben Zakkai, the founder of Yavneh.

Some rabbis in Yavneh had shown signs of annoyance at the presence of Nazarenes during community prayers. Gamaliel II, in order to be sure that none of them would take a turn in leading the prayers, introduced the BIRKAT HA-MINIM, a curse on the heretics in the form of an added benediction. Here is the text according to the Ashkenazi tradition,

> May the slanderers have no hope; may all wickedness perish instantly; may all thy enemies be soon cut down. Do thou speedily uproot and crush the arrogant; cast them down and humble them speedily in our days. Blessed art thou, O Lord, who breakest the enemies and humblest the arrogant.[2]

This text has been used for 18 centuries against all kinds of enemies of Israel. The Sephardi tradition kept the original invocation, "May the MINIM have no hope...." Changes in the text were sometimes intended to avoid offending the Christian political powers. In the beginning the expression the MINIM referred to the Nazarenes and other circumcised heretics; later on it was extended to include the Gentile Christians.

Yavneh was not content with simply introducing this curse into the Eighteen Benedictions. The decision of the Academy was communicated to the Synagogues of the Diaspora. The NASI kept in regular touch with them by sending emissaries who informed the Diaspora of the work of Yavneh and gathered the annual collection. Traditionally this had been used for maintenance of the Temple; now it was used for the works of the Academy. From many references in Justin, Eusebius and Jerome, James Parkes, whose philo-semitism and critical objectivity are widely recognized, tried to reconstruct the letter which transmitted to the Diaspora the official decision concerning the MINIM. He writes,

> It contained a formal denial of the truth of the Christian account of the teaching and resurrection of Jesus. Christianity was a denial of God and of the Law. It was based on the teaching of Jesus, who was a deceiver, and who had been put to death by the Jews. His disciples had stolen His body, and then pretended that He had risen again from the dead and was the Son of God. It was therefore impossible for Jews to have anything to do with such teaching, and His followers should be formally excommunicated.[3]

This is a reconstruction and not a copy of the original, and consequently we cannot ask for details and nuances. The communication to the Diaspora Synagogues was intended to make crystal-clear that the Christian teaching was a denial of the Mosaic Torah, the authority of its teachers being a sham because Jesus of Nazareth was a deceiver and his early disciples deceitful liars. It was at once the condemnation of a doctrine and an exposé of the lack of credibility of its initiators.

The document was directed against the Nazarenes; the Gentile Christians were obviously outside the fold. However, in coming to a decision, the rabbis of Yavneh, who were well informed by the emissaries about all the happenings in the Diaspora, must have taken into consideration the existence of the Gentile Christians, their practices, and their doctrinal statements. They sent the document to the Diaspora synagogues in order to counteract any Christian propaganda among their members.

If there had been any trust between rabbis and Nazarenes in the early history of Yavneh, by the end of the century it was completely obliterated. The BIRKAT HA-MINIM snapped the bond linking the Nazarenes with the House of Israel. In the Diaspora it intensified the rivalry between Church and Synagogue. It succeeded in arresting the hemorrhage of sons and daughters of the Covenant toward the Christian fold, at least in the Land of Israel. But it destroyed any remaining feeling of spiritual kinship. Henceforth it was to be "we" versus "they."

Quite a distance from Yavneh, in Ephesus, on the west coast of Asia Minor, the Community of the Beloved Disciple felt deeply hurt by its official exclusion from the Jewish Synagogue. There is an emerging consensus that the compiling and editing of the Fourth Gospel was an answer to the addition of the curse against the MINIM in the 'AMIDA, and the sending of a condemnatory letter to the Synagogues of the Diaspora. Rather than a few sentences, as in the Yavneh letter, we have in the Johannine Gospel a detailed justification for its rejection of Rabbinic Judaism. For the Johannine community the sages of Yavneh were "The Jews," those who were not receiving Jesus of Nazareth, accusing him of being a deceiver, a seducer of his people.

With its Nazarene roots, its sense of continuity with Jewish history, and its conviction that "salvation is from the Jews" (John 4:22), the Community of the Beloved Disciple was deeply offended that "the Jews had already agreed that anyone who confessed Jesus to be the Messiah would be put out of the synagogue" (John 9:22)—a lapsus of the writer who projects into the time of Jesus the crisis his community had to endure. They will answer Yavneh with all the bitterness of a feud among close relatives.

The spiritual context of the Johannine writings, one generation after Paul, is quite different from the Pauline letters. The messianic fever has very much subsided. Paul's desire to preach to the whole world before the return of Jesus is not present. John certainly believes that Jesus is the Savior of the world, but there is none of Paul's urgency to reach the Greeks, the Barbarians, all nations. There are no Acts of the Apostles in the Johannine literature. The messiahship of Jesus is presented in the framework of his earthly life, but contemplated in the light of his resurrection. It creates an impression of otherworldly reality. The Gospel is totally centered on the person of Jesus of Nazareth, risen and glorified. It is as if God, after choosing Israel among all the nations as his own people, had chosen among all the Israelites Jesus of Nazareth as his only-begotten. In Jesus, God's own Word was made flesh, and the election of Israel had finally been put into focus through the perfect relation of a Jewish mind and a Jewish heart to the living God. Notwithstanding a number of concrete and precise details unknown to the Synoptic Gospels and precious for the historian, the general atmosphere of the Fourth Gospel seems to be a drama at the borderline between this world and the world to come.

John's problem is not how to renew or expand Judaism, nor how to render it messianic; Judaism itself in its essence, which is this-worldly, has become problematic. What is the true Israel? During his night meeting with Nicodemus Jesus had insisted on the need to be reborn from above in order to

enter the Kingdom of God (see John 3:7). Judaism needed to be reborn. It had
nearly perished in the burning of the Temple. Its restoration in Yavneh, in the
framework of the Mosaic Law, was not a real rebirth. Salvation comes from
the Jews. But the hour had come for the Mosaic Law to be impregnated from
above with God's grace and truth through the ministry of the risen Jesus.
Shorn of this gift from above the Mosaic Law would become old-fashioned,
obsolete (see John 1:16–17).

Yavneh had accused the Nazarenes of denying God and the Law. John, in
turn, accused the rabbis of denying the activity of God in the ministry of
Jesus, an activity which was sacred and essential to Christian identity. In the
Fourth Gospel, the rejection of Jesus' authority is not a matter of invincible
ignorance or the result of a proclamation full of ambiguity. Those called
sometimes the chief priests and the Pharisees, and sometimes The Jews, were
not blind. They were seeing but not perceiving, because their hearts were not
attuned to God's activity. Through the centuries Judaism has been rightly
characterized as being indifferent to Christianity. There was a moment,
according to John, when it was not indifference, but a deliberate NO which
was rendered by those who were then leading the renewal of their people. The
Pharisaic NO of the Yavneh Academy was experienced by the Johannine tradition as an echo of the Sadducean NO at the time of Jesus. It was a NO of
certain responsible leaders, but not necessarily of the people. "Nevertheless
many, even of the authorities, believed in [Jesus]. But because of the
Pharisees they did not confess it, for fear that they would be put out of the
synagogue" (John 12:42).

The deep emotional attachment of the Johannine community to its Jewish
roots and to Jesus of Nazareth, risen and glorified, brought a situation not
unlike the bitter conflict, in the second century B.C.E., between the Teacher of
Righteousness and the Wicked Priest, the conflict which gave birth to the
Essene movement. It remained a conflict inside Judaism; the Gentiles were no
part to that conflict. Then it was Qumran versus the Temple priesthood; now it
was the Johannine community versus the Yavneh Academy.

The dualistic framework pervading the Essene as well as the Johannine
writings introduced inside the House of Israel the old attitude of inclusion and
exclusion used to define the relations between Jews and Gentiles. Now it was
used to separate the true Israel from the false Israel. The Rabbinic Jews,
together with sinners and unconverted Gentiles, became "the world," the
realm of darkness opposed to the realm of light. The letter to Smyrna in the
Book of Revelation speaks in the most derogatory manner, "I know the slander on the part of those who say that they are Jews and are not, but are a synagogue of Satan" (Rev 2:9). One more step, and some disciples of Jesus of

Nazareth will demonize all of Rabbinic Judaism, at the same time that they proclaim themselves the true Israel. Anti-Judaism thus becomes the hallmark of genuine Christianity.

It will be John rather than Paul who will shape the Christian attitude toward Judaism and the Jews, in the age of the Martyrs, as well as in the age of the Fathers. Paul's acerbic dispute with the Judaizers will not survive the Bar Kochba revolt. The Law will cease to be the central problem it was in the Church of the Apostles and their immediate successors. Jesus of Nazareth, Messiah, Lord, Son of God, the central figure of the Johannine writings, will become the central problem. John, whose physiognomy quickly faded away, never was a very clear image in the collective memory of the Jewish people, by contrast with Paul, who is remembered as the evil one who blasphemed against Torah and might even be considered the real founder of Christianity as a religion different and separated from Judaism. In fact it is the reading out of context of the Fourth Gospel which will become the main source of the specifically religious anti-Judaism in the life of the Church.

Paradoxically John was the most Jewish of the New Testament writers. His Gospel can be read in an entirely Jewish context. He did not see Israel as only a preparation for, or a prophecy of, the Christian community. Still less did he view Israel as a community to be replaced by the Christian community. Israel was the vine described in Isaiah 5:1–7, which God planted on a very fertile hill, the Land of Israel, and which grew into the true vine, Jesus and his disciples (John 15:1–8). It was the true vine whose time had come to be transfigured in the light of the resurrection.

If it had not been for "the world," the fighting forces of darkness trying to overcome the light, the earthly character of this vine would barely be visible. Paul's universalism had appeared as a denial of the national character of the Sinaitic covenant; now the other-worldliness of the Johannine tradition comes like a radical denial of its earthly historicity. In a still more subtle way the Jewish self-image is totally denied.

The community of the Beloved Disciple was profoundly charismatic, not in the exuberant way of the Pauline Churches, but in a quiet and truly mystical manner. They lived beyond covenant and beyond messianism; they were fascinated by eternal life. By contrast, the Yavneh Academy was in spirit at Sinai, seeking in TORAH the way to become wise and faithful servants in the earthly household of the living God. The twins had grown along very different ways, developing nearly antithetic spiritualities. Were they incompatible? Did they call for mutual delegitimization? Was it God's will that they become so bitter about their mutual rejection? These questions the social scientist could not answer. It is a task for the theologians.

XII. Separation by Mutual Consent

In the beginning, in the very beginning, Jesus' disciples, Jews or Gentiles, were proudly rejoicing in the Jewishness of Jesus of Nazareth. They believed in him as the glory of his people Israel (Luke 2:32). Seventy years later, when the world was passing from the first to the second century, many disciples were already estranged from Jesus' own people. They had become—even some, like the Beloved Disciple, born and raised Jewish—antagonistic to its survival.

Jesus had been received by his own people with great hesitation. The religious establishment had been suspicious from the beginning; the common people, curious, impressed, awed, remained awaiting an imminent messianic event which would liberate them from Roman occupation. After the tragic crucifixion at the hands of the Romans, Jesus' disciples had been conspicuous by their piety, their faithfulness to Temple worship, and their strict observance of the commandments. Jesus, however, had not returned as expected, and the imminent great event turned out to be a catastrophe, the burning of the Temple and the destruction of the Holy City. To Jewish eyes the Jesus movement had become less a blessing than a threat to the religious and national survival of Israel. When the Pauline Churches showed little respect for the Mosaic Law, not only the religious leaders in the Diaspora but even the common people looked askance at the Christians as aliens. In no way could they be considered children of Abraham, a constituent part of God's people; they belonged to the despised Greco-Roman world.

1. CULTURAL KINSHIP AND SOCIAL ENMITY

The relative autonomy enjoyed by the local Jewish Synagogues and the local Christian Churches throughout the Diaspora must have produced many variations in the process of mutual alienation until it became a fait accompli. The addition of a curse against the MINIM to the Eighteen Benedictions at the Yavneh Academy and the publication of the Fourth Gospel probably at Ephesus were enacted under authority, rabbinic or apostolic. However, they were local events which gained acceptance across the Greco-Roman world only step by step.

When we compare the LETTER TO THE CORINTHIANS written by Clement in the name of the Church of Rome during the very last years of the first century with the seven epistles written by Ignatius the bishop of Antioch, about fifteen years later, at the time he was taken under guard to Rome to be martyred in the great Flavian Amphitheatre, we find great differences between the attitudes of these two hierarchs vis-à-vis Judaism.

The Church of Rome seems to have been very comfortable with its Jewish heritage. The quotations from the Hebrew Scriptures in the Letter to the Corinthians are more numerous than the quotations from Christian sources. The Synagogue and the Jews are not mentioned. The letter gives the impression that the entire heritage of the Hebrew Scriptures is now in the hands of the Church. Though the letter was occasioned by a strong party in the Corinthian Church which opposed the local presbytery, the letter's appproach is God-centered rather than Christ-centered. Everything in creation and in salvation history is ordained by God himself through the mediation of the Lord Jesus. Thirty years after the martyrdom of Paul of Tarsus there is not the slightest echo of a potential conflict between Messiah Jesus and the Law. By the end of the first century the majority of the Christians in the Church of Rome were probably uncircumcised; nevertheless, the spirituality expressed in this letter, though sent to one of the main Churches established by Paul, is unmistakably Jewish Christian, in the Matthean tradition.

On the other hand, in two of the seven letters addressed by Ignatius to Churches in eastern Asia Minor and to the Church of Rome, the attitude is definitely and explicitly anti-Judaic. Ignatius was convinced that those who continue to live Jewishly, i.e., in accordance with erroneous opinions and old fables (Mag 8:1), are acknowledging by that fact that they had not received Jesus Christ as sent by God. To the Magnesians he wrote,

> Set aside, then, the evil leaven, old and sour, and turn to the new leaven, which is Jesus Christ. Be salted with him to keep anyone among you from being spoiled, since you will be convicted by your odor. It is ridiculous to profess Jesus Christ and to Judaize; for Christianity did not believe in Judaism, but Judaism in Christianity, into which every tongue that has believed in God has been gathered together (Mag 10:2–3).

Ignatius, probably, would not condemn a believing Jew who observed the Mosaic commandments as a family tradition, but he unquestionably condemned Gentile converts in Magnesia and Philadelphia who wanted to observe, if not all, at least some of the Mosaic ritual commandments.

For Ignatius no community or even no person could be simultaneously loyal to Judaism and Christianity. Paul's emotional attachment to Judaism is nowhere present in Ignatius' letters; he is already a second generation Gentile Christian. He does not argue about any particular aspect of Judaism. It is a clear NO to the Jewish way of life. One can sense in his attitude a certain hostility against anything in the least Jewish.

Nevertheless, the general framework of his religious thinking and spirituality remained profoundly Jewish, with the caveat that the Maccabean devotion to the Law was replaced by a total devotion to the crucified and risen Jesus Christ. Earlier, in sharing the life of the Antiochene Christian community, Ignatius had absorbed unconsciously much of the Jewish religious tradition. Though certain expressions in his letters are in literary Greek, he belonged to a Greek community which culturally lived in the world of the Bible. His anti-Judaism, however, attests to an incipient break between the Hellenistic Synagogue and the emerging Greek Church. Though there was a real cultural affinity between them, as social groups, the two became antagonistic. Some Hellenistic Jews may have been strongly attracted to the new way and some Judaizing Christians to the ancient way; if they desired the benefits of community life, they needed to make a final choice.

In this process of mutual alienation we are dealing principally with a social rather than a cultural hostility. Even siblings who are culturally completely identical may develop bitter feelings of personal hostility. In the beginning of the second century the relations between the Jewish and the Christian communities started to deteriorate significantly, at least in some localities like Antioch. By the time of Ignatius the two siblings had been facing each other for nearly eighty years and much had happened: from mistrust, to contempt, to bruised feelings, to aggressive behavior, and finally to a vicious circle which once started becomes more intense. The living God was silent. There was no higher authority, no arbiter, to initiate a peace process. By the beginning of the second century a new form of antisemitism, Christian antisemitism, was born. It added its own strength to a Gentile antisemitism which was already strong enough to bring Emperor Hadrian, only a few years after Ignatius, to go so far as to declare the ceremony of circumcision a capital offense—an early form of "final solution"! Happily the decree died with him and better days came to the Jews.

2. WHOSE BIBLE?

Ignatius is not an ancestor of Marcion, who 30 years later will reject "in toto" the so-called Old Testament. Ignatius for his part declared the Hebrew Scriptures genuinely Christian, at least the Prophets who "lived according to Jesus-Christ" (Mag 8:2). During the second century the ownership of the Hebrew Scriptures became a bitter subject of controversy between Jews and Christians. Marcion brought the matter to a head by declaring the Hebrew Scriptures are not only non-scriptures for Christians, but in fact anti-Christian scriptures. He had quite a few followers, until the Church of Rome expelled him and his group in 144 C.E. Other Apostolic Churches followed suit. Ignatius' position, however, proved that the rejection of Marcion and the upholding of the Hebrew Scriptures as divine revelation did not necessarily imply a recognition, logical as it would be, of all the values of Judaism, at least for the Jews.

If we could make a content analysis of the way early salvation history was seen at the time by most Christians we would probably detect three categories among the ancestors of Jesus:

1. The Pre-Christians, who will have to wait in Hades until their liberation by the risen Jesus to enter the Kingdom of God, people like Adam and Eve, Abel, Noah, Abraham and the Patriarchs, Samuel, David, Isaiah, Jeremiah, Daniel and the Maccabean martyrs, people who "were living according to Jesus-Christ."

2. The people who are rarely mentioned but were somehow just. They would include people like Enoch, Melchizedek, Moses and Aaron, Joshua, Solomon, Ezekiel, Nehemiah and Ezra. These seem to be more Jewish than Christian and the Christians have no clear notion how to relate to them. Many of these had a special link with the national dimension of Israel's religion.

3. Then there were "the bad guys" whom the Jews themselves despised: Cain and his posterity, Ham, Ishmael, Esau, Saul, Absalom, Jeroboam, Athaliah, Manasseh, the false prophets, and many other sinful Israelites.

It was a very simple vision. All the good people are Christians and are the beginning of the Church. All the very bad people are the Jews. They are the convincing proof that the old dispensation was unable to bring to life a holy people. The people in between do not attract much attention as they are simply the social actors of a period in history that is already totally elapsed. From then on, everything positive in the Hebrew Scriptures will be considered Christian and everything negative Jewish. As the Hebrew Scriptures forcefully condemn any kind of sinful behavior among God's people, the Hebrew Scriptures became paradoxically a source of anti-Judaism among Christians.

It is not surprising that the Jews became extremely angry when they saw that their most sacred sanctity had been purloined by the Christians.

In later periods it was discovered that sinners are as numerous among the Christians as among the Jews. Christianity will have to struggle with human freedom as Judaism had to. But at the beginning, difficult circumstances in which the Church was living, as well as her strong spiritual life during "the age of the martyrs," led to a feeling of superiority. A renewed Testament was supposed to have more spiritual vigor than the ancient ones. This general attitude contributed to a subjective and faulty reading of the Hebrew Scriptures.

Incomplete as it was, the condemnation of Marcion and Marcionism was the most important event in the theological life of the second century Church. It was a partial victory for the Matthean school. Notwithstanding the increasing influence of the Pauline Letters and the Johannine Writings with their strong eschatological framework, so appealing in times of persecution, the Churches had come to realize that the Christians were in the same basic condition as the Jews. In fact they were still waiting for the coming of God's Kingdom at the Parousia of the risen Jesus. They still had to learn to cope with this world and to live religiously in the midst of extremely demanding earthly tasks. The world to come was not yet on earth and this world remained a vale of tears where even Christians were groaning in hope of redemption.

Paul, or at least his early disciples, had been forced to embrace a partial return to the Jewish roots of Christianity in order to stabilize the life of their communities. In the mid-second century the Church read the signs of the times and realized that the experience, wisdom and spirituality of those ancestors of Jesus, who under the guidance of God's Spirit and in loyalty to his Word had been holy and creative, could become a source of strength for the Church in her period of waiting. Then, with a feeling of good conscience, having incorporated into her life the best of the Jewish tradition, the Church turned toward the Jews and saw no justification for their continuous presence. In God's plan of universal salvation they had fulfilled their irreplaceable function. They ought to become Christians or disappear.

3. DEATH OF THE CHURCH OF THE CIRCUMCISION

The first to suffer because of this pervading attitude among many second century Christians was the Church of the Circumcision. In the eyes of many the existence of a Jewish nation, or even of any form of Judaism, after the coming of Christ had become dispensable and perfectly pointless. Jews, who were not believers, had become of no interest to the Church, except as potential converts. The Nazarenes and their offshoots were to be pitied, and encouraged to abandon erroneous opinions and old fables. Still they would be saved because of their firm belief in Jesus Messiah.

With the loss of Hegesippus' five volumes of MEMOIRS we are left very much in the dark on the subsequent history of the mother of all Churches after the martyrdom of Simeon, the cousin of the Lord, who had succeeded James, the hero of Nazarene spirituality. There is no sign that many Palestinian Jews joined the Nazarenes after the Catastrophe of 70 C.E. After the Second Jewish Revolt under Bar Kochba in 132-35 C.E., all Judea was declared by the Romans JUDENREIN, free of Jews, and the Nazarenes survived only in small communities in Galilee, Transjordan and Syria. Unwilling to recognize Bar Kochba as God's Messiah, the Nazarenes in Judea had refused to join the revolt and according to Eusebius some had suffered martyrdom. We do not know how many paid with their lives. The news spread among the Gentile Churches and this rumor contributed to the general feeling that the Church was persecuted by the Jews.

Some sympathy for the persecuted Nazarenes barely retarded the disaffection of Gentile Christians vis-à-vis Jewish Christianity. The mother of all Churches had known a substantial literary activity—a number of gospels written in Aramaic, popular apocalypses, and Christian interpolations in Jewish pseudepigraphia. However, only fragments of the Nazarene gospels have remained, because the Greek Churches had no interest in them. This fact is most significant. It suggests that the young Gentile Churches did not perceive that a unique religious value had survived in the life of the Jewish Christian community. What in their eyes was valid in the legacy of Judaism had already been absorbed by the Gentile Christian communities. The progressive weakening and final extinction after the Muslim conquest of the last survivors of the Church of the Circumcision did not cause the slightest ripple of regret among the Gentile Churches. The Church which in faithfulness to the words of the Master and under the guidance of God's Spirit had transformed Judaism into Christianity, formulating its basic creed and establishing its basic institutions, passed into oblivion without a whimper. From then on the inopportuneness of any form of Jewish Christianity became the only position which Jews and Christians were able to share in complete agreement.

With the hindsight of a few centuries the social scientist is in a better position to study the effects on the life of the universal Church of the demise of the Church of the Circumcision. This demise symbolized and facilitated the progressive alienation of the Church from her Jewish roots. Very rapidly the Gentile Churches had disengaged themselves from the national component always present in the religion of Israel, maintaining solely the fundamental structure and the basic religious values of Temple Judaism. Once their continuity with Judaism ceased to be nourished through close contact with a living tradition, some aspects of the common heritage became weakened while others simply ceased to be transmitted to the following generations. In the second century already we find the beginning of a cultural dejudaization of Christianity. It will become fully apparent at the end of the century in the works of Clement, Origen and Tertullian. What had Christianity lost through this progressive alienation from Judaism?

4. THE LOST HERITAGE

The Apostolic Churches, in the tradition of good Pharisaism, had always considered the oral tradition as important as the written tradition. Once the Christian Churches deliberately tried to express their original semitic tradition in a non-semitic cultural framework, be it Greek, Latin, German, or other, the difficulty of grasping exactly the meaning of the Hebrew Scriptures, which the Churches had vigorously upheld against Marcion, increased substantially.

1. The first element completely lost was the language of Jesus. Saint Jerome could not find one Christian to teach him Hebrew. The Italian adage, TRADUTTORE TRADITORE, reminds us how easy it is for a translation from one language into another (including its cultural presuppositions) to be unfaithful to the original. If God spoke to man in the context of a particular culture—and not through a philosophical or scientific jargon—the well-being of the Christian Church may require the maintenance of close contacts with the people who are keeping alive this religious culture, even if it underwent through time a slow evolution.

2. With the total severance of Jesus of Nazareth from his family, his people and his culture, the realism of God's humanization in the incarnation of God's Word as Jesus of Nazareth lost much of its authenticity. The letters of John had to react against some interpretations of his Gospel that were denying the reality of Jesus' humanity. He felt the need to emphasize "what we have seen with our eyes, what we have looked at and touched with our hands" (1 John 1:1). Docetism, as we noticed, was the first serious heresy the Church had to contend with. Even among the orthodox Christians the humanity of Jesus became more and more apprehended in abstract terms rather than in simple concrete terms. In the middle of the second century the humanity of God's Word became a kind of generalized human being, poorly anchored in history, the kind of indefinite humanity social scientists never meet. The Greek Church increasingly focused her attention on Jesus' divine life as the eternal Logos, and on the relation of the Logos to the biblical God. In the daring speculations of some metaphysical minds, or the ecstasies of a few mystical

souls, the real humanity of Jesus of Nazareth, specifically his Jewish humanity, became completely lost. The story of Jesus of Nazareth had become a divine drama; it had ceased to be a human drama lived by God himself at the heart of history.

3. The good news that the Kingdom of God was drawing near had inserted into Judaism a new hope which was not foreign to Judaism's basic framework of ethical monotheism. This explains that, notwithstanding the great emphasis placed by the Jesus movement on the coming Kingdom, and on the future role of King Messiah, they carefully handed down to the next generations the historical Jewish monotheism which had taken centuries to come to full expression in the life of God's people. But the rabbis in the second century were not so sure that the Christians had in fact remained monotheists. As we noticed, the first developments of Christology inclined them to look at the Christians as duotheists, worshiping sometimes the God of Israel, and sometimes a second God, his eternal Son.

The Church will need a few centuries to develop a conception of the divine origin of Jesus of Nazareth in harmony with her fundamental belief in the oneness of God. During this period of intensive exploration, research, or testing of new insights in the fire of communal devotion, the monotheism inherited from Temple Judaism was faithfully transmitted. However, the positive attitude of the Gentile Churches toward the philosophical and artistic culture of the Greco-Roman world significantly affected the transmission of this religious heritage.

The vivid anthropomorphisms used by the Hebrew Scriptures to describe God's activity in the history of Israel had for a long time puzzled and embarrassed the inquiring minds of some rabbis. Their symbolic nature was obvious. Increasingly, the meaning hidden in, and at the same time revealed by, these anthropomorphisms was perceived in transcendental, i.e., non-representable terms. At the core of Jewish spirituality is God's word,

> You shall not make for yourself an idol, whether in the form of anything that is in heaven above, or that is on the earth beneath, or that is in the water under the earth (Ex 20:4).

The complete absence of any "image" of God is the test of authentic Judaism. To Moses God revealed his existence, not his essence. God is not an idol, but a sovereign presence, a pure mystery, unable to be grasped, or even caught a glimpse of, by tiny human minds.

Though the early Church was losing interest in the humanity of Jesus of Nazareth, being increasingly absorbed in his divinity, the fight against docetism, and the insistence on a real incarnation of the Word of God, led some artists to sketch a pictorial representation of Jesus of Nazareth. Such depictions did not convey an historical memory, but were acts of personal devotion in the midst of a culture prone to depict the form of the human body. Though some Greek philosophers despised matter, the people had a deep longing to see gods through images.

The Epistle to the Colossians had already described Jesus of Nazareth as "the image of the invisible God, the firstborn of all creation" (Col 1:15). When the Christians in the beginning of the second century not only worshiped the living God through the risen Jesus, but worshiped Jesus as God, the slow evolution of Jewish piety toward a greater sensitivity to God's transcendence started to be reversed. The immanence of God in Jesus of Nazareth was not only affirmed, it was experienced by Christian piety. How human the humanity of Jesus remained could be argued by Church Fathers and Councils, but a pictorial representation had been made possible which concretely and immediately was symbolizing the living God. To less sophisticated Jews it looked like idolatry. It certainly weakened the biblical sense of divine transcendence.

4. The greatest loss of all was the final demise of the Church of the Circumcision. It meant the disappearance at the heart of the Church life of one particular charism, the fundamental one: the Sanctification of the Name. From then on, the Christian Church will continue to exist, but severed from the Mosaic Covenant and deprived of the faithful observance of Torah, which according to Jesus' declaration had to endure "until heaven and earth pass away" (Matt 5:18).

Paul had called the Church of the Circumcision the Saints (1 Cor 16:1, 2 Cor 8:4) and had reminded the Gentiles not to boast because "it is not you that support the root but the root that supports you" (Rom 11:18). It was Jewish Christianity which was maintaining the root alive in the Church, offering to Gentile Christianity an organic continuity with the religious life Jesus of Nazareth had experienced during his earthly pilgrimage. This organic continuity finally passed into complete oblivion. During the following centuries any Jew wanting to become a disciple of Rabbi Jesus had to be absorbed into Gentile Christianity. The Christian Churches were insistent in dejudaizing him or her.

The real reason why Gentile Christianity became so quickly alienated from Jewish Christianity remained unconscious at the time and did not surface in any text of the Apostolic Writings. The Gentile Christians were foreign to the Jewish experience of a covenant between God and a nation. They sought a religion of personal salvation. Their faith was in Jesus of Nazareth risen and glorified. They were citizens not of the earthly Jerusalem, but of the heavenly

Jerusalem. Their covenant was essentially eschatological, a membership in the life of the risen Jesus, membership in a born-again Israel. Though they were in this world and had a mission in this world, they were not of this world (John 15:19), in contradistinction to their Jewish brothers and sisters who, even united with the risen Christ, were still of this world, though separated from the other nations. Keeping their Jewish task of sanctifying any righteous aspect of human life to make it holy, they remained God's particular possession, building as a nation an earthly temple to the living God. Evil may have been trying hard to destroy the holiness of this temple from the inside, but Israel could pray and work for wholeness, hoping for a temporary harmony between the earthly and the heavenly.

Jesus of Nazareth, aware of the universal character of the mission he was to entrust to his disciples at the time of his departure, had promised them only the cross and a permanent tension between them and a socio-cultural world redeemed only in hope. Their task would be to prepare as many Gentiles as possible to encounter the risen Messiah, even if they had to live in the middle of a culture and a society which did not know the living God.

With the establishment of a universal and a-temporal monotheism open to the Gentiles, the need for a particular nation totally consecrated to God may have appeared superfluous to some. In the second century many Gentile Christians were remembering the Mosaic Covenant only as the indispensable matrix used by God for the transformation of Israel into the Christian Church. For these Christians the past was no more; the present was fundamentally oriented, not toward the past, but toward the Parousia of the risen Jesus. During the two centuries of frequent persecution by the Roman Empire, the Pauline affirmation that the figure of this world is passing away was easily adhered to. Later, with the freedom given to the Church by Constantine, and the establishment of Catholicism as the official religion of the Empire by Theodosius, a Christian equivalent to the Jewish concept of complete integration between religion and nation started to pervade the ranks of the hierarchy. It will be the first, but not the last, of many great experiments to make Christianity not simply a religious community in this world, but a religion of this world. Some of these experiments have been significant and creative of humanistic values. They did not, however, exhibit strong survival ability and most of them were ephemeral. Today, all have passed away.

An entirely different concept of holiness, of total devotion to the living God, blossomed in the Eastern Churches at the time some were dreaming of a Christian Empire. When pagan Rome became officially Christian, the purity and genuineness of Christian life weakened rapidly. People, and even Church ministers, became more interested in worldly success than in serving God.

Christ's precepts were often displaced by the wisdom of this world. In the presence of such a trend toward secularization, a spontaneous and vital reaction led many religious individuals to turn their backs on Church and Empire, and to withdraw into the deserts of Egypt and Syria in order to live alone with God. Relations with the world, physical and mental, were to be strictly controlled. Everything became sacred, with the regular hours reserved for prayer acquiring primacy of place. At work the tools were to be used as sacred vessels on the altar. The monks were creating a theocratic society in the desert. In time they became a class apart, clearly separated from the rest of the Church, either priests or lay persons. They lived under the law, the monastic law, which they called the Rule. Before long they came to be regarded as a people apart, but superior to the rest of the Church. All was well until some local Churches, impressed by the reputation of holiness attributed to certain monks, elected them as bishops and brought them back into the world. These bishops in turn tried to use some monks for the pastoral needs of their Churches. Eventually a new kind of consecrated life emerged which, like the Church, was in the world but not of the world.

The original monastic exodus into the desert, into a kind of no-man's-land between this world and the world to come, showed striking similarities with the measures taken by Ezra to isolate Israel from contacts with foreigners. The dissimilarities, however, indicate the originality and uniqueness of Israel's calling in comparison with the monastic vocation. The monastic ideal crystallized around three main forms of behavior: celibacy, poverty and obedience. None of these was highly praised in Jewish tradition. Quite the contrary. Marriage and family life were exalted. Wealth was a sign of God's blessing. The Talmud remains the only religious code which carefully notes dissenting opinions. Though Judaism and monasticism each segregated its members from the outside in a highly structured way of life, the spirit pervading each tradition seemed antithetical to the other.

The reason for these profound differences is obvious. Judaism is a covenant between God and a particular nation, isolating it from the other nations in order to bring into a living communion with God not only every aspect of the personal life of each individual, but every aspect of the socio-cultural life of a particular nation. Israel's vocation was a call by God to a religious life circumscribed by the reality of this world. On the contrary, virginity and celibacy, personal poverty and the surrender to the will of a superior, are not realities of this world, but anticipation and foretaste of the world to come, the world of the resurrection, where God is all in all. Such a selfless opening to the activities of God's Spirit looked to some as a denial of God's command to be fruitful, to multiply, and to take full responsibility for achieving with

God the many splendors of his creation. When the population explosion had not yet become an urgent social problem, such an objection had some weight; however, it did not win the day.

In proclaiming among the Ten Words the law of the Sabbath (Exod 20:8), God had asked humanity to consecrate six-sevenths of its time to pursue the goals of creation, but to reserve one-seventh exclusively to his service. In an analogous way he had called a small segment of humanity to be entirely consecrated to him. If the tribe of Levi had been chosen for the service of the tabernacle and the Temple, all of Israel had been called from among the nations to be a holy and priestly nation, to offer herself to God as the first people born to his fatherhood, as the firstfruits of all creation.

When this people, God's particular possession, ceased to be present at the heart of a Church that had become completely Gentile, a monastic people slowly emerged, called to live continually in the presence of God. In a Christian context such a consecrated life became transformed into the life of an eschatological people, a people who not only did not belong to this world, but was already separated from it in spirit. It became a prophetic sign of the world to come. Important as the monastic movement would be in the life of the Church, especially in periods of crisis, its specific charisma was eschatological; the Church, however, had already discovered that she was not yet the Kingdom, and in her present situation could not be purely eschatological.

> Therefore every scribe who has been trained for the kingdom of heaven is like the master of a household who brings out of his treasure what is new and what is old (Matt 13:52).

The Church could not be oriented exclusively toward the future without taking into account the past surviving in the present. She needed to at least sanctify family life and to participate in various affairs of this world; these were areas for which the monks were poor teachers. Consequently her well-being invited her to remain in touch with a spirituality and a tradition anchored in earthly realities.

Harmonious relations between Church and Synagogue after the demise of the Church of the Circumcision could have provided the proper challenge thanks to enriching contacts with a living and expanding Jewish tradition. However, by the middle of the second century, even if many cultural elements were still shared by Jews and Christians, clear religious differences had created a deep antagonism between the two communities. The dream of the Epistle to the Ephesians that the risen Jesus "has made both groups into one and has broken down the dividing wall, that is, the hostility between us" (Eph 2:14), was far from being realized. On the contrary the wall was higher and stronger.

One hundred and twenty years after the tragedy on Calvary well-delineated stereotypes of mutual exclusion had already been formed. They will remain unchanged until our day. It is the nature and the acuity of the painful wounds which Jews and Christians inflicted on each other in this process of religious differentiation which need to be acknowledged by those anxious to overcome and to heal such a long and sorrowful history of inveterate antagonism.

5. THE RESIDUE OF BITTERNESS

To illustrate the anti-Judaic attitude of the average Gentile Christian in the middle of the second century we may draw upon an excellent historical source: the DIALOGUE WITH TRYPHO. Thomas B. Falls in the introduction to his translation of the DIALOGUE wrote, "The DIALOGUE reports a discussion that took place in Ephesus between Justin and the Jew Trypho, shortly after the end of the war instigated by Bar Kochba (ca. 135). While the details of the discussion may be fictitious, the broad outline appears to have been founded in fact."[1]

Justin was a pagan philosopher, a native of Shechem in Samaria, and a recent convert to Christianity. He wrote a courageous APOLOGY to the Roman authorities in defense of his persecuted community. He opened a philosophical school in Rome and had many disciples. The prefect Rusticus sentenced him and six others to death for professing Christianity. They were beheaded circa 165 C.E.

The main interest of this document for us is the possibility it offers to examine the relations between Judaism and Christianity immediately after their parting of the ways, and to do this in a purely religious context. Nobody will deny the role played later by social, political, economic, and even cultural factors in fostering a progressive antagonism between the two communities. These factors became intensified when the Church enjoyed a dominant position in the political structure of the nations. By contrast, in the second century, Judaism and Christianity were in nearly similar positions in the Roman Empire. They were two peoples living apart from pagan society. To the outsider the only important difference was the fact that, from the time of the Maccabees on, Judaism had been recognized by the Roman Senate as a RELIGIO LICITA, a privilege lost by the Christians as soon as they ceased to be recognized as a Jewish sect or did not wish to be so recognized.

The DIALOGUE WITH TRYPHO is a monologue rather than a dialogue. Though most of Trypho's questions are redactional, we may grant to Justin the philosopher a certain respect for objectivity. The way he phrased the questions of Trypho must correspond to the common perception of Jewish attitudes by mid-second century Christians who were still worshiping the God of the Jews and were reading in Greek the Hebrew Scriptures as their own Scriptures. As we do not have access to any contemporary Jewish writing and as the Mishnah and Talmud are silent on Christianity, the DIALOGUE, if critically read, can be used to reconstruct the contemporary Jewish attitude toward Christianity.

Jews were genuinely surprised "that you [Christians] who claim to be pious and believe yourselves to be different from the others do not segregate yourselves from them, nor do you observe a manner of life different from that of the Gentiles" (D. 10).[2] Such a question may sound strange to modern Christian ears. It was already strange to Justin and implies that in the middle of the second century the Christians had ceased to interpret the election of Israel as the status of a priestly nation, destined to live a consecrated life separated from the life of the other nations.

"If you listen to me…first be circumcised, then observe the precepts concerning the Sabbath, the feasts, and God's new moons; in brief, fulfill the whole written law, and then, probably, you will experience the mercy of God" (D. 8). How can you "expect to receive favors from God when you disregard His commandments?" (D. 10). By the time of Justin nearly all the Gentile Christians had ceased to observe the Sabbath and the dietary laws whose strict obligation was enshrined in the Hebrew Scriptures. Trypho, however, nowhere condemns the moral life of the Christians. Concerning the accusations common among the pagans he remarks: "Those other charges which the rabble lodge against you are not worthy of belief, for they are too repulsive to human nature" (D. 10). It was disobedience in everyday life to the Mosaic Law, to God's commandments, which made the Jews recoil from association with the Christians.

Nothing in Jewish eyes justified such blatant disobedience. There had been no visible sign of the coming messianic era, neither during the life and activity of Jesus of Nazareth, nor immediately afterwards which could have convinced the Jews that King Messiah had come. The world around them still looked so unredeemed!

> If the Messiah has been born and exists anywhere, He is not known, nor is He conscious of His own existence, nor has He any power until Elias comes to anoint Him and to make him manifest to all. But you (Christians) have believed this foolish rumor, and you have invented for yourselves a Christ for whom you blindly give up your lives (D. 8).

> The one whom you call Christ was without glory and honor to such an extent that he incurred the last curse of God's law, namely, he was crucified (D. 32).

> Your statement that this Christ existed as God before all ages, and then He con-
> sented to be born and become man, yet that He is not of human origin, appears
> to be not only paradoxical, but preposterous (D. 48).

> We Jews all expect that Christ will be a man of merely human origin, and that
> Elias will come to anoint Him…yet, from the fact that Elias has not yet come,
> I must declare that this man is not the Christ (D. 49).

Justin, the Christian, is now on the defensive. He is far from being a
Marcionite. Not only does he accept the divine authority of the Hebrew
Scriptures; he is familiar with them and possesses a scriptural knowledge
which most Christians, and even many Jews, could envy. More than half of
the DIALOGUE consists of long quotations of these Scriptures, mostly
excerpts from the Prophets and the Psalms. His main problem is how to justify the non-observance of God's commandments by the Gentile Christians.

Justin argues that Christian faith is true circumcision because it is circumcision of the heart (D. 12, 16, 19). Adam, Enoch, Lot, Noah, and Melchizedek
were saved without circumcision of the flesh (D. 19). Ritual prescriptions
were imposed to save people from idolatry (D. 19) and to keep God before
their eyes (D. 20). However, the main assertion which throughout his argument sustains Justin's negative attitude toward the Jewish manner of life is the
transitory nature of the Mosaic Law. One text is particularly revealing.

> Furthermore, we do not claim that our God is different from yours, for he is the
> God who, with a strong hand and outstretched arm, led your forefathers out of
> the land of Egypt. Nor have we placed our trust in any other (for, indeed, there
> is no other), but only in Him whom you have trusted, the God of Abraham and
> of Isaac and of Jacob. But our hope is not through Moses or through the Law,
> otherwise our customs would be the same as yours….I have read, Trypho, that
> there should be a definitive law and covenant, more binding than all others,
> which now must be respected by all those who aspire to the heritage of God.
> The law promulgated at Horeb is already obsolete, and was intended for you
> Jews only, whereas the law of which I speak is simply for all men. Now, a later
> law in opposition to an older law abrogates the older; so, too, does a later
> covenant void an earlier one. An everlasting and final law, Christ himself, and
> a trustworthy covenant has been given to us, after which there shall be no law,
> or commandment, or precept (D. 11).

Discussing the situation of those Christians, Jews or Gentiles, who in the
second century were still observing the Mosaic precepts, while at the same
time placing their hope in the risen Jesus, he acknowledges that there are
Christians who "boldly refuse to have conversation or meals with such persons" (D. 47). Justin disagrees with them. He is willing to receive these obser-

vant Christians and to associate with them in every way as spiritual kinsmen, with the caveat that they will not try to persuade others to be circumcised like themselves, to keep the Sabbath, or to perform any other similar acts. For Justin the so-called Mosaic precepts have lost their binding power, even for Christians born of Jewish parents. They have become a matter of personal devotion.

To understand how Justin can possibly hold such a cavalier attitude toward the Law, the most sacred belief of a Jew after trust in the living God, one must realize that he is wholeheartedly convinced that Jesus of Nazareth is the Messiah of the Jews and the Savior of the Gentiles. "What is the covenant of God? Is it not Christ?" (D. 122). "...he who scorns and hates Him [Christ] clearly hates and scorns Him [God] also who sent Him; and he who has no faith in Him [Christ] does not believe the words of the Prophets who preached his gospel and proclaimed Him to all men" (D. 136).

We have reached the crux of the matter: Who is Jesus of Nazareth and what is the nature of his spiritual authority? Has the divine authority of TORAH been challenged legitimately or not by the divine authority attributed to Jesus of Nazareth by his disciples? Jews and Christians were neighbors in the cities of the Empire; they could not ignore each other. They could observe the slight differences in their customs and life-style. For the Christians the written Law and the oral Law had been at first authoritative, though some points of the oral Law had been contested by Jesus and the Apostles. By the time of Justin the Mosaic Law had become obsolete, something of the past, though the Hebrew Scriptures were still Scriptures. The only existing Law was the Law of Christ as defined by the Church. For the Jews, on the contrary, the authority of Jesus of Nazareth was non-existent. He was simply a man whose messiahship had been invented by some Jews and mostly by Gentiles. His miserable end had proved that he was a false Messiah.

What we find directly expressed in the DIALOGUE is a clear differentiation in the beliefs professed by Jews and Christians at the time of Justin, though the two communities lived, moved and had their being in the same framework of ethical monotheism, worshiped the same Creator, used the same Holy Scriptures (the New Testament was still in the process of canonization) and were waiting for the full realization of the Kingdom of God. Radical differences in the context of great similarity tend to awaken deep feelings of self-justification and strong rejection of the other. Though Justin was writing about belief or disbelief in the messiahship of Jesus of Nazareth, he did so in the matrix of antagonistic feelings which had been progressively gripping the two communities. It is these feelings, their nature and genesis, which we must try to understand. They were in the process of being crystalized and as such they will be the matrix of all future theological interpretations and fateful political decisions.

At that time the Jews appeared religiously secure and confident. They were aware of their unique position in the Empire, and above all they knew they were God's chosen people. Their attitude toward emerging Christianity had changed from annoyed antagonism to serene indifference. This indifference became a deep-seated attitude structuring all religious relations with Christians and Christianity until modern emancipation. It was different from the initial indifference manifested toward the message of Jesus of Nazareth or his disciples. It was the end result of an evolution which had lasted a century.

At first the Jewish masses had been disappointed by the non-appearance of the messianic age. Then the proclamation by Saul of Tarsus that Jesus of Nazareth was the termination of the Law sounded as if Christianity was heralding the demise of Judaism. It was a time when national survival was in jeopardy due to Roman imperialism. An acute sense of self-preservation brought about a religious revival after the destruction of the Temple. Confronting the relative success of Christianity among the Gentiles, the Jewish leaders felt deceived by the Jesus movement, condemned it and tried to purify their ranks from any contamination. They were quite annoyed at the effrontery of uncircumcised Gentiles using their Scriptures and claiming to be the true Israel. According to Marcel Simon, in his thorough study of the period,[3] Judaism kept receiving proselytes, and successfully so, until around 200 C.E. Given this fact, some feeling of competition between Jews and Christians was unavoidable. For these various reasons, between 70 and 135 C.E. the Jewish leadership encouraged an active hostility toward all forms of the Jesus movement.

After the failure of the Second Revolt led by Bar Kochba, the rabbis, who by then were extending their influence to the Diaspora Synagogues, gave up any hope of snuffing out Christianity in its beginnings. They transformed their active hostility into a passive hostility, concentrating their efforts on restructuring communal life and hebraizing synagogal services. For centuries the Jews will develop the art of passive resistance, until finally in modern times Zionism will redirect their energies toward their fatherland.

In certain situations total indifference is the expression and the source of great psychological strength, as well as an efficient tool of survival. However, in the eyes of the one who is trying to establish some kind of relation with the indifferent person, indifference is experienced as a rebuke, a rejection. It is like a declaration of the non-existence of the interlocutor. Individuals, groups and nations are always very sensitive to a recognition of their true self-identity. An enemy acknowledging your identity is more bearable than one who is totaly indifferent to your existence.

Such a strong and unbending indifference must have been the result of a very deep hurt. As long as Jesus of Nazareth and his disciples were bringing hope to the House of Israel, they may not have been followed, but they were never feared and could be lived with. Once Jewish existence was denied and the Jewish sanctities became grossly manipulated by Gentiles, the core of Jewish feelings started to suffer. The Orthodox Jews must have wished that the Christians had never existed. As long as the Christian communities were fledglings, struggling for their survival, it could be hoped that like many similar movements they would be ephemeral. Suddenly, in the second quarter of the second century, it must have dawned on Jewish activists that Christianity was there to stay and was attracting more and more Gentiles to worship the God of Israel. The Jews had just lost their homeland in Judea. Was Christianity going to choke Judaism to death?

If Trypho's attitude had been aggressive during his dialogue at Ephesus with Justin, the latter could not have phrased Trypho's questions in such a non-emotional tone. Trypho expressed strong negations of the Christian claims, but used few pejorative adjectives. He is a good example of the total Jewish indifference to the Christian affirmation that Jesus of Nazareth was sent by God to inaugurate the eternal Kingdom. For him the Christians were building castles in the air that may interest the Gentiles but would leave indifferent any sincere Jew faithful to the Covenant.

The case is different with Justin. He shows great love for the Hebrew Scriptures, especially the prophetic tradition, but his attitude toward the Jews seems to be concealed hatred. Here are some very unfriendly descriptions of the Jewish character under his pen: deceitful (D. 14), forgetful (D. 20), ungrateful (D. 27), hateful (D. 39), obstinate and feeble-minded (D. 44), idolatrous and murderous (D. 93), unjust and sinful (D. 95), prideful (D. 102), stupid (D. 111), faithless (D. 119), fruitless (D. 120), disobedient and unrepentant (D. 120), stubborn, unwise, sly and treacherous (D. 123), a useless, disobedient and faithless nation (D. 130).

From the pen of a philosopher, a rather noble character, who will sacrifice his life to remain loyal to his God, such un-Christian expressions seem very strange indeed. It is true that Jesus of Nazareth had occasionally used sharp words against his contradictors. But Justin is trying to hold a polite conversation with Trypho. Why these invectives? Would the social status of the Christians at the time explain the vehemence of his expression of contempt? Rejected by Jesus' own people, persecuted by the power of Rome, often hated by the populace, and recruiting proselytes mostly from marginal people, they had no status in society except as underdogs. A painful experience of injustice must have nourished a deep resentment toward any kind of religious or political establishment. Like the Jewish attitude of indifference, it was also the end result of a century of history. Resentment had not been the original attitude.

Jesus' first disciples had hoped with all their heart that the House of Israel would recognize in the Nazarene the one sent by God to usher his Kingdom first into Jerusalem and then into the whole world. Israel's repudiation of Jesus' claim to authority, after centuries of preparation, was for the early Christians, Jews or Gentiles, incomprehensible. Their reaction to such ingratitude was a feeling of moral superiority. Underneath, however, lingered a certain sense of insecurity. If God's people, whose Scriptures had become the Scriptures of the Church, had been unable to receive Jesus' message and believe in his victory over death, how could Gentiles believe with complete security what Jesus' own flesh and blood considered to be foolish rumors? This meant that Christian faith had to overcome not only pagan idolatry, but also Jewish blindness.

The unbelief of many Jews had thus opened a small crack in the love and loyalty of the first Christians for their Jewish heritage. The bitter struggle in the early Church between the Judaizers on one hand and Paul of Tarsus and his associates on the other opened permanent wounds in the Body of Christ which will never completely heal. Many Gentile proselytes felt that the Judaizers were trying to impose on them unnecessary obligations. To them and a few liberal Jewish Christians, the integrity of the Jewish heritage had become an obstacle to the proclamation of the Good News. At first they saw in it a superfluous attachment to transitory legislation. Soon it became like a demonic power challenging the Gospel. The opposition of the Synagogue outside and the Judaizers inside the community became like the specter of a Judaism challenging the survival of Christianity.

> You have murdered the Just One, and his prophets before Him.... You dishonor and curse in your synagogues all those who believe in Christ.... You did employ force against us as often as you could (D. 16).

> You dispatched certain picked men from Jerusalem to every land to report the outbreak of the godless heresy of the Christians and to spread those ugly rumors against us which are repeated by those who do not know us. As a result you are to blame not only for your own wickedness, but also for that of all others (D. 17).

> Indeed, your hand is still lifted to do evil, because, although you have slain Christ, you do not repent; on the contrary you hate and (whenever you have the power) kill us who through Him believe in God, the Father of all, and you

cease not to curse Him and those who belong to Him (D. 133).

We are here face to face with a deep hurt and forceful indignation. Recent events in Judea may have been overshadowing the dialogue at Ephesus. In his FIRST APOLOGY Justin wrote,

> These Jews…consider us as their enemies and adversaries, killing and punishing us, just as you do, whenever they are able to do so, as you readily imagine. In the recent Jewish war, Bar Kochba, the leader of the Jewish uprising, ordered that only the Christians should be subjected to dreadful torments, unless they renounced and blasphemed Jesus Christ (F.A. 31).

The Jew had become the persecutor, the wicked one who stands with the sinner and naturally calls on himself the wrath of God.

> The purpose of the circumcision was that you and only you might suffer the afflictions that are now justly yours; that only your land be desolate and your cities ruined by fire; that the fruits of your land be eaten by strangers before your very eyes; that no one of you be permitted to enter your city of Jerusalem (D. 16).

In the eyes of Justin the inexorable link of cause and effect is self-evident: Jewish unbelief had led to the persecution of the Prophets, then of Jesus of Nazareth, and finally of his disciples, which persecution called for divine chastisement. The complete defeat of Judea in her protracted conflict with Rome was interpreted as a solemn verdict of the Lord of history.

For various reasons the early period analyzed in this essay has left few traces in the collective memory of Jews and Christians. Ashkenazim remember Byzantium and Christendom; Sephardim the rise of Islam and 1492; the Talmud in serene indifference ignores Christianity; the Christians on the other hand recollect solely the Roman persecutions and the courage of the martyrs.

After Bar Kochba, for a period of nearly two centuries, the bitter spiritual struggle characteristic of the period 70–135 C.E. subsided into Jewish indifference and Christian resentment. Yet, a psychoanalysis of the Jewish psyche and the Christian psyche would probably reveal the lasting effects of the traumas which marked the twin births of Rabbinic Judaism and Christianity. The bitterness of the early encounter survives as deep wounds that have not yet been healed and create strong psychological blocks to any candid and fearless spiritual exchange in contemporary social circumstances.

A Final Word

Jews and Christians have much to forgive each other. Such forgiveness is beyond the scope of social science, because to understand is not yet to forgive. Nevertheless, a better understanding of the deep-seated attitudes which are the matrix of aggressive behavior, personal or communal, may constitute an important asset in a process of social healing.

The reaction to the Catastrophe of 70 C.E. among Jews and Christians proved to be diametrically opposite. The Jews rejected the NEW and the Christians rejected the OLD. The Jews affirmed that salvation for Israel could be found only by upholding in its pure form the Sinaitic Covenant; the Christians proclaimed that salvation for Israel, and the Gentiles, could be found only in the eternal covenant established through the risen Jesus. Were Jews and Christians giving to the word "salvation" the same meaning? Psychologically, this divergence led the Synagogue to purify itself and to concentrate on its living tradition and led the Christian Church to make that tradition explode from inside toward new horizons.

God had worked centuries to build the religion of Israel, and, after Ezra, Temple Judaism. Culturally, it was unique, clearly distinct from all other religious systems. Totally God-centered, it had a deeply humanistic quality emphasizing ethical and social values. It was a "classical" religion, moderate, measurable, seeking harmony with nature, bursting with love of life and joy— when not punished by the Lord.

Suddenly, the teaching of Jesus of Nazareth with its more radical aspects, the proclamation by the Twelve that the same Jesus was truly risen inaugurating the heavenly Jerusalem, and the reaching out of Saul of Tarsus toward the Gentiles, all seemed to destroy the delicate equilibrium God had built through centuries of patience and inspiration. Not only did these novelties not correspond to the actual messianic expectations of the common people, but they were changing the focus of traditional Jewish life from covenantal justice toward gratuitous love, from concern with this world toward concern with the world to come, and from nationalism toward universalism. Such new perspectives were not essentially anti-Jewish, or completely foreign to Judaism, but they were stretching Temple Judaism to its limits and even beyond its limits.

To understand the reaction of the Jewish people to this new teaching, we must carefully separate the reaction of the Sadducean party in control of the Temple, and indirectly of the nation, from the general reaction of the people. The colonial situation, the fear of the Romans, and the will to maintain a grip on political power, led to an unavoidable conflict at first between the religious establishment and Jesus of Nazareth, and later his Galilean disciples. As the Sadducees lost all power after the burning of the Temple, the general reaction of the Pharisees and the common people remained the most significant response. Originally it was not negative. It was rather a feeling of uncertainty concerning the imminent coming of a hoped for messianic event mixed with a deep uneasiness at experiencing cherished traditions stretched beyond acceptable limits.

It is principally Pauline evangelism which started to transform an attitude of respect, curiosity and distance into a negative rejection. The sense of self-identity and the struggle for national survival in difficult political circumstances brought forth a great fear that the dissolution of Torah Judaism into an a-temporal and universal Judaism would strike down the dividing wall carefully constructed by Ezra and would finally destroy the integrity of the nation. The leaders of the Diaspora dreaded that Paul would attract many Jews to this strange and easier kind of Judaism; they were deeply offended at the manipulation of Jewish sanctities by uncircumcised Gentiles. This time it was not a matter of systematic doubt or suspended judgment, but of a religious injury that needed an antagonistic answer.

Only toward the end of the century, when Christians in worship started to relate to the risen Jesus, less in terms of the coming Messiah—MARANA THA—than the actual High Priest of Israel and all creation, were some suspicions of idolatry and sacrilegious behavior creeping into the Jewish-Christian relations. The Talmud, however, kept the question unresolved. Blasphemy had not been the original cause of the parting of the ways; only subsequently did it become an aggravating factor.

The mainstream of the Jesus movement, around the Petrine tradition, which in the second century became the great Church, the Catholic Church, followed a rapid and extraordinary reversal of its attitude toward Judaism. At first it was a member in good standing of the House of Israel, tolerated at least if not encouraged. But soon it acknowledged Jesus of Nazareth, risen and glorified, as the supreme rabbinic authority, received uncircumcised Gentiles in its membership, refused to acknowledge the emerging authority of the Yavneh

Academy, appropriated the Hebrew Scriptures as its own, declared the unbelieving Jews wicked, cut them from God's covenant and made them fit for shame and punishment.

At the origin of this extraordinary transformation was a grievous spiritual wound which was at the same time a deep hurt and a great sadness. The early Jewish disciples of Jesus of Nazareth had received him not only as the human voice of the God of Abraham, Isaac and Jacob, but after his resurrection as the focus of their religious devotion, the true way to the living God. The fact that the Nazarene was not received by his own people was incredible and profoundly disturbing. This spiritual shock rendered their unquestioned loyalty to Jewish tradition questionable.

Later on, mutual irritation, aggressivity, recriminations and condemnations started on a big scale, not between unbelieving and believing Jews, but among believing Jews themselves, who took different positions concerning the observance of the commandments and the admission of Gentiles into the Christian fold. Some Gentiles were enthused over the observance of the Law, but the majority of the Christian proselytes were not keen to follow that path and wanted to keep their Greek identity. During this protracted conflict Judaism acquired some negative connotations among Gentile Christians. When the Judaizers lost the argument and finally became a voiceless minority, the negative feelings toward a strict observance were transferred to Yavneh and orthodox Judaism.

Obviously the political situation from 60 to 140 C.E. which rendered the Palestinian Jews enemies of the Empire and the Diaspora Jews suspicious to Roman authorities tended to pull the Gentile Churches away from Jerusalem and Judaism. After the exile in Babylon there had been a creeping anti-Judaism present in these localities where the Jewish community was visible and living apart. There is no sign that the local Churches ever tried to stop this insidious anti-Judaism, though they were themselves suffering from many pagan slanders.

By the time of Justin Martyr it was clear that the Synagogue, which soon was to experience a new spiritual efflorescence in Galilee, had no room in its bosom for Messianics believing in the mystical presence of the risen Jesus and his actual influence on the daily life of the present world. On the other side of the street, the Church, i.e., the Messianic Assembly, had no room whatsoever for those Messianics who still cherished their circumcision and were faithfully keeping all the Mosaic commandments. Though the calling and the gifts of God were irrevocable, the Sinaitic covenant was thought of as having ceased to exist the day Jesus of Nazareth died on the cross. The Church did not see the possibility, still less the necessity, to maintain in its bosom a space of freedom for the full exercise of the particular charismata of the Church of the Circumcision—even as a simple gesture of gratitude. Jewish practices, sanctified by Jesus of Nazareth during thirty years of his earthly life, retained only a folkloric interest for the Jewish Christians and were declared detrimental to the spiritual life of the Gentiles. Judaism had been a marvelous creation of God. It had fulfilled its noble role and now its place was in a museum. Such was the spiritual attitude toward Mother Judaism common among the second century disciples of Jesus, the Jew.

The Synagogue had said NO to the divine origin of Jesus of Nazareth and the Church had said NO to the permanent election of Israel as God's holy and priestly nation. Neither had any religious value in the eyes of the other. With such mutual disenfranchisement two religious communities in a context of competition could not easily maintain a pacific coexistence. The strong will dominate and the weak will suffer. The Christians at first were the underdogs. Later, through the accident of the Roman Empire adopting Christianity as its state religion, they felt free to vent their resentment and to humiliate the people of their Lord and Master.

The social scientist is no theologian. As a participant observer, he has to recognize that after nearly twenty centuries the two spiritual heirs of Temple Judaism are still alive and doing well; a surprising fact when we contemplate the field of history covered with institutional corpses. The simple fact of their long survival ought to discourage hasty mutual condemnations.

Israel and the Christian Churches have gone through many crises, divisions, reforms and renewals. Each would like to be recognized and accepted as God's chosen people. The disharmony of their voices makes God's voice hard to be heard in a world in transition, if not in deconstruction. For various social and cultural reasons the bitter animosity which in the past marred Jewish-Christian relations is mellowing. Perhaps the time is approaching when Jews and Christians will realize that the history of their relations in the first century could have been a very different history! Today, in place of fostering an anxiety to diverge, the patient healing of historical wounds might open a path toward creative convergence.

Notes

INTRODUCTION

1. Henry Siegman, "A Decade of Catholic-Jewish Relations," in JOURNAL OF ECUMENICAL STUDIES (Vol. 15:2, 1978).
2. IBID., p. 246.
3. IBID., p. 245.
4. IBID., p. 249.
5. Stuart E. Rosenberg, THE CHRISTIAN PROBLEM (Deneau: Canada, 1986).
6. IBID., p. 12.
7. IBID., p. 8.

CHAPTER I

1. R. Travers Herford, SAYINGS OF THE FATHERS (New York: Schocken, 1962), p. 19.

CHAPTER II

1. Flavius Josephus, ANTIQUITIES OF THE JEWS, Book XVIII, Chp. V,2.
2. E.P. Sanders, JESUS AND JUDAISM (London: SCM, 1985), p. 222.
3. Joseph Klausner, JESUS OF NAZARETH (New York: Macmillan, 1925), p. 374.
4. Sanders, op. cit. p. 232.
5. J. Ramsey Michael, "The Kingdom of God and the Historical Jesus," in THE KINGDOM OF GOD IN 20TH CENTURY INTERPRETATION, ed. by Wendel Willis (Peabody: Hendrickson, 1987), p. 116.
6. Geza Vermes, JESUS AND THE WORLD OF JUDAISM (Philadelphia: Fortress, 1984), pp. 34-35.

CHAPTER III

1, Henry Siegman, "A Decade of Catholic-Jewish Relations," in JOURNAL OF ECUMENICAL STUDIES (Vol. 15:2, 1978), p. 246.
2. THE JEROME BIBLICAL COMMENTARY (Englewood Cliffs: Prentice-Hall, 1968), p. 692.
3. E.P. Sanders, JESUS AND JUDAISM (London: SCM, 1985), p. 174.
4. Judge Haim Cohn, TRIAL AND DEATH OF JESUS (New York: Harper and Row, 1971).

CHAPTER IV

1. Joseph Klausner, JESUS OF NAZARETH (London: Macmillan, 1925), pp. 408-12.

CHAPTER VII

1. DAILY PRAYER BOOK, trans. Philip Birnbaum (New York: Hebrew Publishing Company, 1949), p. 82.
2. WEBSTER'S NINTH NEW COLLEGE DICTIONARY (Springfield: Merriam-Webster, 1991), p. 615.
3. Gershom G. Scholem, MAJOR TRENDS IN JEWISH MYSTICISM (New York: Schocken, Books, 1965).
4. E.P. Sanders, PAUL AND PALESTINIAN JUDAISM (Philadelphia: Fortress Press, 1983), p. 513.
5. Krister Stendahl, PAUL AMONG JEWS AND GENTILES (Philadelphia: Fortress Press, 1980), p. 13.

CHAPTER VIII

1. Edward H. Flannery, THE ANGUISH OF THE JEWS (New York/Mahwah: Paulist Press, A Stimulus Book, 1985), p. 48, revised and updated.
2. Flavius Josephus, ANTIQUITIES OF THE JEWS, Book XX, Ch. IX, # 1.

CHAPTER IX

1. Eusebius, CHURCH HISTORY, Chap. XXIII.
2. Ibid. Chap. XXXII.

CHAPTER X

1. Dom Jacques Dupont, LES BEATITUDES (Louvain: E. Nauwelaerts, 1954).

2. Raymond E. Brown, THE COMMUNITY OF THE BELOVED DISCI-PLE (New York: Paulist, 1979).

CHAPTER XI

1. Josef A. Jungmann, PUBLIC WORSHIP (Collegeville: Liturgical Press, 1957), p. 25.
2. DAILY PRAYER BOOK, trans. Philip Birnbaum (New York: Hebrew Publishing Company, 1949), p. 88
3. James Parkes, THE CONFLICT OF THE CHURCH AND THE SYNA-GOGUE (New York: Atheneum, 1981), p. 80.

CHAPTER XII

1. Justin Martyr, DIALOGUE WITH TRYPHO, in "Writings of Saint Justin Martyr by Thomas B. Falls" (New York: Christian Heritage, 1948), p. 139
2. D.10: References are to the short chapters into which the DIALOGUE is divided.
3. Marcel Simon, VERUS ISRAEL (Oxford: University Press, 1986).

Selected Bibliography

All quotations of the Scriptures are taken from THE HOLY BIBLE New Revised Standard Version (Oxford University Press, 1989).

A scholarly exegesis of the New Testament texts relevant to this essay is to be found in James D.G. Dunn, THE PARTINGS OF THE WAYS (Philadelphia: Trinity Press International, 1991).

The following works have been used as sources:

Boccaccini, Gabriele, MIDDLE JUDAISM (Minneapolis: Fortress, 1991).

Brown, R.E., THE CHURCHES THE APOSTLES LEFT BEHIND (New York: Paulist, 1984).

Brown, R.E., and J.P. Meier, ANTIOCH AND ROME (New York: Paulist, 1983).

Brown, R.E., THE COMMUNITY OF THE BELOVED DISCIPLE (New York: Paulist, 1979).

————, THE GOSPEL ACCORDING TO JOHN (2 vols. Anchor Bible 29, 29A; Garden City, N.Y.: Doubleday, 1955, 1970).

Cohn, Judge Haim, TRIAL AND DEATH OF JESUS (New York: Harper and Row, 1971).

Danielou, Jean, THE THEOLOGY OF JEWISH CHRISTIANITY (Chicago: Henry Regnery, 1964).

Davies, W.D., PAUL AND RABBINIC JUDAISM (Philadelphia: Fortress, 1980).

————, THE GOSPEL AND THE LAND (Berkeley: University of California, 1974).

————, CHRISTIAN ORIGINS AND JUDAISM (Philadelphia: Westminster, 1962).

Dupont, Dom Jacques, LES BEATITUDES (Louvain: Nauwelaerts, 1954).

Evans, Craig A. & Donald A.Hagner, eds., ANTI-SEMITISM AND EARLY CHRISTIANITY (Minneapolis: Fortress, 1993).

Flannery, Edward H., THE ANGUISH OF THE JEWS (New York/ Mahwah: Paulist Press, A Stimulus Book, 1985), revised and updated.

Flusser, David, JUDAISM AND THE ORIGINS OF CHRISTIANITY (Jerusalem: Magnes, 1988).

Grant, Michael, THE JEWS IN THE ROMAN WORLD (New York: Charles Scribner's Sons, 1973).

Grappe, Christian, D'UN TEMPLE A L'AUTRE (Paris: Presses Universitaires, 1992).

Hagner, Donald A., THE JEWISH RECLAMATION OF JESUS (Grand Rapids: Academic Books, 1984).

Hay, Malcolm, THE ROOTS OF CHRISTIAN ANTISEMITISM (New York: Anti-Defamation League, 1981).

Jacob, Walter, CHRISTIANITY THROUGH JEWISH EYES (Cincinnati: Hebrew Union College, 1974).

Jaubert, Annie, LA NOTION D'ALLIANCE DANS LE JUDAISME (Paris: Seuil, 1963).

Klausner, Joseph, FROM JESUS TO PAUL, trans. W. F. Stinespring (New York: Macmillan, 1943).

_____, JESUS OF NAZARETH: HIS LIFE, TIMES AND TEACHING trans. H. Danby (New York: Macmillan, 1925).

Koenig, John, JEWS AND CHRISTIANS IN DIALOGUE (Philadelphia: Westminster, 1979).

Luedemann, Gerd, PAUL APOSTLE TO THE GENTILES (Philadelphia: Fortress, 1984).

McKnight, Scot, A LIGHT AMONG THE GENTILES (Minneapolis: Fortress, 1991).

Manns, Frederic, JOHN AND JAMNIA (Jerusalem: Franciscan, 1988).

Mussner, Franz, TRAITE SUR LES JUIFS (Paris: Cerf, 1979).

Neusner, Jacob, JUDAISM IN THE BEGINNING OF CHRISTIANITY (Philadelphia: Fortress, 1984).

_____, JEWS AND CHRISTIANS (London: SCM, 1991).

Parkes, James, THE CONFLICT OF THE CHURCH AND THE SYNA-GOGUE (New York: Atheneum, 1981).

Paul, Andre, LECONS PARADOXALES SUR LES JUIFS ET LES CHRE-TIENS (Paris: Desclee de Brouwer, 1992).

Rosenberg, Stuart E., THE CHRISTIAN PROBLEM (Canada: Deneau, 1986).

Sanders, E.P., JESUS AND JUDAISM (London: SCM, 1985),

_____, PAUL, THE LAW AND THE JEWISH PEOPLE (Philadelphia: Fortress, 1983).

————, PAUL AND PALESTINIAN JUDAISM (London: SCM, 1977).

Sandmel, Samuel WE JEWS AND JESUS (New York: Oxford University, 1973).

Scholem, Gershom, THE MESSIANIC IDEA IN JUDAISM (New York: Schocken, 1973).

Schurer, Emil, THE HISTORY OF THE JEWISH PEOPLE IN THE AGE OF JESUS CHRIST, rev. and ed. by G. Vermes, F. Millar and M. Black, vols. I and II (Edinburgh: T. & T. Clark, 1973-79).

Segal, Alan E., PAUL THE CONVERT (New Haven: Yale University, 1990).

Shanks, Hershel, ed., CHRISTIANITY AND JUDAISM (Washington, D.C.: Biblical Archeological Society, 1992).

Sigal, Phillip, JUDAISM, THE EVOLUTION OF A FAITH (Grand Rapids: Eerdmans, 1988).

Simon, Marcel, VERUS ISRAEL (Oxford: University Press, 1986).

Siker, Jeffrey S., DISINHERITING THE JEWS (Louisville: Westminster/John Knox, 1991).

Stendahl, Krister, PAUL AMONG JEWS AND GENTILES (Philadelphia: Fortress, 1976).

————, THE SCHOOL OF ST. MATTHEW (Philadelphia: Fortress, 1968).

Theissen, Gerd, SOCIOLOGY OF EARLY PALESTINIAN CHRISTIANITY (Philadelphia: Fortress, 1978).

Vermes, Geza, JESUS AND THE WORLD OF JUDAISM (Philadelphia: Fortress, 1984).

————, JESUS THE JEW (New York: Macmillan, 1973).

Wright, N.T., THE NEW TESTAMENT AND THE PEOPLE OF GOD (Minneapolis: Fortress, 1992).

Wyschogrod, Michael, THE BODY OF FAITH (New York: Seabury, 1983).

Index

Eugene J. Fisher and Leon Klenicki, editors, *In Our Time: The Flowering of Jewish-Catholic Dialogue* (A Stimulus Book, 1991).

Leon Klenicki, editor, *Toward a Theological Encounter* (A Stimulus Book, 1991).

David Burrell and Yehezkel Landau, editors, *Voices from Jerusalem* (A Stimulus Book, 1991).

John Rousmaniere, *A Bridge to Dialogue: The Story of Jewish-Christian Relations*; edited by James A. Carpenter and Leon Klenicki (A Stimulus Book, 1991).

Michael E. Lodahl, *Shekhinah/Spirit* (A Stimulus Book, 1992).

George M. Smiga, *Pain and Polemic: Anti-Judaism in the Gospels* (A Stimulus Book, 1992).

Eugene J. Fisher, editor, *Interwoven Destinies: Jews and Christians Through the Ages* (A Stimulus Book, 1993).

Anthony Kenny, *Catholics, Jews and the State of Israel* (A Stimulus Book, 1993).

Eugene J. Fisher, editor, *Visions of the Other: Jewish and Christian Theologians Assess the Dialogue* (A Stimulus Book, 1994).

STIMULUS BOOKS are developed by Stimulus Foundation, a not-for-profit organization, and are published by Paulist Press. The Foundation wishes to further the publication of scholarly books on Jewish and Christian topics that are of importance to Judaism and Christianity.

Stimulus Foundation was established by an erstwhile refugee from Nazi Germany who intends to contribute with these publications to the improvement of communication between Jews and Christians.

Books for publication in this Series will be selected by a committee of the Foundation, and offers of manuscripts and works in progress should be addressed to:

Stimulus Foundation
c/o Paulist Press
997 Macarthur Boulevard
Mahwah, N.J. 07430